Victory Over Depression

A Complete Guide to Recovering the Joy of Living

Frans M. J. Brandt

Foreword by Earl A. Glosser

BAKER BOOK HOUSE
Grand Rapids, Michigan 49516

Important Notice

I do not encourage anyone to undertake medical or nonmedical
treatment on his or her own. In fact, I urge you to see your family
physician before undertaking any form of medical or alternative
treatment. The ideas, procedures, and suggestions contained in
this book are *not* intended as a substitute for consulting with
professional helpers such as physicians, counselors, and pastors.
All matters regarding your health require medical investigation,
and this is especially true in the case of depression. This does not
mean that each individual does not play a major role in obtaining
victory over depression. In fact, it is not possible to have such
victory without learning to make essential choices in life. The
successful treatment of depression depends on a knowledgeable
and motivated person who works closely with professionals in the
field of mental, physical, and spiritual health. Helpful sources
are only a phone call away, and include counselors, hotlines, pastors, physicians, psychologists, and mental health centers. The
purpose of this book is to educate and inform the reader on some
of the latest information on depression in general, and to explain
the importance of the wholistic, that is, body-mind-spirit approach in particular!

Frans M. J. Brandt

To

my many teachers, especially

Earl A. Glosser, Ph.D.
Maxie C. Maultsby, Jr., M.D.
Janet Stevenson, S.R.N.

and to all physicians, pastors, counselors, and others who are
promoting the treatment of the whole person: body, mind, and spirit.

Contents

Part Three
The Treatment of Depression

Part Four
Appendices

Tables and Charts

Foreword

Dr. Brandt has written an exceptional book! He does a superb job of presenting state-of-the-art information on depression. He also correctly, in my view, identifies the tangle of symptoms we associate with the depression label as just that, namely, as "symptoms" of underlying biological, personal, social, and/or spiritual malaise. I think that Dr. Brandt's system merits the kind of empirical research that recently has been given only to cognitive and pharmaceutical therapies in the treatment of depression. In fact, the well-known Swiss theologian Professor Hans Küng has called for precisely this kind of investigation at a recent meeting of the American Psychiatric Association.

Here Dr. Brandt deals first with that range of depressed behavior primarily caused by physiological and neurological deficits. He then correctly distinguishes this from the more reactive forms of depression. He again correctly pursues the idea that balanced nutritional intake, and/or carefully controlled medically prescribed drugs, are the treatment of choice primarily for certain biologically based depressions. Psychotherapy, especially cognitive therapy, is seen as the best possible form of treatment for the overwhelming majority of depressed people. Spiritual

11

growth, on the other hand, is seen as the primary form of treatment for those who are suffering from a spiritual deficit.

All types of depression receive the same careful diagnostic planning. Full use of the medical profession is strongly encouraged, with the provision to alert physicians to special issues such as allergies, endocrine disorders, or any of a wide range of physical possibilities. Again and again Dr. Brandt suggests a wholistic model to help the individual gain power and control over his/her symptoms by treating root causes such as poor diet, irrational thinking, and its concomitant behavior, as well as shallow or ignorant spiritual, philosophical, and religious development.

Fortunately Frans Brandt is not struggling alone in his efforts to treat and encourage depressed people. I believe he stands in the company of Scott Peck, Richard N. Bolles, and other superior communicators such as Robert Schuller, Lloyd Ogilvie, Fulton Sheen, and Norman Vincent Peale, who for years have urged us to look to our relationship with God as the greatest source of inspiration and help in dealing with life's problems.

What Dr. Brandt does for us here is to show us specifically how we can help ourselves with God's help to take effective responsibility for our lives, and to stop depending merely on drugs, prescribed or illicit. His message is crystal clear: "Stop being personal and spiritual sluggards and dilettantes. Stop poisoning yourself with improper diet and dangerous substances. Let me show you exactly how. This is the structure. You fill in the content. Do it now!"

Now are you ready for an exciting journey through the scientific, mental, emotional, and spiritual sides of depression? Are you ready to learn even more than you thought you wanted to know about this complex topic? Well, then, read on.

Earl A. Glosser, Ph.D.
Director, University Counseling Services
University of Virginia

Acknowledgments

I am extremely grateful to the many people who have directly, or indirectly, contributed to *Victory Over Depression*. It is impossible to mention all by name, for the list includes counseling clients, college students, colleagues, seminar participants, and many others who have helped me to realize that the wholistic—body, mind, spirit—approach is the most effective way to health and happiness.

Nevertheless, I would like to mention a few people by name: Dr. John R. Lixey for placing his work facilities at my disposal and helping me in numerous other ways; Eunice and Nelson Good for earnest caring, sharing, and daily prayers; Sue Davis for understanding, love, and encouragement; John Solomon for setting an example of unselfish devotion and providing assistance whenever needed; Shari Maharg for administrative and personal assistance and loyal friendship; Clay Busha for his valuable assistance at seminars and with a heavy workload in the office; John D. Drummond for a long and lasting friendship and continuous inspiration; Mike Cornelius for perpetually setting an example to follow; Peter Vellenga for solid advice, assistance and friendship; Peter G. Brandt for unwavering devotion and support;

13

and Shirley Bender for believing in my work and making it so widely available.

I am also very thankful to the many people who have critically read and evaluated the manuscript: William C. Adamson, M.D.; Karen Beach, R.N.; the Rev. George A. Boutieller; the Rev. Gerald Derstine, D.D.; the Rev. Mario Cuppetelli; Patrick V. DeMay, M.A.; the Rev. Edward Glotfelty; the Rev. Jack Fowler; Earl A. Glosser, Ph.D.; Nelson Good, M.A., Psy.S.; Kathy Hill, R.N.; the Rev. Edward Holsworth; Karen Kirschner, B.A.; Michael K. Lake, Ph.D.; John R. Lixey, D.C.; Maxie C. Maultsby, M.D.; John Maxwell; Gail May, M.S.W.; Bill Mitchell, D.C.; Dennis Mollard, D.D.S.; the Rev. Clifford Molnar; Josip Petani, M.D.; the Rev. Jack Pepple; Belle Prescott, R.N.; Paul Rajashekar, M.D.; the Rev. Ronald Scheer; the Rev. William Stone; General Doyle Varvel; Peter Vellenga, J.D.; and the Rev. John Vriend.

For typing assistance I am indebted to Bonnie Smith and Gail Wacker. Gail's incredibly positive attitude has made it possible to keep things on a steady course. Without Gail, once again, there would not have been a book. Blessed indeed is the man who has friends that bring the best out of him!

                                                    Frans M. J. Brandt

The Total Person
Body—Mind—Spirit

And the very God of peace sanctify you wholly; and I pray God your whole spirit and soul and body be preserved blameless unto the coming of the LORD Jesus Christ (1 Thess. 5:23).

Part **1**

Understanding Depression

Introduction

We live in an age of sadness. Depression—our most prevalent emotional disorder—has assumed such epidemic proportions that we have 35 million sufferers in this country. The extent of the problem is grimly reflected in a few simple statistics: 25 percent of the beds in public mental-health facilities, and 50 percent of the beds in private mental-health facilities are occupied by those who have depression. Outpatient facilities are equally strained by this epidemic of sadness. Nearly half of the patients in outpatient mental-health facilities have depression. The story is no different in general medical practice. Seven out of ten patients seen by medical practitioners for emotional problems are diagnosed to have depression.

Although observed for thousands of years, there has never been a greater incidence of depression. Democracy, freedom, opportunity, affluence, medical advancements, and major industries geared to the pursuit of pleasure, have not been able to stem a growing tide of unhappiness, sadness, and despair. And with or without professional help, all too many people have been unsuccessful in overcoming their difficulties. We have failed to provide adequate measures for the prevention and treatment of depression.

19

The reasons for our failure are many. It has been difficult to define accurately and classify depression. There has also been much confusion because of differing theories provided by authorities within the field. The biggest problem, however, has been the widespread use of "singular" treatment methods for different types of depression; that is, treating all forms of depression in one manner. This book addresses the problem of single modality treatment and stresses the importance of a wholistic approach, as well as other factors pertaining to this vast and important subject.

Body, mind, and spirit are the tripartite makeup of man. Yet, most of today's treatments are directed to heal only one of these parts. Modern treatment of depression has become compartmentalized and fragmented to the detriment of millions of sufferers. One fact, in particular, has become clear: drug treatment is definitely *not* the only, nor the primary solution for depression. The majority of depressed persons—about 75 percent—suffer from so-called mild and moderate depression.

A 1986 six-year-research project (Collaborative Research Treatment Program) conducted by the National Institute of Mental Health showed psychotherapy as equally effective as drug therapy for most forms of depression. And that is very good news, especially in light of side effects and adverse effects that are associated with drug treatment. On the other hand, it is also good news that in certain cases of severe depression—depressive illness—medical treatment can be extremely helpful.

Neither psychology, nor medicine, however, can resolve the spiritual malaise that is contributing to an age of sadness. Depression is multifaceted and treatment must be wholistic— *body, mind,* and *spirit.*

Although depression is a complex disorder, lasting solutions can be discovered through the careful application of faith and reason. Depressed people are in need of both positive and rational thinking. They need to believe that victory over depression is possible, and know how to obtain it.

This book presents a wholistic three-step approach to physical, psychological, and spiritual problems. All of the following observations regarding depression are valid in part:

1. In simple terms, depression is merely a negative emotion due to self-defeating perceptions and appraisals. However, it may also be a sign of serious, even malignant disease.
2. Depression can either be a description of the "blahs" or "blues"; or it can be a description of a neurotic or psychotic disorder. Depression can be mild, moderate, or severe. It can be harmless or life threatening.
3. Depression can be caused by physical, mental/emotional, and/or spiritual problems.
4. Depression can be found in babies less than one year old, or in people who are over one hundred years old.
5. Depression can be caused by our self-defeating thinking or by separation from God, but it can also result from a shortage (or malfunctioning) of essential neurotransmitters in the brain. It can result from major variables in atmospheric pressure, or perhaps lack of sunlight during the late fall and winter. The latter depression known as seasonal affective disorder (SAD), is possibly the result of underproduction of melatonin. Depression can also result from "rare" conditions such as mercury leaking from fillings in our teeth.
6. Depression can be an inspiration to some creative people, or it can end in suicide for many others.
7. Depression can be a disorder, or merely a symptom of a disorder. For example, any of the symptoms of stress can be indicative of depression, and any of the symptoms of depression can be indicative of stress, or some other specific ailment.
8. Depression may be readily observed by any lay person in some individuals, or be so masked that only experts can recognize it.
9. Depression has been treated with dozens of different drugs, shock treatments, psychotherapy, and a host of other treatments. Many of these have proved inappropriate and of little or no value.

A brief review of these divergent observations emphasizes why depression is often misunderstood and misdiagnosed. The bottom line is that depression is a multifaceted disorder, which can result from personal choice, physical disorders, loss of spiritual direction, or may simply be inherited through the genes. Yet each individual plays a major role in cause, cure, and prevention of this universal disorder.

The good news is that depression can often be prevented, and with proper diagnosis and treatment, nearly always be cured (Pfizer Health Care Series, "Health" September 1986). A great danger to effective treatment is getting stuck in a one-sided approach and becoming blinded to other more appropriate treatments.

If this book helps the reader understand that depression is not necessarily caused by flu, self-pity, or sin, but that any one of these, or any one of hundreds of other sources, could be involved as primary stress factors contributing to depression, it will have made a major contribution.

The book does more, however. It shows that we can be *victorious over depression if we deal with it from a wholistic point of view*. Hundreds of possible stressors found in our physical, psychological and/or spiritual life may be sources of depression. Properly identifying and removing these stressors will help a person achieve full victory. The following are some *random* examples of specific stressors and what can be done about them:

1. If the depression results from low norepinephrine levels in our brain due to the use of reserpine, we may be able to substitute this drug, or use a lower dosage.
2. If the depression is caused by leaking mercury from fillings in our teeth, then we may have the fillings replaced or repaired.
3. If the depression is caused by allergies to milk, chocolate, chemicals, or other substances, then we simply eliminate them.
4. If the depression is caused by low blood sugar, we may change our diet, take food supplements, and begin a more relaxed lifestyle.
5. If the depression is caused by self-condemnation, then we'd better remember that there is no condemnation for those who are in Christ Jesus (Rom. 8:1).
6. If the depression is caused by self-defeating thinking, we can learn to replace this kind of thinking with life-enhancing thinking.

As you go through *Victory Over Depression,* you should take the steps of obtaining medical advice and professional counseling. You may also consider additional specialized help such as vocational and spiritual counseling.

It is not easy to find a physician to help you consider all three areas of body, mind, and spirit. Therefore, you may need to consult with several persons. There is no objection to this approach as long as you let each person know who you are seeing. This assures that consultation between different specialists will be coordinated. On occasion, you will experience opposition, particularly from those who might wish to cling to a singular approach. This should neither surprise you nor cause discouragement. Remember that each of these specialists are your employees; treat them with respect, for each provides valuable assistance in their specialty.

This book will widen your horizon and increase your choices for the best possible treatment of depression. It will help you to have a greater understanding of depression, a deeper commitment to personal change and growth, and a more successful participation in the treatment program of your choice. Professionals in the field of mental health will also benefit, as well as pastoral counselors and others who deal with depressed persons.

Because this practical handbook is comprehensive and up-to-date, it is important to become acquainted with the Appendices, Glossary, and Index at the end of the book. Here you will find features on diet and medications, a directory of organizations, hundreds of definitions of terms, and quick references to every important aspect of depression as it affects body, mind, and/or spirit. Twenty years of experience has brought me to the conviction that the wholistic approach is the sanest, safest, and most effective way to treat depression. May God bless you as you study this book.

1

What Is Depression?

$\mathbf{B}$ecause of the increasing incidence of depression over the past several years, a balanced approach is urgently needed in the understanding and treatment of depression. This is particularly true in our present writings, where there appears to be a great lack of a balanced approach. Practitioners who have written in this area tend to present only a singular point of view, based on their own particular theoretical orientation.

The Psychological and Spiritual Models

An example would be those who believe with Sigmund Freud that depression is primarily "anger turned inward," as the result of an ongoing war between the id, ego, and super-ego. For treatment they may employ such psychoanalytical methods as free association. On the other hand, those who believe that depression is "learned helplessness" may use behavior modification as their treatment of choice. Others who believe that depression is exclusively caused by a separation from God employ strictly spiritual-treatment methods.

The Medical Model

In the medical world, where depression is usually seen as a biochemical reaction (Fieve 1975; Greist and Jefferson 1985; Kline 1974), the treatment often consists of powerful drugs such as *Lithonate,* or turns to *tricyclic antidepressants* such as Aventyl, Elavil, Norpramin, Sinequan, and Tofranil. Medical treatment may also consist of antidepressant drugs known as *MAO Inhibitors,* such as Marplan, Nardil, or Parnate. Less frequent use has been made of *sleep treatment.* On the extreme in the medical model, we find limited use of *shock treatment,* and various experimental treatments such as *insulin coma therapy.*

Nature of Depression Not Fully Understood

The treatment of depression is often haphazard because it is difficult to construct a reliable picture of the causes of depression.

Dr. H. Keith Brodie, president of the American Psychiatric Association, stated in *U.S. News & World Report* (January 24, 1983) that even in those cases where a biochemical abnormality was found to accompany depression, it was not determined what caused this abnormality. Said Dr. Brodie, "We don't know if the mind thinking depressed thoughts causes these bio-chemical changes, or whether the chemical imbalance in the brain is what causes the depression."

Hypothesis of this Book

This book views depression as a multifaceted psychosomatogenic (body, mind, spirit) stress disorder, characterized by self-defeating perceptions, thoughts, and emotions.

It is essential to recognize that we have many types of depressions, with varied sources and complexities. The use of singular explanations applied to all types of depression simply does not work. Before commencing with an analysis of the origins and symptoms of depression, keep in mind the following observations:

1. *Depression is a disorder of the total person.*

Depression is a disorder affecting the total person. The signs and symptoms of depression are only a reflection of an underlying illness which touches body, mind, and spirit. Before victory over depression can be gained, we must discern how the illness affects each component of body, mind, and spirit.

When practitioners follow a single treatment modality, they often fail to recognize that depression might be a manifestation of a number of somatic and psychogenic disorders, resulting from specific social, mental, emotional, spiritual, and/or physical stressors.

The tendency at one end of the spectrum is to deal only with "feelings." This is particularly dangerous, as was pointed out by Brandon (1969): "Those who are most prone to rhapsodize about their emotions and to speak disparagingly of reason, are those who are most incompetent at introspection and most ignorant of their emotions."

A lot of deception (both of themselves and of those they treat) results when counselors are not aware of the complexity of the problem. Many people, including Christian practitioners, make claims which, on careful examination, cannot be substantiated by either the Bible or by science. We should constantly remind ourselves that God is a God of wisdom and that his people "are destroyed for lack of knowledge" (Hos. 4:6).

Some people reject reason; others reject faith. But the Word of God stresses a marriage of faith *and* reason. Victory over depression can more readily be achieved when faith and reason are joined together.

Although depression is more prevalent than ever before (as mentioned earlier, 35 million sufferers in the USA), we now also have more knowledge about how people can be helped. Depression has plagued mankind for thousands of years. We find various accounts of it in the Bible, and in massive books, such as Robert Burton's *Anatomy of Melancholy,* which was written in the early seventeenth century. Although we now have a better grasp on the subject, the development of new theories regarding causation and techniques for treatment still tend, unfortunately, to be myopic in their approach.

Recent books tell of those who through one approach or another, obtained personal victory over depression. A word of caution is necessary. Although these books are generally of value to the reader, they almost universally tend to generalize that what happened to the authors will also happen to others. They reach this faulty conclusion by assuming that all depressions and depressed people are alike. But we are dealing with a complex and multifaceted problem, where no singular approach is satisfactory and often is dangerous.

Many people suffer not only from a clearly defined depression, but also from long-standing personality disorders, or from social and spiritual problems. Each case must be individually analyzed (considering the whole person) to reach an accurate diagnosis and to treat the particular type of depression. The starting place must be to consider the individual's spiritual, psychosocial, and medical background.

2. *Depression is a stress disorder.*

Depression is a multifaceted general stress disorder, resulting from excessive physical, emotional, spiritual, mental, and/or social stress. Excessive stress is the amount of stress an individual is unable or unwilling to deal with in one of the three main components of his or her makeup: body, mind, and/or spirit. Researchers have discovered that spiritual problems, lack of sleep or essential nutrients, or loss of loved ones could all become sources of excessive stress that can prove disastrous to any individual at any given time. Depression is no respecter of persons: we are all subject to an attack.

Hans Selye in his classic textbook *The Stress of Life* (1978) lists "depression" as one of the first observable indicators of excessive stress. This excessive stress, according to Selye, is due to deranged hormonal secretions. Interestingly, virtually all observable stress signs are manifested in various types of depression. The interrelationship of excessive stress and depression, and vice versa, is obvious. Hans Selye (1978) points out that stress is "the non-specific response of the body to any demand made upon it." He makes it clear that any stressor, whether pleasant or unpleasant, produces a certain general demand on the body for adaptation.

Stress cannot be avoided. The production of this book would have been impossible without some stress. There is no life without stress. It is part of normal living. The key is how the entire person reacts to a given stressor. There are both positive and negative reactions.

"General stress disorder" refers to excessive stress; that is the amount of physical, emotional, mental, social, and/or spiritual stress we are unable or unwilling to deal with. Indeed, when excessive stress is negative, damaging, unpleasant, or disagreeable, it is "distress."

Also, stress as well as distress has a physical involvement regardless of its source. It is impossible to experience stress or distress, or any emotive feeling, other than biochemically. This does not mean that we do not have mental anguish, worry, or sorrow, but there is always measurable or observable physical involvement.

Selye's general adaptation syndrome (G.A.S.) consists of three steps, or reactions, namely, (1) *alarm,* (2) *resistance,* and (3) *exhaustion.* Dealing with this stress syndrome also involves three steps, namely, (1) *discerning* (being aware of the stressors); (2) *deciding* (setting up a treatment plan); and (3) *doing* (following up on the decisions).

The G.A.S. shows that the body adapts only for so long and only for so much. Every person has a definite breaking point. We have a limited amount of energy for adaptation. How long our body and mind will be able to adapt to or resist stress depends on the intensity and duration of the given stressors, our physical condition, and our value system. Sooner or later exhaustion, which is physical and psychological illness, takes place. Stages of exhaustion are reversible only for given periods of time, and complete exhaustion will eventually lead to death.

The general adaptation syndrome is the opposite of homeostasis (specific body responses to specific stimuli) which is designed to maintain our body's internal physiological environment. In the G.A.S. there is an absence of constancy and initially blood pressure and blood glucose are higher than normal. The G.A.S. is designed to deal with ongoing emergencies. Too many real or imagined emergencies will eventually exhaust our bodies, especially our endocrine system, and in particular our adrenal glands.

Depression is a general stress disorder because of the intimate connection of proper brain functioning with the proper functioning of the endocrine system. We know that the hypothalamus, adrenal glands, pituitary gland, and other glands play a major role in a number of endogenous depressions, and some role in "all" forms of depression. This will be discussed in greater detail later in this book.

3. *Depression is a thinking disorder.*

In the Bible it is clear that depression is a thinking disorder—that we are what we think (*see* Prov. 23:7). Some specialists in the field of depression have come to similar conclusions and maintain that most depressive illness is the result of thought disturbances such as magnification, misinterpretation, and negative interpretation (Beck 1979; Burns 1980).

Other mental health experts like Maultsby (1984) and Hauck (1976) emphasize that self-defeating thinking precedes depression. Regardless of the theoretical persuasion followed, or whatever treatment modality is employed, self-defeating thinking is a definite component of depression.

Jesus stated that we are condemned or justified by the way we speak (Matt. 12:37), and a proverb states "Pleasant words are as an honeycomb, sweet to the soul, and health to the bones (Prov. 16:24)." We determine our emotive feelings and actions by the way we perceive, think, and speak. Along with this, thinking is also a physiological activity. Whenever a negative physical factor interferes with the brain cells, clear thinking is disrupted. For example, disease, physical trauma, nutritional deficiencies, or toxicity impair the ability to think rationally.

Nevertheless, the most reasonable view of depression is that it invariably involves self-defeating thinking (Beck 1979; Burns 1980; Maultsby, 1984). This holds true for exogenous (externally caused) as well as endogenous (internally caused) depressions, whether primarily from major illnesses, metabolic disturbances, physical trauma, nutritional deficiencies, biochemical disorders, poisoning, or allergies.

4. *Depression often seems to disappear without treatment.*

Some depressions disappear without any observable treatment. This is another reason to go slow in giving a certain approach credit for a so-called cure. Many depressions might have cleared up a lot faster without interference. It is no mystery that every approach and every practitioner can claim various degrees of success in helping depressed people. This is especially so when they are dealing with exogenous depression.

There is often little reason to believe that a particular treatment was responsible for success. I have seen depressions prolonged by the misuse of various therapies, such as talk therapy, when people excessively dwell on the past. Frequently recreating the problems of the past can lead to dysfunctional emotional relief. One of my clients had previously gone to a clinic for two years, and every week (following the visit to the clinic) would be in tears for a day. How many times do people go for "counseling" only to feel worse?

Why depressions sometimes disappear is not mysterious. Individuals by a natural inclination for health and survival, consciously or unconsciously, begin to apply positive measures to reduce stress. If an individual was suffering from a chemically (such as natural gas) induced depression, then merely leaving the house (or other source of the problem), would alleviate the depression. If the depressed person has been on a wrong diet, then a change in diet would help relieve the depression (Philpott and Kalita 1980). If the person is suffering from a certain lack (such as, recreation, socialization, or stimulation), then any positive change in these areas, for example, dining out, jogging, swimming, walking, or joining the choir, could have a beneficial effect. The latter holds true primarily for the milder forms of depression. Depressions primarily related to a loss usually disappear when this loss has been compensated.

5. *Depression is often mistreated.*

The mistreatment of depression has been discussed by a number of authors, such as Abrahamson and Pezet (1977); Cleave (1974); Lesser (1981); Mackarness (1976, 1980); Newbold (1975); and Sheinkin and Schachter (1980).

Certain treatments are counterproductive, and could be dangerous or even life threatening. Depressions should never be treated with the use of alcohol, sinful escapes, retreat in seclusion, or by any other obviously dangerous method. Frequently overlooked, but very wrong, is the treatment of depression without a thorough physical examination. *Any person who is suffering from depression needs a thorough physical examination by a competent physician.* A complete physical examination must include a review of systems as well as laboratory tests. A complete blood profile, including a GTT (Glucose Tolerance Test) and possibly further studies for chemical and food allergies, and for metabolism, might also be indicated. Unfortunately, some general practitioners and psychiatrists prescribe antidepressants and antipsychotic drugs without a proper physical examination and a reasonable diagnosis of the problem.

Obviously all these tests might not be necessary for people with identifiable serious losses who are clearly undergoing exogenous depressions. Nevertheless, whenever *any* depression continues beyond a few days, then it is necessary to see a physician. As you study this book, you will understand that medical advice and drug treatment are not necessarily synonymous. The treatment of depression must first of all start with the depressed person who, whenever possible, should insist on playing the primary role in the treatment and resolution of the depression.

The treatment of depression with antidepressants can make a person dependent on the drug, less able to think rationally (and make sound decisions), and less capable of dealing with objective reality. Many patients have started with a mild antidepressant drug, only to become more and more ill and to eventually have psychotic symptoms. Treatment for these symptoms could then mask any of the original sources.

Through the use of drugs (legal and/or illegal) a mild case of depression can actually turn into a serious one. No tranquilizers or antidepressants are harmless. The use of these drugs must be closely supervised and undertaken only for short periods of time and always in conjunction with other forms of treatment. (Read carefully the section entitled *Special Care Is Required in the Use of Drugs for Depression,* beginning on page 101).

Mistreatment of depression can occur not only under physicians and psychiatrists, but also under teachers, pastors, psychologists, and counselors. I have seen cases where depressed persons suffering from endogenous depressions received only spiritual counseling and found themselves more depressed and even suicidal. Obviously the feelings of worthlessness, self-blame and guilt will increase when our faith seems to fail, and it appears that we are outside the will of God.

On the other hand, the reverse holds true. I have seen people treated with various forms of psychotherapy and/or drug therapy who only got worse. What such people really needed was a relationship with God and meaning in their lives. They suffered from spiritual depression. Drugs in those cases only made the situation worse.

6. *Depression is a complex disorder.*

Most depressed people suffer from multiple symptoms, due to psychological, social, metabolic, nutritional, spiritual, and other problems. It matters little in this case if we have a specific answer to the question (which has been posed by Dr. Brodie, *U.S. News & World Report,* January 24, 1983, as mentioned earlier) whether biochemical changes come first or if self-defeating thinking comes first.

Massive evidence collected in the field of psychosomatic and somatopsychogenic medicine, clearly indicates that physical disorders can lead to mental and emotional disorders and vice versa. A healthy spiritual life also requires a healthy mind. Neither the seriously impaired mind nor the unrenewed mind shows spiritual discernment and/or discretion. We need to pay attention to the total person. Anything less is not good enough.

In a narrow sense depression is a negative emotive feeling, manifested by angry helplessness, despair, and dependency. Depression thus defined is directly related to our perceptions and cognitions. In a broader sense, however, depression is a multifaceted general stress disorder that is manifested in numerous mental, emotional, social, intellectual, physical, and spiritual symptoms. In the narrower definition of depression, we tend to deal with one aspect of human behavior. In the broader and more appropriate definition, we deal with many aspects of human behavior.

7. *Depression often responds to psychotherapy or drugs.*

The 1986 six-year, ten-million-dollar *Collaborative Research Treatment Program,* conducted by the National Institute of Mental Health (NIMH), has shown that psychotherapy is equally as effective as drug therapy for most forms of depression, with the exception of depressive illness (*see* Glossary) such as bipolar depression and unipolar depression. This research data supports day-to-day clinical and other empirical findings that there is little justification for the use of drugs for the overwhelming majority of people who are depressed. Considering the many *side effects* and *adverse reactions* that the manufacturers report in the *Physician's Desk Reference* (1986), the use of drugs for depression must not be the first, or certainly not the only, approach to the problem. Drug treatment, however, has proven important in the treatment of *depressive illness* (*see* Glossary).

8. *Depression has many sources.*

Because of the many types of depressions, *true* depression can be difficult to identify. For that reason, depression is sometimes called "the great imposter."

Rarely do we find only one symptom in true depression, and therefore we look for clusters of symptoms called "syndromes." A typical depressive syndrome consists of sadness, pessimism, and slowness of thought, speech, and movement. In association with this syndrome, various mental, spiritual, emotional, social, and physical variables can be identified, such as those listed on page 35.

9. *Depression can be fatal.*

Although the majority of depressed people do not attempt suicide, nevertheless a large number of depressed people of all ages do so. Fortunately the number of attempted suicides far outweighs the number of actual suicides; yet the real tragedy is that virtually all suicide *can be prevented.*

Suicide in Adults. Every day about one thousand people in the world commit suicide, and daily as many as eight thousand people attempt to kill themselves. In the USA it has been estimated that from twenty to fifty thousand people of all ages each year succeed in committing suicide. They have fallen prey to an alternative that is no alternative at all.

Contrary to popular opinion, most suicide does not occur in the dreary winter months, but rather in the springtime. In the USA male suicide outweighs female suicide three to one. The reason for this difference may well be found in the fact that 75 percent of the women who try to kill themselves do not succeed, while 75 percent of the men who try to kill themselves do succeed.

Most suicide in this country is directly related to serious depression. It is the ultimate expression of feeling totally lost. We find "loss" at the center of all depressions, whether this is loss of physical balance, psychological integrity, or loss of spiritual direction. Serious depression is also behind the higher-than-average suicide rates among professionals. This is a particularly frightening phenomenon among physicians, especially American women physicians. Sixty-five percent of American women physicians are said to suffer from mood disorders, reflected in a suicide rate four times as high as that of other females. Psychiatrists, too, are at great risk, with a suicide rate that is the highest

Loss of Physical Balance

Physical Variables
Allergies
Bacteria
Chemical imbalances
Metabolic deficiencies
Trauma to central nervous system
Viruses
Weather conditions

Loss of Psychological Integration

Emotional Variables
Anger
Anxiety
Fear
Guilt

Mental Variables
Lack of knowledge
Lack of love
Lack of self-esteem
Perfectionism
Thinking disorders
Other pity
Self-blame
Self-pity

Social Variables
Divorce
Lack of friends
Overcrowding
Physical isolation
Separation
Unemployment

Loss of Spiritual Direction

Spiritual Variables
Lack of fellowship with God
Lack of fellowship with other believers
Lack of meaning in life
No assurance of salvation
Various forms of bondage

Note: These are only a few of the hundreds of possible physical, emotional, mental, social, and spiritual variables.

among medical specialists (*The Merck Manual* 1982). These statistics highlight my observations about drugs: they are not the widely heralded solution to unhappiness and despair, especially if the source of sadness is psychological or spiritual.

In the USA, suicide is currently the tenth leading cause of death. Because of an ever-growing increase in the suicide rate among all age groups, we may expect this to change again in the future. It could change for the better, however, once we start to deal wholistically with our mental-health problems. Historically, suicide has been defined as an aggressive or hostile act against oneself. This is really not a good definition, as most of the people who attempt suicide, or those who succeed, did not really want to die at all. Rather than a hostile act, it is the ultimate irrational act. It is an irrational act to be self-defeating or self-destructive, for everything in nature and in man cries out for perpetual life-enhancement.

Physical, mental, and spiritual stress lies behind every form of depression and also suicide. There are at least two questions to be considered in every case of suicide: *What kind of life style did the person have? What kind of thinking was predominant?*

Suicide involves not only psychological and spiritual factors but very real (and ultimately measurable) biological factors as well. Loss of physical balance, which plays such a significant part in many forms of depression, is undoubtedly also involved in many cases of suicide. The warning signs for suicide overlap to a great extent with the signs and symptoms of depression. Here are some suicide warning signs:

Mental-Emotional Indicators.
Any of the symptoms listed in the section entitled Symptoms of Depression in Adults (chapter 3), and in particular, despondency, hopelessness, loneliness, and worthlessness.

Behavioral Indicators.
Excessive use of alcohol or other legal or illegal drugs. Giving away valued possessions. Talking about death and/or suicide. Abrupt changes in behavior, including aggressiveness, insomnia, lethargy, withdrawal, lack of interest in personal appearance. Sudden euphoria following a period of utter hopelessness. Difficulty relating to others. Inability to cope with stressful job or marriage situation.

Suicide in Children and Adolescents. A sad phenomenon in our modern society is the steady increase in childhood depression and suicide. Feelings of alienation and desperation plague our youth, who seek escape through substance abuse, delinquency, crime, and violence. Perhaps nowhere do we find a greater expression of the unhappiness and sadness of our youth than in the cold suicide statistics. Teenage suicide has gone up by 66 percent in the seventies and is still climbing in the eighties. The suicide rate for children, ages five to fourteen, has *doubled* from three-tenths per one hundred thousand in 1970 to six-tenths per one hundred thousand in 1985.

Every year about half a million young people try to kill themselves, and more than five thousand succeed in doing so. This means every two hours a child commits suicide in the USA! Children as young as five years old have committed suicide. Reports on two-and-a-half-year olds probably are not true suicides.

I disagree with those scientists who tell us we don't know why we have so much suicide. The truth is that we are breeding despair and reaping the fruits thereof. We are raising our children in a magical make-believe world of television, instant happiness, power, and wealth, and are imparting unrealistic, irrational, and dangerous values. The responsibility for our present sick society is totally that of the adults. Excessive stress factors are constantly building up in the lives of our youth. An endless cycle of excessive competition alternates with escape in questionable music and entertainment.

Children kill themselves because they are excluded from the world of responsible adults. They feel lost and see no way out of their anxieties, fears, frustrations, and feelings of worthlessness. They have not been taught how to have a sense of personal worth, and they have no idea about their inner resources. They lack proper role models, wholesome direction, spiritual guidance, and discipline. There are scores of reasons why our youth can easily depress themselves. Merely living in our self-seeking society is enough to depress anyone who does not know about the higher reasons for living. Life without God and goals is meaningless indeed.

Children find themselves in an exceedingly competitive but meaningless struggle for survival. It is not the dread of nuclear annihilation but the loss of meaning, love, hope, opportunity, and manifold other losses that lead to the psychological disintegration of our youth. Add to this the absence of any spiritual direction and the disintegration of the family, and we have plenty of ingredients for depression.

Vulnerability for suicide is not necessarily related to the degree of depression. A child can be very depressed and have little, if any, vulnerability for suicide, while another less-depressed child may have great vulnerability for suicide. The main reasons for this seem to be of a biological nature, for example disturbed hypothalamic-adrenal functioning. The dexamethasone test (mentioned in Appendix 3) might be helpful in identifying depressed children who are more vulnerable to suicide.

Whereas social-environmental, as well as some genetic factors, are responsible for increased "vulnerability" to depression and suicide in our youth, we must not overlook two facts:

1. Whatever the motivation for child suicide, be it escape, revenge, manipulation, or some form of avoidance, it is still based on *irrational thinking*.
2. Thinking (rational and/or irrational) has not only psychological and spiritual aspects, but also physical aspects.

Major sources for childhood depression and suicide may also be found in physical disturbances that are directly related to improper diet. Dr. Laurence Schwab (1984) looked for a common denominator among those who had committed suicide and those who had tried to commit suicide. He described the common denominator as "rotten nutrition and an imbalanced body." His findings confirm my theory about depression, that is, that it is a body-mind-spirit stress disorder. Excessive stress may lead to depression, and unbearable stress may lead to suicide. Dr. Schwab tells us that "inadequate nutrition was the predominant factor. Sugar was a constant companion. Eighty-nine percent said 'yes' to caffeine. Alcohol was a must for 76 percent. Drugs, especially among seventeen- to twenty-four year olds, ranked high. Eighty-five percent had experimented, and 78 percent were deeply involved with very heavy drugs."

Youth suicide is the normal and logical outcome of an irrational lifestyle, one which is only a reflection of our sick society.

In this country we have about 1.3 million teenagers (ages twelve to seventeen) who have a serious drinking problem, and many more who get involved with some kind of crime. Suicide is the "ultimate" irrational act that can only be committed by a person who is in an irrational frame of mind.

Later in this book I will explain how food influences mood, and how shortages of essential vitamins, minerals, and amino acids may make it difficult for a child, adolescent, or adult to think rationally. Drugged, glucose-imbalanced, and neurotransmitter-depleted brains cannot think rationally and cannot cope with the excessive stresses of our competitive and conflict-ridden society. Depression in children and adolescents is the outcome of vulnerability and choice.

Any evaluation of depression must recognize the potential seriousness. It can be a matter of life or death. Following are some warning signs of suicide in children and adolescents:

Mental-Emotional Indicators
Any of the signs and symptoms of depression described in the section entitled Signs and Symptoms of Depression in Children and Adolescents, (chapter 3), and in particular anger, apathy, despondency, feelings of inferiority, and denial of objective reality.

Behavioral Indicators
Disobedience, drug or alcohol use, dropping out of activities, disruptiveness, difficulty in communicating with family, friends, and peer group, cutting classes in school, giving away valued possessions, sexual promiscuity, previous suicide attempts, temper tantrums, truancy, running away, withdrawal from family and friends.

I have taken some extra time to discuss suicide so as to emphasize the seriousness of many depressions. *Depression can be fatal.* The good news is that it does not have to be so at all. I will show that unhappiness of any kind or severity is a problem of body, mind, and spirit, and that treating the "total" person will bring the needed results.

Throughout I also remind the reader that treatment of depression requires professional help, and this holds especially true for those who are suffering from suicidal thoughts. There are many sources for help in every community, and these include physicians, ministers, and specialized agencies, for example, mental-health centers. The telephone book usually provides hotline or crisis center telephone numbers which are answered twenty-four hours a day. There are also suicide crisis centers and during business hours the American Association of Suicidology (303-692-0985) will provide the address and telephone number of the nearest suicide prevention center in any given area. Any hospital emergency room may also be contacted for assistance, day or night. For parents of depressed teenagers I recommend a book by Kathleen McCoy, *Coping With Teenage Depression* (New American Library, 1982). The book has a lot of good practical advice, although it fails to recognize spiritual problems and the myriad of problems caused by hypoglycemia, inadequate nutrition, and sensitivity or intolerance to foods, and/or food additives. Of value is the Appendix in Kathleen McCoy's book, which lists counseling centers, suicide-crisis intervention centers, hotlines, medical clinics for adolescents, and special help resources.

10. *Depression defies singular explanations.*

Depression is not a straightforward problem. We must not underestimate the complexity of depression. Extensive medical tests will indicate whether or not there is a biochemical basis for the depressed person's symptoms.

Even without positive test results from a medical examination, a person can still suffer from depression due to a faulty diet, lack of sleep, or allergies, and it is important not to overlook this. Finally, people can become depressed over injustices, loneliness, grief, unemployment, and numerous other sources. Hundreds of potential stressors could eventually lead to depression.

Whatever the stressors, however, there is always a thinking or attitude component involved in every case of depression. What is depression? From a narrower point of view, it is a negative emotive feeling manifested in angry helplessness and despair. From a broader point of view, depression is a multifaceted stress disorder manifested in numerous symptoms that are directly related to perceptions and cognitions, as well as neurobiological stimuli.

2

The Classification
of Depression

Because depression is such a multifaceted disorder, it is no surprise to find lack of agreement among experts in regard to causes, treatment, classification, and diagnosis of depression. This lack of agreement was highlighted in an excellent study conducted by Heather Wood MacFayden (1975) who reviewed seventy-nine scientific reports and concluded that "the reliability of most diagnostic labels is low and varies according to the frequency with which it is used and when it is used."

That so many people are confused about depression is understandable, for it is truly one of the more complex disorders. In describing depression it is best to avoid underestimating or overestimating the problem. A balanced approach is needed to help the millions of sufferers. We must be careful not to label the slightest case of the blues as depression, nor to ignore a serious case of depressive illness and see it merely as a passing midlife crisis. There are obvious differences in age of onset, origin, occurrence, and severity among various depressions. It is undoubtedly helpful to briefly consider depression by severity, origin, and type.

41

Classification by Severity

Mild Depression. Although it is frightening that perhaps as many as one in seven people in this country suffer from depression, we need to realize that most of them suffer from *mild depression.* This depression is the result of misinterpretations, negative interpretations, exaggerations, and other misperceptions and misappraisals, as well as a host of self-defeating ideas, attitudes, feelings, and actions. Usually depression is self-induced and self-maintained. People learn to be depressed, and they can learn to undepress themselves. The identifiable sources of mild depression include bitterness, greed, jealousy, resentfulness, hatred, self-pity, other pity, and self-blame.

Depression might be rampant in this country, however, not primarily as a physical disorder (although we have plenty of that), but rather as a disorder of mind and spirit. Mild depression can be eradicated by a healthier and more spiritual lifestyle. Drug treatment is often counterproductive, and at times leads to more serious forms of depression.

In mild depression there is plenty of sadness, unhappiness, bitterness, and anger. However, psychomotor retardation (slow, physical and mental responses), or serious physical complaints are usually less prominent. Mild depression is *primarily* of an exogenous nature and is sometimes referred to as normal depression.

Moderate Depression. No clear-cut line divides mild and moderate depression, as many of the symptoms overlap. In the case of moderate depression, however, we usually find people who have suffered serious disappointments and unfortunate (unhappy, negative, and hurtful), events in their lives. Whereas reactions to these events will involve perceptions and appraisals, we can usually identify real sources that would result in a traumatic effect on most people anywhere.

Other identifiable sources include such endogenous factors as diet, hormonal disorders, and allergies. It is not always possible to clearly separate mild depression from moderate depression. There are, however, definite characteristics to look for in moderate depression. These include such physical signs as a furrowed forehead, a rather serious facial expression, a stooped posture, and/or sudden weepiness. Psychological characteristics include self-defeating thinking as manifested in feelings of worthlessness, guilt, hopelessness, helplessness, self-pity, other pity, self-blame, and lack of self-esteem. In addition, we might find psychomotor retardation, a slowness of mental and physical responses (slow talking and moving). We also might find somatic complaints, including headaches, fatigue, and sleep difficulties. Drug treatment, if any, should be administered with care, as most cases of moderate depression will respond more permanently to psychotherapy. Moderate depression is *primarily* of an exogenous nature and is sometimes referred to as reactive or neurotic depression. (*See* the Glossary for a description of neurosis and neurotic depression).

Severe Depression. Most depressions are mild or moderate and the least number of depressions are severe. This type of depression is usually referred to as depressive illness. Severe depression can be distinguished from mild and moderate depression not only by the severity of the depressed mood, but also often by a lack of identifiable sources. A primary feature of severe depression is its endogenous nature. Yet, on other occasions some environmental stress may herald the onset of depressive illness. Symptoms of severe depression, also known as major depression, include severe sadness, and feelings of helplessness and hopelessness. In about 25 percent of the sufferers we also find hallucinations, such as hearing voices. Thoughts of worthlessness and suicide are frequently present. Severe depression includes agitated and involutional depression, but especially bipolar and unipolar depression. Both of these illnesses are described in more detail in the Glossary and Appendix 1. While clearly identifiable stressors are often absent in unipolar or bipolar depression, we find the opposite in the socalled *psychotic depressive reaction.* Here stressors are clearly identifiable. The main distinguishing feature between severe depression of a nonpsychotic nature, and severe depression of a psychotic nature is found in the absence or presence of serious perceptual cognitive distortions. For example, in psychotic depression we can usually identify hallucinations and delusions.

In schizophrenic depression we find perceptual-cognitive, and other distortions that might involve the auditory, olfactory, sight, tactile, and taste senses, as well as time and position.

Bipolar depressions, characterized by major up and down mood swings as described in Appendix 1 and the Glossary are usually considered psychotic depressions, but I believe we must be careful here. When a person does not lose touch with reality, I do not think it is proper to make a diagnosis of psychotic depression.

Drug treatment is often appropriate for severe depression; however, other treatment methods must also be applied, in particular psychotherapy, as well as somatic, spiritual and other treatment modalities, all of which will be discussed later. Remember, that as a rule, *severe depression is primarily of an endogenous nature and is often referred to as depressive illness.*

Classification by Origin. Two main divisions in depression are commonly accepted: an endogenous (internal) and an exogenous (external) one. Endogenous depression is primarily related to hereditary, to metabolic, toxic, or other factors within the body. In its most practical sense, the term *endogenous* refers to that which comes from within as opposed to that which comes from outside ourselves.

In the case of exogenous depression, we usually find that the depression is a mental/emotional reaction to something which has occurred in the environment (Hurst 1962). The term *exogenous depression* is often best reserved for those depressions that have a clear environmental basis.

Exogenous depression, however, is not necessarily the direct result of some real loss. Rather, general thinking habits (attitudes, beliefs, and cognitions) are primarily responsible for determining depressive reactions to real or perceived facts and/or events. Most mild and moderate depressions fall into the exogenous category. However, sometimes these depressions may also have primary endogenous sources.

The endogenous and exogenous divisions are used only in a pragmatic sense, to help identify the primary source of a depression. Ultimately, depression is a disorder of the whole person and whereas treatment might have to emphasize the primary source, we must not overlook secondary sources and reactions.

Classification by Type. In addition to considering *origin* (exogenous *versus* endogenous) and *severity* (mild, moderate, and severe), it is also useful to consider depressions by *type*. Depression and other mood disturbances, however, have been difficult to describe and classify. Ideal "textbook" cases are rare, and heterogenous symptoms are common. Observed behaviors are often most suitable for a classification system. Nevertheless, knowledge of origin, severity, and age of onset are helpful for the classification of depression by type.

The exact percentages of depression by type are not available. It is also unknown what exact percentages of depressions are primarily of a physical, psychological, or spiritual nature. Yet it is a fairly safe assumption that as many as 75 percent of depressions are primarily of a *psychological* nature. They are the result of self-defeating perceptions, thoughts, and behaviors (Brandt 1979, 1984). The other 25 percent are primarily the result of physical factors. All depressions, however, have a perceptual-cognitive component. Regardless of the origin, severity, or type of depression, and regardless of how limited, inaccurate, or otherwise impaired, perception and appraisal are involved.

Many types of depression can be distinguished. (Those identified with an asterisk* are commonly seen as a *depressive* illness. *See* Glossary.)

*Agitated depression

*Bipolar (manic) depression
   (manic phase, depressive phase, or mixed type)

Brain-allergy depression

Childhood depression

Climacteric depression

*Involutional depression

Metabolic depression

Narcissistic depression

Nutrient deficiency depression

Postnatal depression

Premenstrual syndrome depression

Psychosocial depression

Reactive depression

*Schizophrenic depression

Secondary depression

Senile depression

Spiritual depression

*Unipolar depression

Appendix 1 provides descriptions of these listed types of depression. Additional information may also be found in the Glossary, for example, under DSM-III.

The Symptoms of Depression

Before describing the symptoms of depression in adults and children, it is useful to keep in mind that depression is a *body-mind-spirit* disorder. Consequently we can identify various signs and symptoms that are specific to each area of our tripartite makeup. For example, in the *physical* area we might find depressive facial features, such as a furrowed forehead, drooping corners of the mouth, and/or a stooping posture. In addition there might be such physical symptoms as fatigue, or problems with eating, crying, sleep, or weight. In the *psychological* area we might find rather obvious changes in a person's usual behavior, such as lack of interest, lack of enjoyment, feelings of hopelessness, worthlessness, self-pity, self-blame, other pity, and remorse. In the *spiritual* area we might find a feeling of being separated from God, or feelings of condemnation, confusion, and/or guilt.

In this discussion the symptoms of depression in adults and children are listed separately.

48

Understanding Depression

Symptoms of Depression in Adults

Because of the many possible symptoms related to depression, only a total evaluation of physical, mental/emotional, and spiritual health will give a true picture of depression. Over one hundred possible symptoms of depression are listed below in alphabetical order. Of course, many of these symptoms pertain to other disorders, and it requires training and experience to make a proper diagnosis. A few of the more common symptoms are identified by an asterisk (*).

Agitation
Alcohol abuse
Allergies
*Anger
Anorexia
*Anxiety
*Apathy
Bacterial disease
Bitterness
Boredom
Chemical imbalances
Chest pains
Coldness of extremities
Constant need for
  reassurance
Constipation
Crying spells
*Decreased activity
Decreased breathing
Decreased heartbeat
Delusions
*Despair

Despondency
Difficulty concentrating
Difficulty facing new day
Difficulty falling asleep
Difficulty in comprehending
Difficulty sitting still
Difficulty staying asleep
Difficulty with decision
  making
Difficulty with job,
  housework, and so forth
Discontent
Disheveled appearance
Dislike of cooking
Dislike of eating alone
Dislike of going out
Dislike of physical
  appearance
Dislike of self
*Distress
Drug abuse
Dryness of mouth

Dullness
Excessive guilt feelings
Facial pains
*Fatigue
Fear of losing one's mind
Fear of others
Fear in general
Feelings of
    depersonalization
*Feelings of worthlessness
Financial worries
Forgetfulness
Friends are not important
*Future looks hopeless
Gastrointestinal difficulties
*General gloominess
Grief
Habitual underachievement
*Hallucinations
Headaches (band around the
    head, and so forth)
*Helplessness
*Hopelessness
Hostility
Hypochondriacal
    preoccupation
*Hypoglycemia
Hypomania
Inability to explain fears
Indecisiveness
*Insomnia
Irritability

*Irrational ideas
Irresponsibility
*Isolation
*Listlessness
Loneliness
Loss of appetite
*Loss of energy
*Loss of enjoyment
*Loss of interest
*Loss of libido
Loss of memory
*Loss of pleasure
Loss of self-confidence
Loss of self-control
*Loss of self-esteem
*Loss of self-respect
Loss of weight
*Magnification
*Misinterpretations
*Negative thinking
*Noticeable changes in
    behavior
Numbness in hands and
    feet
Nutritional deficiencies
*Overeating
*Pessimism
*Physical changes, aches,
    pains, and so forth
Preoccupation with death
*Pressure in head, neck, and
    so forth

*Procrastination
 Rejection of opportunities
*Retarded thinking
*Retardation (slowness)
*Remorse
*Ruminations
*Sadness
 Search for relief
*Self-accusation
*Self-blame
 Self-centerdness
*Self-denegration
*Self-deprecation
*Self-doubt
*Self-hatred

*Self-pity
*Sleep disturbances
*Social withdrawal
*Somberness
 Sorrow
 Suicidal attempts
 Suicidal thoughts
 Swollen, drooping eyelids
 Tingling of hands and feet
 Undereating
 Unusual thoughts
 Unusual urges
 Viral disease
*Waking up too early

Even if only a few of the items pertain to a given individual, the possibility of depression exists. In any case, whether symptoms are few or many the individual needs a thorough physical and psychological examination before an accurate diagnosis of depression can be made.

Symptoms of Depression in Infants, Children, and Adolescents

Depression strikes all age groups, and it is unfortunate that most books on this subject do not mention this. It is commonly believed that depression is peculiar to adults; nothing is further from the truth. Depression can start in babies less than one year old.

Known as anaclitic depression, it is usually the result of maternal deprivation. Babies deprived of affection from a mother or mother substitute for periods of less than three months usually recover without any detrimental effects. However, babies who suffer maternal deprivation for more than three months might suffer irreversible developmental damage.

Babies might also suffer from depressions that are not necessarily related to maternal deprivation. A number of babies born to loving parents might suffer from various forms of physical and/or psychological stress. Such stress might stem from prenatal, natal, and/or postnatal conditions. This could include physical problems of the mother, including poor health, the use of addictive substances, and/or psychosocial problems. Both the parents and the baby need to be seen by specialists as quickly as possible. The earlier corrective measures are instituted, the more reversible the condition will be.

More common, however, is depression in childhood and adolescence, where we find many of the symptoms previously described in adults. In addition, we usually find serious "behavioral problems," such as disobedience, temper tantrums, truancy, running away, feelings of inferiority, and denial of objective reality. Sexual promiscuity is also a likely symptom of depression in adolescents. The following are some common symptoms of depression in *children* and *adolescents:*

Agitation

Anger

Anorexia

Anxiety

Apathy

Boredom

Chemical imbalances

Constant search for new
    activities

Crying

Decrease of drive

Delinquency

Denial of objective reality

Difficulty in concentration

Diminished activities

Disobedience

Excessive compulsive
    behavior

Fatigue

Feeling isolated

Feelings of helplessness

Feelings of inferiority

Gastrointestinal difficulties

Guilt

Headaches

Hallucinations

Hyperkinesis

Hypochondriacal
    preoccupation

Ideas of self-accusation
Isolation
Lassitude
Low self-esteem
Paranoid delusions
Poor parental relationships
Poor peer relationships
Poor teacher relationships
Procrastination
Reluctance to be alone
Restlessness
Retardation of expressive
    motor responses
Running away

School phobias
Self-blame
Self-doubt
Self-pity
Sexual promiscuity
Sleep difficulties
Suicidal attempts
Suicidal gestures
Suicidal thoughts
Temper tantrums
Truancy
Withdrawal

This brief review of the signs and symptoms of depression underscores that it is a complex, multifaceted stress disorder. Knowledge of signs and symptoms, and information about severity, origin, types, age of onset (*see* Appendix 1), are all helpful in determining what specific type of depression a person might be suffering from. The sources of depression, as discussed in Part 2, provide further helpful guidance in the proper identification and successful treatment of depression.

Part **2**

The Sources of Depression

4

Physical Sources and Aspects of Depression

Our physical well-being is directly influenced by our emotional and spiritual well-being. Although many books have been written on this subject, not enough attention has been placed on the great influence our body has on the functioning of our mind.

Millions of people are suffering from a variety of mental-emotional disorders that are primarily physical in origin. Of all the varied types of depression listed in this book, the majority of them (fifteen types) are either primarily biochemical or have a major biochemical component.

About 25 percent of the depressed people in this country suffer from depressions that are primarily physical in nature. The 75 percent of the depressed who suffer from primarily perceptual-cognitive depressions are best helped by psychological and spiritual therapy, as explained in chapters 8 and 9.

Why We Need to Look for Physical Sources First

Victory over depression can be ours if we learn to apply three sequential steps to the three parts of our personality. The three steps are: learning to *discern* what the problem is; *deciding* how we can overcome the problem; and *doing* what we have decided needs to be done. In other words, don't start doing anything unless you have an insight into the problem and have developed a plan for dealing with it.

It is necessary that the steps are applied in the specific order of *physical, psychological,* and *spiritual* sources. First, we check our physical life. What physical symptoms do we have? Second, our mental/emotional life. What kind of self-defeating beliefs and attitudes do we cling to? Third, our spiritual life. Do we have meaning in our life because we know God? Have we walked away from fellowship with God? Are we confused about God?

Therapists must inquire into the physical history of the depressed person, such as lifestyle and eating habits. *Also, in every instance, the person must be referred for a complete physical examination and laboratory tests.* It is irresponsible for a therapist who deals with anyone suffering from depression not to refer that person for a physical examination. Fifteen of the twenty *types* of depression have a physical basis, and several of these are in the form of depressive illness, which require medical assistance. Some depressed people even suffer from malignant diseases or other less severe but nevertheless debilitating illnesses. These might have nothing whatsoever to do with their spiritual life or their perceptual-cognitive field. Allergies, the common cold, broken legs, and any other disorder, including depression, might come to any one of us.

In the majority of cases, people suffer from depression that is self-induced and self-maintained. They can be helped only by a new way of thinking and a new lifestyle. It is, however, a sign of good management to *first* eliminate the basics. If our TV set does not work, we first check the plugs, fuses, and wires before we tackle the big tube. If our car does not start, we check the battery, starter, and carburetor before taking the engine apart. If someone suffers from depression, we must not commence to take the psyche apart, but check into the basic essentials first.

It is of the utmost importance to deal with the total person (body, mind, and spirit), and for the sake of safety, effectiveness, and efficiency that we follow the steps exactly as discussed.

The Obvious and Not So Obvious Physical Sources

Hundreds of varied physical stressors could start the physiological-mental-emotional chain going that leads to depression. It is not feasible to list all of them, however, as we pay attention to the obvious, we must not overlook the not-so-obvious.

First and foremost, poor eating habits can be a major source of trouble. Food substances are grossly misused and abused in our society. Sometimes we get either too much or not enough of needed foods, but more frequently, we consume the wrong kinds of food. We need to know the following:

1. What we eat and drink affects our brain and, therefore, our moods, memory, pain threshold, and ability to reason.
2. What and how much we eat affects the blood glucose levels in our brain. When they are too high, too low, or change too abruptly, our ability to think, feel, and act rationally is altered. Glucose and oxygen are the fuels for our brain.
3. For proper functioning of our neurotransmitters, it is essential that we have certain nutrients circulating through our brain at all times. Some of these nutrients penetrate the brain cells and are necessary for the manufacture of neurotransmitters.
4. More than thirty different neurotransmitters enable the 100 billion nerve cells in our brain to communicate with each other. Some of these chemicals have been identified as playing a crucial role in the creation and elimination of some forms of depression. They include such important neurotransmitters as serotonin, norepinephrine, and acetylcholine.
5. The brain needs certain nutrients from the bloodstream to manufacture neurotransmitters. For example, serotonin requires the amino acid tryptophan. Norepinephrine requires the amino-acid tyrosine, and acetylcholine requires the B-complex vitamin choline.
6. A well-balanced diet and healthy lifestyle are essential to

get the necessary nutrients in our bloodstream to enable
our brain to function at optimum levels at all times. Many
people who suffer from depression also may need to supplement their diets as explained in chapter 7, and Appendix 7.
7. Not only what we eat, but also how we eat affects our ability
to provide essential nutrients to our brain. The digestive
process starts in our mouth.
8. Our overall health greatly affects the ability of our body to
manufacture essential nutrients. Of great concern are the
endocrine and gastrointestinal systems.

From the foregoing, it makes sense to apply the "three-step
formula" first to the body. No wonder we see such startling results
when this is done.

Many times excellent relief was obtained from various depressive symptoms by considering some obvious and sometimes not-
so-obvious physical sources. Let us examine some case histories.

Case History #1   The Depressed Woman
Who Wanted a Divorce

A young woman came in the early afternoon one day in an
agitated state. She had left her husband that day, wanted a divorce, and was making plans to leave for her parents' home in
another town. She told me also of several problems she had with
her four-year-old son. She talked in a high-pitched voice, trem-
bled and shook visibly, looked disheveled, and had a painful
expression on her face, and in general presented a picture of
sadness and helplessness. Upon inquiry, I found that she had not
had breakfast or lunch, that she did not usually eat breakfast or
lunch, and that she consumed much caffeine and nicotine.

I decided not to deal with this young woman unless she promised to go home, eat a good meal, and to do the same thing the
next day before seeing me. The next day I faced a well-composed
young woman, a smiling husband, and a playful young boy of
four years old. What happened? Had all the problems disap- ➤
peared? Were there no longer areas of friction in the marriage?

Of course there were still problems, and there were many areas
of friction; but in this case unusually rapid progress was made
in only a few sessions, and a happy family life was re-established.

The client's main problem was a low blood-sugar level, due to faulty eating habits and excessive stress. A rare case? Not at all. These cases happen with a steady frequency.

Case History #2   The Depressed Man in Prison

One day I visited a young man who was in jail because he created disturbances in public places, abused drugs, resisted arrest, and struck a police officer.

I found him to be anxious and depressed, but also friendly, intelligent, sincere, and eager to get out of "the mess." What had happened? Now in his early twenties, he had been in trouble since his late teens. I inquired into his lifestyle, including his eating habits. What did I find? An addiction not only to alcohol and other drugs, but also to nicotine, caffeine, and sweets. I suggested to one of his relatives that a Six-Hour Glucose-Tolerance

The Depressed Man in Prison

The glucose tolerance curve helped to reveal reactive hypoglycemia, which was eventually brought under control.

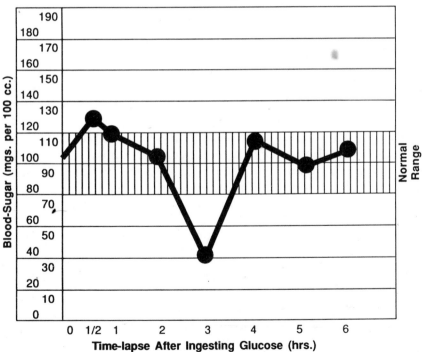

Test (GTT) be obtained (*see* Appendix 3). This was done with some difficulty. The results of this young man's GTT indicated a serious problem with hypoglycemia (*see* Glossary).

Further medical studies indicated there was no organic disease, but that he was indeed suffering from reactive hypoglycemia. After a number of setbacks and difficulties, the hypoglycemia was eventually brought under control with the proper diet, and this young man is now happily employed and has had no further difficulties. The results of this young man's Glucose Tolerance Test are on page 59.

Case History #3   The Middle-Aged, Depressed Client Who Wanted to Die

This client had several times attempted to commit suicide. These attempts, over several years, included drug overdoses and ingesting other poisons. The last attempt had once again been unsuccessful.

In great despair, the client asked me for help. The client had been ill for about twenty years, and had been treated with a long list of drugs, including Sinequan, Valium, Dilantin, Thorazine, Haldol, Elavil, and many others.

The client had been hospitalized on several occasions and traveled to some of the top clinics in the country for treatment. All had been to no avail, and the client remained suicidally depressed. To eliminate all doubts, I referred the client to a major diagnostic center. The report indicated nothing wrong except for agitation, anxiety, and depression found on a standardized psychological test. But a GTT had *not* been performed.

Although this client had demonstrated a mixture of symptoms and possible disorders, I was impressed from the beginning that there was both an organic and perceptual-cognitive disorder involved. Upon return from the diagnostic center, I insisted on a Six-Hour Oral Glucose Tolerance Test, which was performed locally. The test revealed reactive hypoglycemia. (Reactive hypoglycemia usually consists of an insulin sensitive response to certain nutrients or drugs. Hypoglycemia, however, is a complex subject and is discussed in greater detail in the Glossary.)

Some of the very best clinics in the country as well as many physicians during a twenty-year period had failed to administer this simple test. Result: (1) A depression seriously aggravated by the administration of wrong treatment: drugs that led to serious physical and mental side effects, including tardive dyskinesia (*see* Glossary); (2) Removal of hope and faith ("it is all in your head and you don't cooperate with us"); and (3) a continuation and aggravation of the original predisposing source of the depression.

By instituting corrective measures, which included a diet free of refined carbohydrates, megadoses of vitamins, minerals, and tryptophan, as well as regular scheduled exercise, dramatic results were obtained. It was too late to completely cure the tardive dyskinesia (a serious physical side effect of certain drugs), but the client recovered sufficiently to function relatively well at home and in daily surroundings. A stunning transformation indeed! Drug-free treatment proved to be the most successful method. Previously either hospitalized or housebound, the client was now free to move about.

The Middle-Aged Depressed Client Who Wanted to Die

The glucose tolerance curve helped to reveal reactive hypoglycemia, and borderline diabetes, both of which were readily controlled by diet.

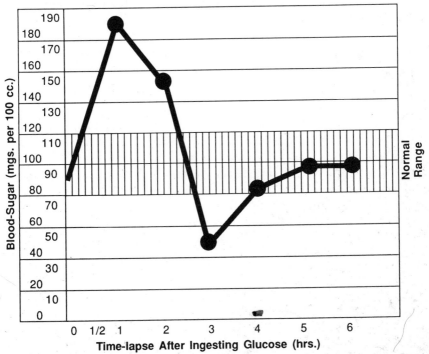

Case History #4   The Woman With Recurrent Depression

A young woman in her early thirties was seen for recurrent depressions that allegedly stemmed from several traumatic incidents in childhood and adolescence. She had been seen over the last fifteen years by several professionals, tried to commit suicide several times, and had been hospitalized on a number of occasions. Her symptoms were indicative of bipolar depression and schizophrenic depression. Treatment with drugs had been unsuccessful.

A review of her lifestyle and thinking patterns indicated self-defeating thinking, feelings, and actions. Her diet was poor. She was advised to make major changes in her overall lifestyle, including her spiritual, physical, mental/emotional, and social life.

The Woman with Recurrent Depression
The Glucose Tolerance Test revealed hypoadrenocorticism and anorexia nervosa, controlled by lifestyle changes, including emotional reeducation, healthful diet, food supplementation, and exercise.

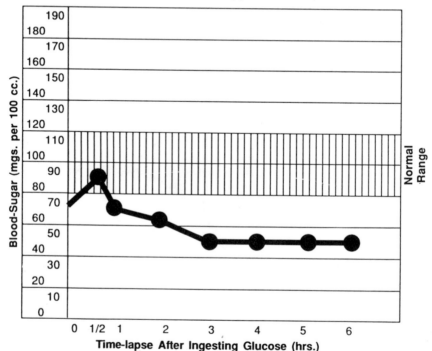

After a number of visits, however, she made only sporadic attempts to stick to any program of reeducative therapy, and she was not given a GTT. After many psychosocial problems and a severe marital crisis, followed by further hospitalizations and drug treatment, finally the GTT was obtained. The test results helped reveal hypoadrenocorticism and anorexia nervosa (*see* Glossary).

The client is doing well as long as she sticks closely to her diet, participates in regular exercise, and obtains sufficient sleep and rest. She is fully employed and completely able to function in society without hospitalization or drug treatment.

Case History #5   The Depressed Woman Who Believed She Was Going to Hell

A middle-aged woman believed that she had violated a religious custom of her particular church. Her minister reinforced her beliefs and called for repentance. She misunderstood the Scriptures and believed that she could not be forgiven and would surely go to hell. She was in a seriously agitated state and had a typical depressive syndrome including sadness, pessimism, slowness of thought, slowness of speech, and slowness of movement.

She presented a coherent picture of her troubles, both at home and with her church, and tenaciously clung to a number of distinctly self-defeating beliefs. I nevertheless elected to proceed first with the customary medical referral. A detailed medical report, including full laboratory analysis and a Six-Hour Glucose Tolerance Test, revealed no organic basis for her depression. However, the GTT showed findings consistent with reactive hypoglycemia.

I immediately suggested the proper diet, and enough progress was made within forty-eight hours to help her better understand some of her self-defeating beliefs. She rapidly gained insight in her physical, mental/emotional, and spiritual condition. Unfortunately, she did not receive necessary support and positive reinforcement at home or from her church, and failed to follow up with the wholistic program. She went to a psychiatrist who placed her on drug therapy. This greatly exacerbated her problems. It was not until she returned to the proper diet that her symptoms abated.

I have seen many people with suicidal depressions, psychosocial depressions, bipolar depressions, and even the common house-town-garden variety of the blues and the blahs who needed to make major changes in their diet before they were able to use their brains in a more self-enhancing manner.

We need drug-free brains to counsel ourselves in a more rational manner.* But we also need brains that have the proper quantity and quality of nutrients for the manufacture of essential neurotransmitters and the maintenance of proper levels of glucose.

The clients just discussed are some of the more obvious cases

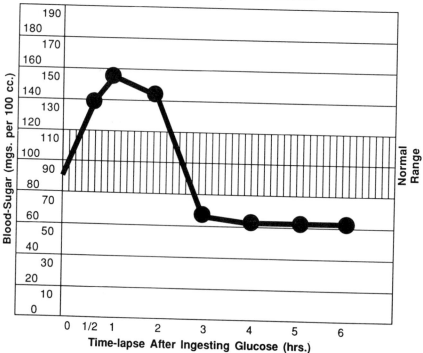

The Depressed Woman Who Believed She Was Going to Hell
The Glucose Tolerance Test revealed reactive hypoglycemia, which was eventually brought under control.

*An exception, of course, is the person who is on medication for depressive illness (see Glossary) precisely to help him or her to think better.

where it became quickly evident how powerful the interrelationship is between our body, mind, and spirit. Yet several physicians, psychiatrists, psychologists, and ministers had missed the obvious in these cases. I believe the reason for this is to be found in the singular approach that keeps many professional helpers short-sighted.

We often miss the obvious while searching for the complex. Be especially alert to the fact that our endocrine and central nervous systems are intimately connected with each other. What affects the one will affect the other. Newbold (1975) has pointed out that "any emotional symptom may be caused by low hormone levels." The same sentiments are echoed by many other experts, including Langer (1984).

The most prevalent physical sources center around metabolic disturbances, which in turn are primarily related to our lifestyle, and in particular our diet. Many depressions are primarily biochemical.

About 75 percent of our depressions are primarily of a non-organic nature. Of the remaining organic 25 percent only 10 to 15 percent are beyond personal control. In other words, we might rightly be held responsible and accountable for about 90 percent of our depressions. What's more, we can do *something* for all depressions.

Specific Physical Sources of Depression

The case histories discussed in this chapter show how glucose disturbance can be a primary physical source of depression. It must be stressed, however, that a glucose disturbance is only *one* of a large number of possible physical sources. In turn these are only *potential* stressors for depression. Physical sources include allergies, amino-acid deficiencies, disease, drugs, glandular dysfunction, heredity, malnutrition, mineral deficiencies, neurotransmitter deficiencies, overstimulation, poisoning, trauma, understimulation, vitamin deficiencies, unfavorable weather conditions, and yeast infections. (*See* Appendices 1 and 2.)

Poor diet is a common potential physical stressor for depression. For example, diets devoid of essential nutrients such as the amino-acids tryptophan, tyrosine, or phenylalanine, might lead to a shortage of the neurotransmitters serotonin, norepinephrine, and phenylethylamine respectively. A shortage of these neurotransmitters is believed to play a role in many cases of depression. Food allergies too, have been implicated as potential physical stressors for depression.

Chemical imbalances usually resulting from faulty nutrition or other physical factors play a major role in many depressions. These chemical imbalances, however, might also be caused by severe emotional stress (or a combination of physical, emotional, and/or spiritual stress). For example, severe emotional stress can, among other things, raise cortisol levels. This, in turn, might lead to an increase in tryptophanase. This enzyme helps split tryptophan into other chemical substances, and in the process lowers tryptophan levels and ultimately serotonin levels. Whenever a person is under heavy mental/emotional stress and also has a poor diet, the chances of chemical imbalance and depression are greatly increased.

Appendix 2 describes such potential physical sources of depression as pancreas, adrenal, pituitary, and thyroid dysfunction, as well as vitamin, mineral, amino acid, and neurotransmitter deficiencies, diet, malnutrition, food and chemical allergies, and candidiasis. A review of Appendix 2 will help you better understand chart #1, Physical Sources and Aspects of Depression.

1. Physical Sources and Aspects of Depression

Potential Stressors

Allergies, amino acid deficiencies, disease, drugs, glandular and glucose disturbances, heredity, malnutrition, mineral and neurotransmitter deficiencies, overstimulation, poisoning, trauma, understimulation, vitamin deficiencies, weather sensitivities (seasonal affective disorder), faulty diet, and so forth.

Actual Stressors

Potential stressors, such as faulty diet, may eventually lead to a loss of physical balance, due to an excessive number of alarm calls to and from the hypothalamus in the brain. This may result, for example, in *overfunctioning* of the adrenal cortex, creating high levels of cortisol, which, in turn, results in lowered levels of the amino acid tryptophan and the neurotransmitter serotonin. Eventually this may lead to *underfunctioning* of the adrenal cortex and reduced levels of cortisol. The latter may cause excessive glucose utilization and low blood sugar (hypoglycemia). Too many stress calls may also develop into an *underfunctioning* of the adrenal medulla and decreased levels of the neurotransmitters epinephrine and norepinephrine. In summary, excessive stress may result—among other things—in low levels of blood sugar, cortisol, epinephrine, and norepinephrine, or increased levels of cortisol. Any of these conditions may predispose to depression.

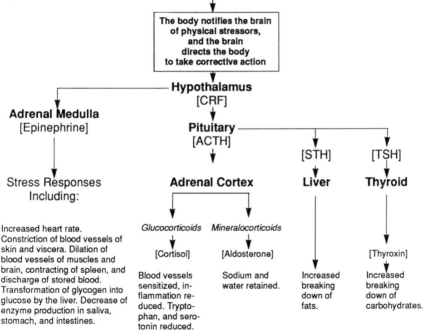

Psychological Sources and Aspects of Depression

Wrong Thinking Leads to Depression

Because of the extensive interrelationship between body and mind, most types of depression are of a physical nature. Nonetheless most people (75 percent) create their own depression. Consequently, the most common kind of depression is exogenous depression, which results from our value system. We create most of our own depressions because of self-defeating attitudes and beliefs. Wrong beliefs and wrong attitudes lead to self-defeating thinking, and we literally work against ourselves.

This may lead to emotional problems, and to any one of hundreds of different so-called psychosomatic diseases, including asthma, allergies, headaches, sinusitis, bronchial troubles, female problems, stomach ulcers, and heart disease. Even cancer is, to a certain extent, the result of our self-defeating psychological, as well as physical, and spiritual lifestyles (Padus 1986; Pearce 1983).

The power of our mind is so incredible that we actually receive what we can conceive and believe. This holds true especially for those who believe in God, for they have his special promise that he will give them "the desires of thine heart" (Ps. 37:4). In chapter 6, "Spiritual Sources and Aspects of Depression," I deal more extensively with this subject. For now, let it suffice to say that the majority of depressed persons believe that they are far removed from God and his blessings.

How do people create their own depressions? It's done in such a simple way that they are usually unaware of it. They really fall for a set of lies. They do it by saying what is not true and then believing every bit of it. They lie so much that eventually it seems to be the truth for them.

Chart #2 Psychological Sources and Aspects of Depression on page 81, lists some potential stressors that could lead to depression, but they do not have to. Stressors are only powerful opportunities to make ourselves depressed; however, there is no law that says that anyone must become depressed over them. Although loss is behind almost every kind of psychological depression, it will not automatically lead to depression.

We can become depressed over a loss only if our value system decides it. Our attitudes and beliefs toward the loss will determine how we perceive it, talk about it, and feel about it. Potential psychological stressors, however, usually lead to depression because of cultural factors. Most people in a given culture share similar self-talk habits about similar events. To a great extent our self-talk is learned, and consequently most of our depressions are learned behavior. It is not the event that makes us depressed, but we make ourselves depressed over the event.

This holds true even for physical stressors. For example, just because a person has hypoglycemia, low thyroxine, *or whatever,* does not mean that this person automatically becomes depressed. There might, however, be a physical effect on the brain cells, all depending on the status of our body systems. It has been noted repeatedly that people with similar physical disturbances frequently have dissimilar emotional reactions (AMA *Family Medical Guide* 1982; Stearns 1972).

Thus one person with hypoglycemia might show mental/ emotional symptoms of depression; another person may show extreme anger; and yet another may have less noticeable mental/

emotional symptoms. This has to do with the way in which our body and mind interprets a given situation, fact, or event.

We are, of course, also dealing with various levels of disturbances and a myriad of other factors. Yet, ultimately the Word of God wins out: "As a man thinketh in his heart so is he." Let's take a closer look at how we form our own emotions and rejoice that we have an opportunity to obtain the emotions we desire.

Scripture reminds us that we create our own feelings. "A word fitly spoken is like apples of gold in pictures of silver (Prov. 25:11). If what we say is positive, uplifting, kind, loving, friendly, considerate, and joyful, then both mind and body feel better.

Negative self-talk, however, leads to depression. From the Book of Psalms, David shows how he talks himself into and out of depression:

> How long wilt thou forget me, O LORD? Forever? How long wilt thou hide thy face from me?
>
> How long shall I take counsel in my soul, having sorrow in my heart daily? How long shall mine enemy be exalted over me?
>
> Consider and hear me, O LORD my God; lighten mine eyes, lest I sleep the sleep of death;
>
> Lest mine enemy say, I have prevailed against him; and those that trouble me rejoice when I am moved.
>
> But I have trusted in thy mercy; my heart shall rejoice in thy salvation.
>
> I will sing unto the LORD, because he hath dealt bountifully with me.   Psalm 13

Here is what David does:

1. He *believes* wrongly that God has forgotten him.
2. He *complains* about this.
3. He *accuses* God of hiding from him.
4. He *pleads* to be heard.
5. He *calls out* to be rescued from his depression.
6. He *recognizes* his use of wrong beliefs (lies).
7. He *changes* to the right beliefs (truth).
8. He *reminds* himself of God's mercy.
9. He *rejoices* in happy thoughts of salvation.
10. He *recovers* totally and begins to sing.

Read this psalm out loud and check on how you feel when you apply these words to yourself. It is precisely as the Scriptures tell us: "Choose you this day whom ye will serve . . . (Josh. 24:15). Do you say as Joshua did ". . . as for me and my house, we will serve the LORD?"

We Create Our Own Emotions

Emotions are not given to you by someone else: you give them to yourself. No one upsets you, makes you angry, depresses you, or elates you.

You are the only one who controls your brain and consequently, you are the only one who can create your feelings. You do this by perceiving something and telling yourself something about it, which can be good, bad, and/or neutral, and which will always be in accordance with *your* value system (attitudes, beliefs, opinions, prejudices, fantasies, hopes, dreams, and biases). Following all this you begin to experience emotions.

Some people refuse to believe the process is that simple and believe their lives are far more complex. It is true that living can be very complex indeed, and from the discussion of physical factors in many types of depression, it should be clear that we must not take anyone's emotive feelings lightly.

Nevertheless, it is true that most of the time people create their own emotions based on the simple formula that perceptions lead to cognitions and then to feelings. Of course, other factors are involved that freely intermingle in this process. For example, emotions feed on themselves not only because of the full cycle of perceptions, cognitions, feelings, but also because endogenous stimuli begin to intermingle, as explained in the chart Psychological Sources and Aspects of Depression (*see* page 81).

It is a fact that we can choose our own thoughts and create our own emotions. We can even select the frame of mind we want to have, be it a blinded or renewed mind. We have been given brains to use, minds to select, and opportunities to create emotions within ourselves. Happiness is something we choose for ourselves.

The Way We Think and Speak Determines the Way We Feel

Our self-talk leads either to justification or condemnation. Our words express our value system, consisting of our attitudes, beliefs, opinions, wishes, dreams, hopes, biases, and prejudices.

The Bible and many secular findings remind us that throughout history people have concluded that happiness, unhappiness, success, or failure are often the outcome of the way in which we have learned to think. Because of the way our brain operates, our thinking precedes our feelings. The thinking portion (cortex) of our brain receives messages, sorts them out, and relays them to the feeling portion (limbic system) of our brain. We first think, then feel, then act. Although many of our actions (and our emotions, too) seem automatic, they "primarily" reflect our well-learned behavior.

The stoic philosopher Epictetus said in his *Enchiridion (The Manual),* "It is not things themselves that disturb men but their ideas about things. When we meet with troubles, become anxious or depressed, let us never blame anyone but our opinions about things. The uneducated person blames others when he does badly; the person whose education has begun blames himself; the already educated person blames neither another nor himself."

In short, if we are depressed, it might be the result of how we look at our circumstances through our "value system," which uses an evaluative/interpretative process. Abraham Lincoln realized how the process worked when he said, "Most folks are as happy as they make up their minds to be."

The majority of depressed people (about 75 percent) suffer from self-defeating thinking, which is simply the wrong kind of thinking. It is not based on truth and goes directly against their dearest wishes for a long, happy, and godly life. Self-enhancing thinking, on the other hand, is based on truth and is the kind of thinking that God wants them to have.

Specialists in the field of depression such as Beck (1979), Burns (1980), Hauck (1976), and Maultsby (1984), have shown for many years that depression is primarily a thinking disorder. Over the years, I have learned to see depression as a psychosomatogenic stress disorder (Brandt 1983, 1984), while not overlooking that there is a thinking component involved in depression. At times this component might seem negligible, for example, when people become rapidly depressed on certain medications and undepressed when these medications are withdrawn.

The best approach to depression is the wholistic approach, where proper attention is given to body, mind, and spirit—*because that is the way God has created us.* Even with this wholistic approach, however, we are in need of a minimum amount of motivation and rational thinking to start us on the path of constructive change. Only a change in our thinking will change our feelings and actions.

Specific Mental/Emotional Sources of Depression

Over the years authors have repeated *ad infinitum* various so-called psychological causes of depression. This list includes lack of self-esteem, rejection, loneliness, lack of friends, perfectionism, boredom, lack of stimulation, overstimulation, guilt, self-pity, other pity, self-blame, other blame, anger, anxiety, fear, worries, marital difficulties, and unemployment problems. It is more correct, however, to emphasize that psychological depressions are the result of how our value system deals with real or imagined losses. Out of "sources" we make "causes."

In every case of exogenous (reactive) depression, we are dealing with attitudes and beliefs by which we perceive and interpret real or imagined losses. These losses as first perceived are only potential stressors that must be filtered through our perceptual-cognitive field where they might (or might not) become actual stressors.

A loss in and of itself does not cause depression. Rather it is how we deal with a loss that determines our depression and its extent. The chart Psychological Sources and Aspects of Depression verifies this on page 81.

The aforementioned so-called psychological causes for depression are only *potential* stressors, and our attitudes, beliefs, and other cognitions determine whether they become *actual* stressors. What definitely obstructs our ability to deal more effectively with potential stressors is our fallibility. The Scriptures remind us that we see and know only in part. It is not possible for us to see clearly (1 Cor. 13:12). More often than not we see, hear, or experience things differently than they are. Dealing with human fallibility requires patience and tolerance for others and ourselves.

Wrong Thinking Versus Right Thinking

Wrong thinking leads to depression, and about 75 percent of depressed people suffer from this problem. What is wrong thinking? It is synonymous with (1) irrational, (2) self-defeating, (3) erroneous, (4) subjective, (5) incorrect, (6) untruthful, and (7) sinful thinking.

There *is* good and bad behavior, and there *is* right and wrong thinking. In *The Way to Wholeness* (1984) I said this about behavior:

> It is clear that our past is important and that there are many factors in both our past and present environments that we allow to influence us. Nevertheless, we are, to a very great extent, free to choose how we feel! Although there are no bad or good people (those with *only* bad or *only* good characteristics), there nevertheless are bad and good behaviors. This is not the kind of badness or goodness which is based on subjective evaluations, but rather those which can stand the test of time, and of all civilized cultures and societies. For example, good behavior is the kind of behavior that is constructive. It shows practical love—that is, understanding, acceptance, and respect. It is the kind of behavior that inflicts no harm of any kind on anyone, that does not trespass, but rather helps to enhance the happy survival of others. Bad behavior is the other kind of behavior. It is not love, but rather hatred and hostility that is practiced. It does inflict harm on others, it does trespass, and it hinders or prevents the happy survival of others. Having these behaviors does not make us good or bad, for as long as we are in our mortal bodies we remain fallible. Clearly there is not one of us who can point a finger at anyone else. The Scriptures tell us that "all have sinned, and come short of the glory of God" (Rom. 3:23).

Right thinking, like good behavior, is constructive. It helps us to survive happily. It is the kind of thinking by which we do not condemn ourselves or others, and which inflicts no harm. Right thinking helps us grow in a positive direction, to be sensible and realistic, and live in accordance with the admonition of the apostle Paul:

> Finally, brethren, whatever things are true, whatever things are honest ... whatever things are lovely, whatever things are of good report; if there be any virtue, and if there be any praise, think on these things (Phil. 4:8).

We are to think truthfully and honestly about subjects worthy of our thoughts. Right thinking leads us into a closer relationship with God himself, for it heals rather than hurts, brings light rather than darkness, lifts up, rather than presses down. The ultimate in self-enhancing thinking is to love God and others as ourselves (Matt. 22:36–40). This will be further discussed in chapter 6 on "Spiritual Sources and Aspects of Depression."

Virtually all depressed people suffer from wrong impressions through misunderstanding, misinterpretations, misconstructions, or misapprehensions. Their value system (perceptual-cognitive field), filled with misbeliefs, prevents them from more appropriately dealing with actual or imagined losses in their lives.

Such negative thinking is geared not for survival but destruction, not for happiness but unhappiness, not for joy but sadness. Perceptions and cognitions are too often preconditioned by the twin self-fulfilling prophecies of failure and illness. Thus our whole value system might come to rest on lies and distortions, and our way of thinking not only reflects this but also reinforces it. It is essential, therefore, to discover what is going on, to make sound decisions, and to speak in a positive and realistic manner. Right thinking requires the use of logic and other principles that help us make objective inferences.

It is best to be as reasonable, logical, sensible, judicious, and clear-headed as we possibly can be. Of course, we start with a handicap, for as Scripture warns us, "Every man is right in his own eyes ..." (Prov. 21:2). We need to go against this by questioning our thoughts, and to ask where is the evidence that what I am saying is really true? Can I prove what I believe? Where did I get my ideas? On what am I basing them?

It is particularly important to challenge the concept of "allness." Examples of self-defeating allness statements include:

I am "always" left out.

I am "never" appreciated.

"Everybody" is smarter than I am.

"Nobody" is as ugly as I am.

"Every" time I mess up.

I am "forever" stuck with the past.

"All" the time I am being picked on.

Each of these statements lacks common sense and is improper, imbalanced, or plain foolish. This kind of thinking goes against the rules of logic and objective reality and becomes so prevalent in most cases of depression.

Depression in a "narrower" sense is only a negative emotive feeling, and this feeling is mainly the result of our thinking. We can distinguish happiness and depression thoughts. Have a look at the following:

Happiness Thoughts	*Depression Thoughts*
I accept myself.	I dislike myself.
I respect myself.	I hate myself.
I am tolerant of myself.	I am stupid.
I can laugh at myself.	I am ugly.
I am a creative thinker.	I am no good.
I am hopeful.	I am hopeless.
I am self-motivated.	I don't believe anybody.
I like to take responsibility.	I don't trust anybody.
I don't always have to succeed.	I am a loser.
I cannot always succeed.	I never do anything right.
I like other people.	I am always the last to know.
I am worthwhile.	I am a failure.
I am self-directed.	I know that I will never change.
I have several talents.	
I like myself.	I am powerless over everything.
I am a doer.	
I have plenty of choices in life.	I never say anything right.
I accept my limitations.	I lack willpower.

I look forward to the future.
I like changes and new ideas.
I am a winner.
I have the power to choose.
I have faith.
I believe in God.
I enjoy the beauty of nature.
I respect differences in people.
I accept the fallibility of
  others.
I can associate with lots of
  people.
I don't have to control
  anybody.
I don't demand that others
  make me happy.
I don't blame others for my
  feelings.
I accept as calmly as possible
  what cannot be changed.
I welcome new experiences.
I like to use my talents.
I look for opportunities.
I enjoy life.

I doubt most things.
I am a born loser.
I really don't like people.
I have no talent at all.
I need somebody to take
  care of me.
I hate to get up.
I am worse off than others.
I am stuck with my past.
I don't think anybody likes me.
I suffer because of other
  people.
I don't want to be
  responsible.
I cannot face difficulties.
I am afraid that I will fail.
I should be better qualified.
I should be more intelligent.
I should have achieved more.
I will always suffer.
I must have perfect control.
I cannot change.
I hate life.
I see no meaning in life.
I see no purpose in anything.

The Bible, Stoic philosophers, cognitive psychologists, poets, statesmen, and philosophers have stressed over and over that our thinking determines our feelings. It is time to listen.

Once people realize that good thinking leads to good feelings, they are more ready to go for the good thinking. Many, however, never get to that stage because they are bound not only to erroneous thoughts but also to erroneous perceptions. They won't accept their fallibility. Most people can agree with that, but they don't think that it pertains to them. They foolishly persist that it is the other person who cannot "see" things as clearly as they do.

It is time to rid ourselves of this delusion. Take a simple test. Read the statement below and after having done so, count the number of Fs. Having done this, write this number on a piece of paper and *only then,* proceed to the end of this chapter where you will find further instructions. Start reading and counting the Fs.

> FINISHED FILES ARE THE RE-
> SULT OF YEARS OF SCIENTIF-
> IC STUDY COMBINED WITH THE
> EXPERIENCE OF MANY YEARS.

The simple test you have just taken tells a lot about human fallibility. It tells about psychological set, that is, getting into a certain frame of reference and measuring all that follows on that reference. It also shows how we habitually perceive things, and highlights the use—or less than full use—of the left hemisphere of the brain. The left cerebral hemisphere is more objectively descriptive and analytical. Even in newborns the left hemisphere is more active than the right hemisphere in processing speech. The right hemisphere is more subjectively descriptive, artistic, intuitive, and visual. While both hemispheres process thoughts, each hemisphere is more proficient with certain kinds of thoughts. For example, the right hemisphere only affirms, it does not process negations, and uses evocative (responsive) thinking. The left hemisphere affirms and negates. Most people fail to make the best use of the left hemisphere, although they are able to learn to do so, and consequently when they take this simple test do not, at first, come up with the correct answer. Simply stated, our perceptions and interpretations are usually that imperfect.

If we acknowledge our fallibility and inability to perceive and reason accurately, then we are more able to do something about our problems. Chapter 8 presents a simple program to help us with that.

In summary, most of us who suffer from depression do so primarily because of the way in which we interpret events. This interpretation depends very much on our perceptual-cognitive field, which in turn, is based on training, education, and experience. As we make rational changes in our value system, we can develop attitudes and beliefs that are self-enhancing and that will propel us to health and happiness. Although distinct psychological sources for depression are presented in this chapter, it is important to realize that these sources only reflect their primary nature. There is no depression that is only physical, only psychological, or only spiritual. As long as there are no "zippers" between body, mind, and spirit, when one part suffers, all parts are affected. I agree with Dr. Menninger (1958) who said, "We have to treat the man, not pieces and parts."

The Cause of Psychological Depression

Psychological depression cannot take place as long as our perceptual-cognitive field is (1) rationally, (2) realistically, and (3) positively integrated. As can readily be seen from the chart at the end of this chapter, it is *value system disintegration* that leads to *psychological* depression. The primary determinant is choice and the secondary determinant is vulnerability.

As long as value-system integrity is maintained, depression will not result. It is loss of psychological integrity that enables potential stressors to become actual stressors, and for negative emotive responses (including depression) to take place.

This loss of psychological integrity reflects an absence of necessary *rational, realistic,* and *positive* choices. The cure for psychological depression is emotional reeducation and spiritual regeneration, which are discussed in chapters 8 and 9.

Note: *The Mini-Perception Test.* Most people count only three Fs. The correct answer, however, is six Fs. If you found only three, you probably missed the three *of* words.

2. Psychological Sources and Aspects of Depression

Potential Stressors

Loss of acceptance, achievement, challenge, confidence, employment, energy, faith, familiarity, goals, health, hope, independence, love, loved ones, memory, opportunity, respect, self-esteem, self-sufficiency, security, stimulation, trust, and numerous real or imagined losses.

↓

Actual Stressors

Potential stressors, such as loss of employment, may eventually lead to a loss of psychological integrity, that is, the disintegration of a rational, realistic, and optimistic value system into an irrational, unrealistic, and/or pessimistic one. The chart shows that a loss in and of itself cannot cause depression. It is our evaluation/interpretation of facts and events that determine a depression and its extent. Sources of depression, however, only reflect their primary nature—be it psychological, physical, or spiritual. There is no depression that is only physical, only psychological, or only spiritual.

↓

Perceptual-Cognitive Field

↓

| Heredity and social, cultural, and other experiences | Value system affected attitudes, beliefs, cognitions | Religious beliefs and spiritual experiences |

↓

Loss of Psychological Integrity

Specific Thinking that Leads to Specific Emotions

| What will happen now?
I will be badly hurt!
Things will get worse!
= Anxiety | Nobody loves me.
I am a loser.
I am worthless.
= Depression | How could they?
They are bad!
They should not!
= Anger | I shouldn't have.
It's my fault.
I am bad.
= Guilt |

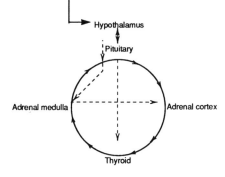

Spiritual Sources and Aspects of Depression

The Loss of an Illusion (God-Void)

Spiritual depression—like all other forms of depression—is characterized by an awareness of loss. The primary source of spiritual depression is loss of direction. Spiritual depressions differ greatly in severity and type. But the more common form of spiritual depression is based on the loss of an illusion: it is found in people who—often despite all sorts of wealth, health, and power—find themselves anxious, lonely, empty, and experiencing a general void within themselves.

For years, perhaps even decades, they clung to the belief that fulfillment could be found in a materialistic or hedonistic life. Slowly—and sometimes suddenly—they came to realize that the material and transient things of the world by themselves cannot give meaning, and found themselves lost like a ship without a rudder or compass.

These people are miserable. Having lost faith in the meaningfulness of their lifestyle, they now also lose faith in themselves.

This may spell the end of an illusion; it does not mean the end of life. It may, in fact, signal a new beginning if in this crisis they are made willing to listen—perhaps for the first time—to the gospel. Once under conviction, they may in their misery cry out to the Lord (Ps. 107:6, 13, 19, 28), be set free from their turmoil, and find new direction.

At this point I should like to stress the close relationship between *mind* and *spirit*. Our spiritual awareness is directly tied in with knowledge, and knowledge is bound up with our intellectual/emotional makeup, perceptions, attitudes, beliefs, and so forth. When God speaks to us, he addresses our hearts and minds. He teaches and—through his servants—explains his Word in ways our minds can grasp and respond to.

God's people have special status in the world. They are called by such lofty titles as "a chosen generation, a royal priesthood, an holy nation . . ." (1 Peter 2:9). They are a privileged people with a special calling: to declare the wonderful deeds of him who called them "out of darkness into his marvelous light" (v. 9). When God called them—using his servants whoever they were—he invited them with great love and sincerity to enter his kingdom, and they had a decision to make. No one is forced into the kingdom from without; even when God draws us by his love, we can resist—or we can yield.

We do not profess to understand the mystery and miracle by which a person gives up his or her misguided autonomy. But we do know that when the Spirit of the Lord works in people's hearts they are made free to choose to be subject to him. The more powerful the working of God's Spirit in their hearts, the freer they become (intellectually and emotionally and in all ways) to respond to the gospel.

The Gospels show us how, in the days of his earthly ministry, Jesus always addressed people in terms of their needs. The striking thing is that he chose to connect with them at the point where they were most powerless. Blindness embarrasses us when we meet people who pick their way down the sidewalk with the help of a white cane. Jesus, however, made blindness his point of contact with people. In one instance he anointed a blind man's eyes with a mixture of spittle and clay and told him to go wash in the pool of Siloam (John 9:1–11). The man came back seeing! On another occasion he told a lame man to take up his bed and to walk—but that was precisely what he could not do! No matter: when Jesus spoke to him, his words carried power and healed the man. And the man, trusting Jesus and sensing a surge of new power in his legs, got up and walked (John 5:2–9). His very paralysis was for him the beginning of a new life.

So it is also on the deeper levels of the human heart. People may be totally powerless to do precisely what they *must* do to find new direction in life. They may not have it in them at all to believe the good news about Jesus. Yet millions have come to believe in Him. That is to say, when Jesus comes into people's lives he comes with power and persuasion and transforming grace. He heals human hearts and redirects human wills in a way that is overpoweringly real and marvelously gentle.

As a result human beings move from an illusion of spiritual freedom to the reality of spiritual freedom. Having made people free, God calls them to use their freedom (*see* Gal. 5:1), employing all their faculties. Within the context of this great liberation, God mightily stresses the importance of human choice and decision making (Deut. 30:19, 20; Josh. 24:15; Isa. 7:15). And in this context one can never again separate spiritual problems from one's mental faculties—faculties such as the will and the intellect.

The apostle Paul once put it unforgettably: ". . . work out your own salvation . . ." he told the Philippians, "For it is God who worketh in you both to will and to do of his good pleasure" (Phil. 2:12, 13). With all the energies at their disposal, says Paul, people must work out their salvation. How can they when they are powerless? Ah, says the apostle, but they are not powerless. For God works in them both to will and to do.

I know that in a book on depression these statements do not sound totally convincing. Too many fine Christians have suffered—and continue to suffer—crippling depressions. For them, despite their longing for good health and faith in God, it seems the heavens *are* closed and a hell of nothingness yawns at their feet. That fine Christians have deep depressions, however, does not invalidate what Paul is saying. The causes of depression are many, and though depressions affect our spiritual outlook, the cause is not always spiritual—it may be physical or psychological. But it *may* also be due to a loss of meaning in life. And when this is demonstrably the case, one needs to act. Passivity is death.

Life in God's world awaits our full and deliberate involvement. God calls *and* empowers.

Spiritual depression—resulting from the loss of illusion—is very much like psychological depression. It is ultimately, I believe, the result of wrong thinking. Most depressions, in my opinion, can be traced to wrong thinking.

Right thinking is constructive. It is based on reality, truth, reason, logic. It impels us to deal with life's problems, and so to grow, and be in health. It is right thinking that insures our long-term happy survival.

Wrong thinking, by contrast, is the fountainhead of the illusions to which people cling. Wrong thinking is based on the mistaken premise that the self is the center of the universe, a premise that makes us ethically unreliable and blind to the real Center. Because such self-centered thinking runs against the deepest grain of life, it is a source of endless frustration, isolation, and misery. The end of that road, in many cases, is depression.

Right thinking—thinking rooted in God's perspective on human life—is oriented to truth. It does not wish to wear blinders. It is open to the reality which heals body, mind, and spirit. The ultimate in right thinking is to think as God thinks. "Let this mind be in you, which was also in Christ Jesus" (Phil. 2:5). Christ did not stand upon his privileges but, as the Bible vividly puts it, "took . . . the form of a servant" (v. 7). This is the model for right thinking.

When a lawyer (probably a pretty good thinker!) asked Jesus: "Master, which is the great commandment in the law?" Jesus replied: "Thou shalt love the LORD thy God with all thy heart, and with all thy soul, and with all thy mind. This is the first and great commandment. And the second is like it, Thou shalt love thy neighbor as thyself. On these two commandments hang all the law and the prophets" (Matt. 22:35–40).

To love, therefore, is the ultimate in right thinking and right feeling. Although love is an emotion, it is far more than *just* emotion. Love is also thought and action. For to love, as Jesus teaches, is the ultimate expression of doing things right. To love, in this context, means to understand God's love, accept God's love, respect God's love, and express God's love. Love for God, for others, *and* for ourselves (yes, *that* too!), leads to right thinking, whereas "love" without God leads to wrong thinking and, inevitably, to disillusionment and depression. It is here that the awareness of loss is potentially an asset, for the realization that we are "lost" can stir up a desire for a saving knowledge of Jesus.

The Scriptures tell us that "But if our gospel be hidden, it is hidden to them who are lost, in whom the god of this [world] hath blinded the minds of them which believe not, lest the light of the glorious gospel of Christ, who is the image of God, should shine unto them" (2 Cor. 4:3, 4). What a blessing to receive mercy, to be saved by grace through faith (Eph. 2:8), and to shed our blindness as we come into that light!

On the basis of a fundamental reorientation to the gospel of Jesus Christ, we also discover the imperatives of that gospel: the call to be transformed by the renewal of our minds (Rom. 12:2). Once this begins to happen we increasingly broaden the circle of our love, which is the highest form of reason. Love as a superior form of reason breaks the powers of darkness and doubt. It is a constant challenge to the mind to love God above all, and to love others as well as ourselves.

What higher reason can there be than to choose life over death, blessing over cursing, light over darkness, joy over sadness, hope over despair? What better choice is there than to opt for love over fear?

To love God is to do the will of God, and to do the will of God is to keep his commandment to love one another (1 John 4 and 5). This kind of thinking and doing is so important that Jesus tells us to give it everything we have: heart, soul, and mind; that is, every aspect of our being (Matt. 22:37).

The Loss of a Sense of Fellowship With God (God-Neglect)

Earlier I said that love without God leads to wrong thinking, self-worship, self-deification, and sheer selfishness. It is a condition of those who have never turned their lives over to God. But it is also possible to experience the love of God and then, through neglect, to lose the awareness of that love. From here it is only a short step to spiritual depression. This experience comes not as a result of the loss of an illusion but as the product of neglect— a failure to practice the presence of God. At the heart of it very often is willful disobedience to God's commandments with the result being true guilt and depression.

Wrong thinking gets people—including God's dearest servants—into trouble every time. Neglect of "love" thinking invariably makes way for "fear" thinking and consequently depression.

The Scriptures tell us: "There is no fear in love, but perfect love casteth out fear, because fear hath punishment. He that feareth is not perfect in love" (1 John 4:18). Whereas God has given a spirit "of power, and of love, and of a sound mind" (2 Tim. 1:7), we may lose it through neglect, and neglect is the product of wrong thinking. Wrong thinking easily leads to depression: witness Jonah (4:3, 8), David (Ps. 13:1–3), Job (3:25), and Moses (Num. 11:11–15).

Wrong thinking is often reflected in unresolved guilt, anger, and other negative emotions, as we saw in the previous chapter on the psychological sources and aspects of depression. *Christians are no different from other people when it comes to their ability to make themselves depressed.* I often think that many Christians are particularly prone to depression precisely because they imagine themselves immune from it. Claiming the wonderful promises of God, they think they can ignore the laws that pertain to the sound operation of their bodies and minds. But these laws are as relevant to Christians as the law of gravity is to all creatures here below. Failure to recognize them spells disaster.

I believe that spiritual depression is best understood from the principle of free choice. Only freedom of choice permits growth, challenge, responsibility, accountability, victory. It is a truism that the human mind thrives on proper stimulation. Our minds would soon disintegrate if deprived of encouragement to use them to the full in making choices. A mind that is not allowed to choose is bound to shrivel from sheer boredom. It atrophies—like a muscle that is not used. Boredom entails sensory deprivation. Carried to an extreme this condition ends with a mind that ceases to function at all.

A break in one's awareness of God's presence is sufficiently serious to lead to depression. As depressed people well know, this loss is often compounded by the loss of fellowship with other believers, the loss of friends, and estrangement from family members. And the love, joy, and peace we come to expect as the fruits of the Spirit are eclipsed by the inner darkness of depression.

The Loss of Peace (God-Confusion)

What about those who suffer from "pseudo-spiritual depression," a condition based mainly on misunderstanding? Christians sometimes experience a depression in which they find themselves saying and doing things contrary to their own noble desires, true nature, or calling. Just what is going on here?

I have counseled some very depressed Christians who were not aware that one's spiritual nature is of a piece with the mind and that the mind is interwoven with the body. They have lost sight of the totality of their personhood. Under these circumstances Paul's prayer that "your whole spirit and soul and body be preserved blameless . . ." (1 Thess. 5:23) is forgotten and the implied imperatives are neglected.

Given this neglect, strange behaviors, including feelings of anger, depression, or panic reactions, are all too readily blamed on lack of spirituality. As a result, because of these negative emotive feelings some Christians regard themselves as spiritual weaklings. On closer examination one usually finds that there are perfectly logical explanations for their behavior. Very often such feelings stem from physical problems—including dangerously poor diets. Once the diets are corrected, marvelous changes in attitude and behavior can be seen to occur.

It cannot be stated too often that one's spiritual nature is of a piece with one's psychological nature (perceptual-cognitive field) and that the latter depends on well-functioning central nervous and endocrine systems. In a nutshell: when our bodies do not work properly, our minds cease to work properly. We are psychosomatic organisms that have no dividing walls between spirit, mind, and body. A failure in one part of one's existence can bring on great stress, not to say *dis*tress, in another.

Many Christians, for example, allow themselves to get physically and mentally too tired. They become overstressed and eventually their mental and spiritual well-being is gravely impaired. They think they have a spiritual problem whereas actually their circuits are overloaded and their generator cannot keep up with the requirements. A different lifestyle and a sound diet would have prevented this whole sorry state of affairs.

Summary

The most prevalent type of spiritual depression is due to the loss of illusion and an increasing awareness of a great void. This void exists where people have not yet met Jesus. A second common form of spiritual depression comes from a self-induced unawareness of closeness with God, a loss which is reinforced by a lack of assurance, purpose, and meaning. Thirdly, there is a pseudo-spiritual depression resulting from a loss of peace. In this case, physical or psychological dynamics cause confusion that prevents people from taking corrective steps.

Eating junk food and thinking junk thoughts will blind us to the truth. Again, *passivity* in the face of these habits *is death*. We need to rouse ourselves, immerse ourselves in Scripture, ask God for guidance, knowledge, and wisdom and if need be seek professional help. "God is not the author of confusion but of peace . . ." (1 Cor. 14:33).

Spiritual depression comes in various degrees and is the result of a general loss of spiritual direction. Not all depressions are of a spiritual nature. Most depressions, however, regardless of their source, benefit from spiritual treatment, administered in conjunction with physical and psychological treatments.

Please review table 3, *Spiritual Sources and Aspects of Depression* (p. 94) and compare it with the previous charts on physical and psychological sources and aspects of depression. Note that in "all" forms of depression a loss is "perceived"—perceived by our physical, psychological, and/or spiritual value systems.

Now What? I shall assume that you have by now made a thorough study of the charts and have some notion of the interrelationship of body, mind, and spirit. Do not skip this stage: it could mean the difference between being set free or remaining in bondage.

Next, recognize that to be human is at some times to be deeply troubled. Anxiety is part of the human condition. The poet of the Book of Job is sure of this: ". . . man is born unto trouble as the sparks fly upward" (Job 5:7). The apostle Paul confessed: "We are troubled on every side . . ." (2 Cor. 4:8). And Peter assured his readers: ". . . for a season, if need be, ye are in heaviness through manifold trials" (1 Peter 1:6).

But the Scriptures also show that, as long as believers look hourly to God for help, they can overcome troubles, trials, temptations, and whatever other difficulties they encounter. Knowing the goodness of God, they also know that God does not force depression on them. To the contrary: God would have them be well and whole. He is their healer.

Thus the threat does not come from the side of God. Nor does the threat arise from the fact of our losses. Any loss—of our possessions, friends, health, loved ones, or whatever—by itself cannot bring us to despair. *It is what we tell ourselves in the situation of loss that makes the difference.* People, events, Satan— they all have influence, and sometimes that influence is powerful. But none can dictate to us what we must think or feel. Not even the power of political dictatorship is such that it can determine what people think in their hearts and tell themselves when they are under pressure. Ours alone is the privilege of deciding how to respond and what to tell ourselves.

The privilege of decision is ours but that is not all. The Lord has also granted us the resources for making sound decisions. He has surrounded us with his self-revelation in Scripture and in the world around us. He has provided us with numerous helpers, including the Helper within, the Holy Spirit. He has set us free from the whole dismal legacy of sin. He has conferred on us the gift of faith, be it ever so weak (Eph. 2:8). By God's grace, we are not powerless.

Potential stressors that can lead to an awareness of loss and eventual depression are plentiful; but none of them can become an actual stressor (through our mental value systems) unless we let it.

Perhaps it would be helpful to look up the following "potential sources" of depression in the Scriptures:

1. Bereavement (Ruth 1:20, 21)
2. Discouragement (Jon. 4:3, 8)
3. Disaster (Job 1 and 2)
4. Excessive burdens (Num. 11:11–15)
5. Fears (2 Cor. 1:8)
6. Frustrations (2 Cor. 12:8)
7. Misbeliefs (Ps. 13)

8. Oppression (Ps. 42:9)
9. Persecution (2 Cor. 12:8)
10. Sickness (Isa. 38:9–15)

No one can claim that God will see to it that no Christian will ever be sick, poor, or hungry. Nor, as we have seen, do the Scriptures teach that, and life as we live it bears out the contrary. There is trouble in the world, and Christians are not exempt. Some of this—perhaps most—is the result of violating God's laws, the laws of nature, and the laws of common sense. Other difficulties descend upon us involuntarily or even because we have been faithful. ". . . In the world ye shall have tribulation . . ." (John 16:33).

Thus, as we experience serious situations, from bereavement to sickness, we do not need to act as if something strange had happened to us, nor as though we were powerless. We are not merely the outcome of some accident in the night as some evolutionists would have us think, nor are we the victims of an angry God as some believers would have it.

Every trouble in this world can be traced back to the fall of Adam and Eve. Man, under Satan's seduction, brought ruin into this world and man's continued disobedience is still the source of a vast amount of sorrow. The greed, bitterness, hatred, ignorance, and willful stupidity of many people, in authority or as private citizens, is often behind the hunger, diseases, and death that affect hundreds of millions of people. Human enslavement to evil impulses is manifest in the destruction of the soil in which crops are grown, the contamination of the water we drink, and the pollution of the air we breathe. It is evident in the destruction of human bodies through the abuse of addictive substances. It is obvious in the billion-dollar industry of pornography in this country. It is seen in rock music that promotes the occult and other perversions.

But we are not as those who decry these evils and offer no remedy. Nor do we look to ourselves for the cure of all these ills. We look to him who said: ". . . In the world ye shall have tribulation: but be of good cheer; I have overcome the world (John 16:33). "And the ransomed of the LORD shall return, and come to Zion with songs and everlasting joy upon their heads; they shall obtain joy and gladness, and sorrow and sighing shall flee away" (Isa. 35:10).

Consider again table 3, *Spiritual Sources and Aspects of Depression* and note the importance of choice. Remember: passivity is a negative choice and an unworthy response to the goodness of the Lord who "giveth us richly all things to enjoy" (1 Tim. 6:17).

3. Spiritual Sources and Aspects of Depression

Potential Stressors

Loss of belief in a meaningful existence, faith, fellowship with others, hope,. purpose, peace, love, and similiar losses.

Actual Stressors

Potentials stressors, such as loss of peace, may eventually lead to a loss of spiritual direction, that is, the disintegration of the spiritual value system. Spiritual depression is much like psychological depression, for it is ultimately the result of wrong thinking, the kind that is based on the premise that the self is the center of the universe. Such self-centered thinking is a source of endless frustration, isolation, and misery. The end of that road, in many cases, is depression. Spiritual depression is experienced in the total person. Once the neocortex (thinking portion of the brain) registers a depression, the limbic system (feeling portion of the brain) is also alerted. Here the hypothalamus will activate various stress responses.

Spiritual Perceptions and Cognitions

Heredity, and social, cultural, and other experiences	Spiritual value system affected attitudes, beliefs, cognitions	Religious beliefs and spiritual experiences

Loss of Spiritual Direction

Specific Thinking that Leads to Spiritual Depression

The world is an illusion. There is no meaning in life. There is no purpose in living. I am lost.	I am too busy to go to church I don't want to forgive him or her. I refuse to obey. I must take care of myself first.	God does not care for me. God hides from me. God no longer loves me. God is out to get me. God is too busy for me.
= God-Void	= God-Neglect	= God-Confusion

Depression

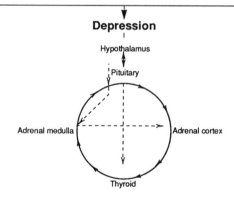

Hypothalamus

Pituitary

Adrenal medulla

Adrenal cortex

Thyroid

Part 3

The Treatment of Depression

7

The Physical Treatment
of Depression

The Medical Model: Restoring Homeostasis

The physical treatment of depression can be either simple or complex, and definitely requires discipline. In the physical treatment of depression the main problem is loss of physical balance. Homeostasis is lost and must be restored. The very best way to do this is to help our bodies do the work that God designed them to do. Our bodies are self-healing, and we have a built-in system of making needed corrections, fighting off germs, cleansing the bloodstream, and revitalizing our cells.

The physical treatment is simple in that God requires but a few tasks from us to keep our bodies in good condition or to help restore them. On the other hand, healing is infinitely complex because our bodies are infinitely complex. It is only because of the self-healing and self-regulating aspects that God has provided for us that we can do so well. No physician on earth can heal anybody. Only God can do this. We stand amazed in trying to appreciate the complexity of the body's chemical makeup.

Dr. Jerry Bergman (1985) describes the human body:

> Chemically, the body is unequalled for complexity. Each one of its 30 trillion cells is a mini-chemical factory which performs about 10,000 chemical functions. And every cell has 10^{12} (one trillion) bits of data—equal to every letter in ten million books! Each one also replaces itself every seven years. Each one is independent, yet cooperates with many millions of other cells.
>
> Even though there are over four billion people alive today, each body is exorbitantly expensive (and about 50 billion humans have been born since Adam). If its chemical elements were bought on the open market, a medium-sized human body would cost at least six million dollars.

We need to have greater appreciation for our bodies and consider them as "temples" of the Holy Spirit. As long as we live in accordance with God's laws, respect and appropriately deal with the needs of our bodies, and have no serious hereditary problems, then the necessary physical balance will be maintained. Many of us, although born with healthy bodies, are in trouble because of our self-defeating and even self-destructive lifestyles.

Most diseases are the result of neglect, abuse, or wrongful interference all culminating in a kind of toxemia, which is finally manifested as excessive physical and psychological stress. Too much stress will make our bodies and minds bend toward disease and ultimately will bring on premature death. Because of our increased understanding of the physical sources of depression, we are now in a position to do much more in the way of physical treatment.

Victory over depression frequently depends on the proper diagnosis and selection of appropriate treatment methods. Two facts come immediately to mind. First, manifold physical factors are likely involved in any given case of depression. Second, some diagnostic data is needed as quickly as possible. The best way to do this is via a thorough physical examination and laboratory studies.

The Physical Examination

The physical examination consists of a subjective and objective investigation. It requires lengthy questioning by the physician. It also involves looking at, and listening to, various aspects of the body, and evaluating the body in its totality. A physical examination means precisely what it says. It provides an assessment of the overall health of the individual concerned.

This examination cannot be done during just a fifteen-minute office visit, regardless of the skills of the physician. Part of the examination must also include an in-depth personal history, as well as a review of family history, including parents, siblings, and children, as applicable. Overlooking this can make the difference between right or wrong diagnosis and treatment.

Even a thorough physical examination, however, provides only a partial picture. It is essential to obtain certain minimum laboratory studies; additional studies usually depend on the outcome of the minimum studies. The physician wants to know something about both blood values and blood chemistry. These studies are important but too often are neglected. I have seen people who for decades endured numerous depressive episodes without obtaining necessary laboratory examinations.

The Laboratory Examination

Obviously only a physician can determine what special studies are to be included for each individual patient. For example, a person who is depressed but who also has heart disease and is taking a certain medication for high blood pressure, may require special laboratory studies to rule out any possible relationship between the depression and the medication.

Nevertheless, certain tests have universal value. They are applicable to all persons who suffer from depression and especially those who are suspected to suffer from endogenous depression. The Glossary provides definitions for most of the tests, including:

1. *Blood values,* such as hematocrit, hemoglobin, and blood counts.

2. *Blood chemistries,* such as glucose (FBS), total serum protein, albumin, globulin, albumin-globulin ratio, nonprotein nitrogen (NPN), urea nitrogen (BUN), creatinine, calcium, phosphorus, sodium, potassium, chlorides, cholesterol, total lipids, serum alkaline phosphatase, etc.
3. *Special blood chemistries,* for "adrenal cortex functioning," for example, cortisol; for "thyroid functioning," PBI, T_3 and T_4; and for "pancreas functioning," the Glucose Tolerance Test (GTT).
4. *Complete urinalysis.*
5. *Urinary 17-Ketosteroids,* for "adrenal cortex functioning." (*See* Glossary under *Ketosteroids.*)

The physician needs to evaluate the results of these tests in conjunction with the results of the physical examination, history, and the patient's complaints. The practice of medicine is a time-consuming art and science. The person suffering from depression needs to be at least as interested in the physical findings and their meaning as the physician.

Clients need to play as active a role as they possibly can in the evaluation and treatment of their depression. Certainly, it is important that counselors and therapists take a serious interest in all of the data that is being compiled on their clients, and this includes the laboratory findings.

It is helpful to know something about the so-called "normal range" of blood chemistries. These are listed in Appendix 3, and described further in the Glossary.

Special Tests that May Be Helpful

Sometimes clients go to various practitioners for years without a definite diagnosis being made of their particular type of depression. Often they do not receive an in-depth (physical, mental, emotional) workup, or laboratory tests.

Many of these people believe that helpful tests are not available for the investigation of depression. They often think that a specific diagnosis is, more or less, a hit-or-miss psychological affair. Fortunately the overwhelming majority of depressions can be diagnosed and treated successfully. Much can also be done to pinpoint potential sources for the depression and prevent the disorder from occurring in the first place.

Thorough physical examinations and laboratory studies are important for most depressed people to find or to rule out physical disorders. When standard tests are unsatisfactory, then a number of special tests can be ordered. Extremely important is the *Six-Hour Oral Glucose Tolerance Test (OGTT,)* which is the most common clinical-chemical investigation (Haneveld 1982). The results obtained on a OGTT are fairly independent of sex and age and are universally recognized as a major diagnostic tool. Because of its great importance in the proper diagnosis and treatment of depression, the OGTT is described in detail, along with a discussion of other tests for the investigation of endogenous depressions in Appendix 3.

Special Care Is Required in the Use of Drugs for Depression. I believe that the overwhelming majority of people are far better off without antidepressant medication. This opinion is not shared by all physicians, as they are well trained in the prescribing of drugs and usually lack time to deal with depressed people in any other manner. On the other hand, it is true that those who suffer from severe depression often derive great benefit from certain appropriately administered medications. Yet, this treatment is best undertaken in conjunction with psychological and/or spiritual counseling, preceded by physical and laboratory tests. (*See* Appendix 4 for drugs commonly used in the treatment of depression.)

There are some dangers attached to the taking of antidepressant medications. A long list of *adverse effects* goes with virtually every antidepressant. The adverse effects of various antidepressants include even some of the very symptoms they are supposed to control, for example, anxiety, disorientation, excitement, delusions, hallucinations, panic reactions, changes in sex drive and sleep patterns, and a host of other problems. These include heart attacks, stroke, dangerously low, or dangerously high blood pressure (the latter often caused by combining, for example, Monoamine Oxidase Inhibitors with certain foods), which can even cause death. The drug manufacturers warn about these many dangers at great length in the *Physician's Desk Reference* (PDR). A copy of this book can be found in most public libraries. Another useful book is *The Essential Guide to Prescription Drugs,* by James W. Long (1985).

Patients should be told of possible *side effects* (these are usually *not* dangerous) and so-called *adverse effects* (these usually *are* dangerous). If the physician does not discuss this then it is the responsibility of the patient to ask questions. Self-medication or using previously prescribed medications in addition to a more recent prescription can be fatal. Never mix antidepressants with amphetamines, alcohol, anticonvulsants, antihistamines, other antidepressants, barbiturates, sleeping pills, sedatives, tranquilizers, and similar drugs.

Antidepressants should not be taken without a physical examination, appropriate medical history, and possibly laboratory studies. There must also be an inquiry into other prescribed, over the counter, and/or illegal drugs that are now being taken. The patient needs certain warnings about *adverse* and *side effects,* and to know what to do should they occur. The Glossary in this book includes information on *lithium* and other drugs used for depression.

Most physicians are extremely busy, so it is important that patients play an active role in their own treatment by freely sharing information about their lifestyle and personal concerns. It is essential that patients strictly abide by the instructions they receive from the physician, especially adhering to the proper dosage of the drugs that are being taken. Adverse side effects should be promptly reported. It is also important to know that antidepressants are often started in small quantities and gradually increased to a safe as possible and effective dose. Then the smallest possible dose is used for a maintenance period. Likewise it is not usually safe to abruptly stop antidepressants. Only the physician can advise in these matters.

The Use of Nonprescription Drugs and Depression. Some of the medications commonly prescribed by physicians for the treatment of depression have been briefly mentioned. Because we live in a drug-oriented culture, however, the majority of people in our society, often unknowingly, use mood-altering substances every day. These include the following common depressants and stimulants:

Alcohol. To help elevate moods of sadness and unhappiness, millions of people resort to dangerously erroneous methods. For example the use of alcohol as a mood elevator is common. Unfortunately this drug is in actuality a depressant. At first it affects the cortex of the brain and helps lower inhibitions, and seemingly elevates our moods. Soon, however, the limbic system of our brain becomes involved and now emotion, rather than reason, begins to rule our life.

The more alcohol we consume the more areas of the brain will become involved, and eventually the cerebellum and reticular formation of the brain will be affected. This results in irrational behavior, physical disturbances, such as loss of coordination, loss of consciousness, or—all too often—death.

A variety of mental/emotional, but also physical reasons lead people into the excessive use of alcohol. Many alcoholics suffer from hypoglycemia. This may be a source of their alcoholism or the result of it. Most of these people will foolhardily refuse to even take the Glucose Tolerance Test. Months and even years of persuasion may go by before they finally start to investigate possible physical sources of their problem.

Reaching for the bottle when the chips are down, when the blues and blahs occur, is all too common. Many people who are depressed foolishly believe that alcohol can help them. The bitter truth is that it does so for only a little while, and then the depression comes back with a vengeance. The additional stress on both body and mind makes matters far worse.

Alcohol and many other drugs might look good, smell good, taste good, and feel good, but yet are deadly. The temptation is truly satanic. The damage is progressive and, at first, hardly noticeable. Slowly, however, both brain and liver suffer the harmful effects of alcohol abuse.

Many bipolar depressives also suffer from hypoglycemia and alcoholism. This triad ought to tell us something. For one thing, I do not believe that every one who has a genetic predisposition (as seems to be the case in bipolar depression and schizophrenia) needs to develop serious forms of pathology. Genetic predisposition is only one factor in the development of depression. We can work ourselves into the pit, and we can also work ourselves out of it. Regardless of vulnerability, choice is still involved.

From my experiences, those on medication for bipolar depression but who pay proper attention to body, mind, and spirit as outlined in this book have far fewer and less severe depressive episodes than those who take only medication.

Nicotine, Caffeine, and Other Stimulants. Alcohol is by no means the only nonprescribed drug that is frequently abused in the self-treatment of depression. Other commonly abused drugs for mood elevation include the stimulants nicotine, caffeine, theobromine, and theophylline.

Nicotine is, of course, found in tobacco, and caffeine is found in coffee and many cola drinks. Caffeine, plus the stimulant theobromine, is found in cocoa. Both caffeine and theophylline are found in tea. These stimulants are drugs and many people are addicted to them, including many self-righteous people who look down on those who have alcohol or other addictions. No one has the right to throw a stone at those who suffer from addictions, least of all those who have addictions of any kind themselves.

These stimulants work on the hypothalamus (a small portion of the brain that helps regulate motivation and emotion) and the reticular formation (the center of consciousness) of our brain, and help people to be more alert. Especially the depressed will reach for anything that will give them a lift. Unfortunately these stimulants also increase heartbeat and respiration, and often result in physical problems such as insomnia and heart palpitations.

In addition, these stimulants are sources of stress (precisely what depressed people do not need), for they alert the hypothalamus in the limbic system of our brain to send out messages to our adrenal glands, and this activates the fight or flight stress mechanism.

The use of stimulants also increases sugar production. One symptom of low blood sugar is hunger, and when we smoke or use coffee, this hunger temporarily disappears. For this reason we are usually well advised not to take any kinds of stimulants—legal, or illegal, prescribed or nonprescribed. A temporary mood elevation will be followed by a more serious mood depression. This can become part of a vicious self-defeating cycle of ups and downs, without a long-term resolution of the depression.

The Mixing of Various Drugs and Food

It is extremely dangerous to mix barbiturates, tranquilizers, amphetamines, MAO inhibitors, tricyclic antidepressants, or lithium carbonate, with one another or with alcohol.

It is perhaps less well known that MAO inhibitors and tricyclic antidepressants (or DL-Phenylalanine) are not to be taken at the same time, and that many common prescription and nonprescription drugs do not mix. It is extremely important to question the physician, and/or pharmacist, to be sure that dangerous mixing of drugs does not take place.

In the case of the MAO inhibitors it is essential to follow special diet restrictions (as given by the physician) as these drugs are dangerous in combination with certain foods, for example cheese, chocolate, and bananas. Likewise, no one who uses MAO inhibitors must take any tricyclic antidepressants. The best policy is throw away old drugs and avoid any self-medication.

The Use of Drugs and the Wholistic Approach

Whereas it is important to recognize the function and contribution of some medications in treating depression, it is even more important not to lose sight of the overall picture. We need to recognize the serious limitations of drugs, their adverse and side effects, and remember that they never solve any mental/emotional or spiritual problem. Yet, the overwhelming majority of depressions are of a mental/emotional and spiritual nature. Consequently, any practice is incorrect that does not provide treatment for the total person—body, mind, and spirit.

The percentage of people who suffer from such disorders as bipolar depression is small compared to the number of those who suffer from other forms of depression. The national figures show that only about 1 percent of the population (2.5 million people) suffers from bipolar depression (Mears and Gatchel, 1979). These 2.5 million people in turn represent only about 7 percent of all the depressed. Since people with bipolar, involutional, schizophrenic, unipolar, and agitated depression are main candidates for drug therapy, about 85 to 90 percent of the depressed most likely do not need drugs.

My belief that no more than 10 to 15 percent of the depressed are good candidates for medications is also partially based on the belief that roughly 75 percent of the depressed suffer perceptual-cognitive problems (misperceptions and misbeliefs), and that the rest suffer from a variety of depressions, whose main sources lie in a faulty lifestyle, such as lack of exercise, lack of stimulation, overstimulation, lack of proper rest and recreation, lack of proper diet, loss of spiritual direction, organic disorders, or genetic predisposition.

If drugs are prescribed, they should be administered only after a thorough physical examination and laboratory workup. Physically based depressions are primarily the outcome of excessive physical and psychological stress, and treatment must be aimed at restoring physical homeostasis.

As mentioned earlier, The National Institute of Mental Health study showed that drug therapy and psychotherapy (actually cognitive therapy and very similar to the method described in this book) were *equally* effective for various forms of depression. Excluded from this study is bipolar and unipolar depression for which it is believed that drugs are an essential part of the overall treatment program. This study confirms that no more than 10 to 15 percent of the depressed are valid candidates for drug therapy, although certain drugs do have value in the treatment of schizophrenic, bipolar, agitated, unipolar, and involutional depression. In general, the greatest value of drugs is primarily for so-called depressive illness (*see* Glossary).

It is best to restore physical homeostasis (for example, by raising norepinephrine and serotonin levels) through natural healing methods such as (1) reducing stress; (2) increasing vitamin, mineral and amino-acid levels; (3) eliminating or reducing certain medications (if at all possible) such as, reserpine and cortisone; and (4) following a wholistic, rational lifestyle.

In summary, the use of drugs is appropriate for only a small percentage of depressed people. These people also need counseling or psychotherapy, and apply the 3 × 3 formula of learning to discern, decide, and do, whatever is necessary for the body, mind and spirit. Above all, they need to look to God for all their needs. Depressed persons need to recognize, that regardless of vulnerability, they can choose to become well.

Thus far our discussion of the physical treatment of depression has been limited to the medical model which reaches only a small number of the depressed people in this country. Regardless of success or failure, the overwhelming majority of depressed people do *not* seek professional help from physicians, psychologists, counselors, or pastors.

The next section will deal with the nonmedical approach to

overcoming depression. It includes physical lifestyle changes that are necessary for anyone who suffers from any form of depression. Unfortunately, few people are taught to change their lifestyle so that the God-given natural healing capacity of the body might be put to work most effectively. I do not know anyone who has followed the guidelines in "The Nonmedical Model" who has not benefited from them.

The Nonmedical Model: Reducing Stress

Excessive physical stressors are potential sources that might eventually lead to loss of physical balance and various forms of depression. It is our objective, therefore, to develop a new physical lifestyle that not only reduces excessive stress but also prepares the body to deal with unforeseen stressful events in the future.

This new lifestyle requires special attention to diet, food supplements, exercise, addictive substances, and the three *Rs* of stress reduction (*rest, recreation,* and *relaxation*). One of the most overlooked potential sources of excessive stress is *diet* and we do well to start with that subject.

A Healthy Diet Is Essential for Stress Reduction

Diet is not only the most overlooked source of many physical and mental/emotional troubles, but it is often ridiculed by those who oppose it for a variety of reasons. Some do so because it goes directly against their own lifestyle of addictions, indulgence, or gluttony.

Others oppose it because they were taught to oppose it, or did not learn about it at their various universities; or, some do not find it profitable to teach people a more natural and healthy lifestyle.

Still others, perhaps misinterpreting the Scriptures, believe

they can eat whatever they please and see no relationship whatsoever between diet, emotions, and spiritual wellness.

All of these assumptions, however, are false. First of all, what
we eat *does* determine our physical health. Second, what we think
(certainly how we think) is greatly influenced by what we eat
and drink as I have explained in some detail in chapter 4 *Physical
Sources and Aspects of Depression*. Third, scientific evidence is
rapidly piling up to show that even serious degenerative diseases
are intimately related to diet. Fourth, a proper diet is essential
for manufacturing those chemical substances necessary for a
healthy physical, mental, and emotional life.

Our bodies need to be preserved and well cared for if our minds
are to function right. We also know that we need well-functioning
minds for our spiritual life. God wants to live in our bodies, and
we are told that they are temples, "Know ye not that ye are the
temple of God, and that the Spirit of God dwelleth in you? If any
man defile the temple of God, him shall God destroy; for the
temple of God is holy, which temple ye are" (1 Cor. 3:16–17).

Paying attention to our diet is scriptural and essential. Our
diets above all other things are responsible for much ill health
and the reason behind many mental, emotional, and even social
and pseudospiritual problems (*see* chapter 6).

One of the more common denominators in the lives of depressed people is that many live on junk food. Another common—
and somewhat startling—denominator is the rapid progress many
depressed people make once they begin to eat balanced and nutritionally healthy meals.

Many types of depression, as discussed in Appendix 1 and 2,
are directly related to such primary potential stressors as glandular dysfunction, glucose disturbances, amino-acid, mineral and
vitamin deficiencies, and malnutrition. They are the result of our
bodies' loss of homeostasis. Excessive and prolonged stress eventually takes its toll, and depression manifests itself.

Whatever we do, it is best to include good nutrition as one of
the very first steps toward recovery. The dietary recommendations to be outlined here are based on the findings of experts in
both Europe and the USA. The suggestions, if properly followed,
will allow us to feel better physically, improve our longevity, and
reduce overall physical stress, which is so essential to combat
depression.

Follow these general rules:

1. *Avoid processed foods.* These are foods that are no longer in their natural state. They are usually canned, smoked, pressure-cooked, pouched, bottled, preserved, irradiated, salted, cured, or colored.
2. *Avoid overeating.* Avoid eating more than your body needs. You need only so many calories and no more. Never eat to the point of feeling stuffed. It is better to eat six small meals rather than three large ones. It is unwise, however, to snack in-between these small meals.
3. *Avoid self-poisoning.* We often poison ourselves with the use of addictive and other substances. Avoid nicotine and caffeine, and be especially careful with alcohol and prescription and nonprescription drugs.
4. *Avoid obesity.* Obesity is a main source of poor physical health, and contributes directly to poor mental and emotional health. Depression is fairly common among overweight and obese people.
5. *Avoid refined carbohydrates.* Carbohydrates consist of sugars, starches, and fibers, and are made up of carbon, oxygen, and hydrogen. Although carbohydrates are essential for our bodies, refined carbohydrates, however, are bad for our health. Excessive use of refined carbohydrates, such as white-flour products, white rice, and sugars (white sugar, brown sugar, raw sugar, syrups, dextrose) is not only a major health hazard, but "contributes" directly to many types of depression. The excessive use of refined carbohydrates is very stressful to our bodies and minds (Abrahamson and Pezet 1977; Airola 1971; Cleave 1974; Yudkin 1972).
6. *Avoid excess fat and fatty foods.* Highly publicized research on the dangers of using excessive amounts of fats and fatty foods should make it unnecessary to remind anyone. But remember that clogged arteries, heart disease, and other stressful conditions are directly related to the excessive use of fat, saturated fat, and cholesterol.
7. *Avoid excessive use of food supplements.* I believe that food supplements are important for just about everyone in our society because most Americans have poor diets and the

majority of our foods have much of the nutrition processed out of them—but the danger of abusing vitamins and minerals remains. Vitamins and minerals are to be taken as "supplements" with balanced meals. They must never take the place of food. Also, they must not be taken in dosages that exceed the standards set by experts such as Airola (1974), Kirschman (1973), Lesser (1981), and Newbold (1975). An excellent guide on this subject is *The Right Dose,* by Patricia Hausman (1987).

8. *Avoid too much sodium.* A major relationship exists between sodium and stress, and resultant disorders such as hypertension (Whittlesey 1978). A better "salt" to use, in limitation, is half-sodium and half-potassium, for example, Morton's Lite Salt. Hypoglycemics, however, may need some salt with their meals because there is some evidence that salt may either improve the digestion of food in the intestine, and thus release more sugar, or to stimulate the intestine to absorb sugar more efficiently (British Medical Journal, 292: 1697, 1986).

9. *Avoid eating the same foods over and over.* For balanced nutrition and good physical and emotional health, it is important to consistently eat a variety of foods. This will help insure that you get more of the essential nutrients.

10. *Avoid those foods for which you have a craving.* The reason for this is primarily that we often crave precisely what we are allergic to or what's not good for us. As a rule, these are commonly used products, such as sweets, milk, eggs, oranges, or chocolate. Investigate if you are allergic to any of these substances. (*See* Appendix 2)

The Wellness Diet

Most health diets share significant similarities in what they recommend for such diverse disorders as cardiovascular disease, depression, diabetes, cancer, hemorrhoids, and kidney malfunctions.

Many so-called high-risk foods are recognized as the cause of a number of disorders. Diet, perhaps more than any other part of our lifestyle, is to blame for much ill health. It is widely recommended that we leave sugar and other refined carbohydrates out of our diets, and especially out of the diets of arthritis and cancer patients, or of those suffering from anxiety, lack of emotional control, or depression. Nearly everyone who has closely looked at nutrition (and who is not in bondage to tradition or to special interest groups) recognizes that it is important to eat foods in their natural state as much as possible.

Many experts over the past half-century have urged us not only to avoid refined carbohydrates but to eat a lot of living foods, such as raw fruits and vegetables. Likewise, we have been warned for decades to limit our intake of meat, table salt, alcohol, and caffeine (decaffeination of coffee started in Europe more than fifty years ago).

Even our government is getting the word out about these concerns. These attempts, however, have been lukewarm and fiercely opposed by powerful special interest groups. Diet recommendations made by independent researchers and practitioners can be ignored only at our peril. Ignorance is not bliss, but is supremely destructive. Pay special attention to the recommendations in this chapter and follow them as closely as possible.

Because I can give only basic ideas and food recommendations, it is important that you continue to study nutrition in greater depth as much as possible. Among the helpful books in the reference section, several deserve special mention: *The Bristol Diet,* by Dr. Alex Forbes, as well as the following books on natural healing and nutrition, Dr. Paavo Airola's *How to Get Well* (1974), Kirschmann and Dunne's *Nutrition Almanac* (1984), Mindell's *Vitamin Bible* (1985), and Dr. M. L. Newbold's *Mega-Nutrients for Your Health* (1975).

We find virtually universal agreement that certain diets are healthy while others promote disease. Here are some basic suggestions for anyone who is even remotely interested in physical and mental health (they overlap somewhat with the previous listings of foods to avoid).

1. *Reduce intake of foods of animal origin.*
Be extremely careful with red meat and fats, as well as sausages, egg yolks, and hard cheeses (especially colored cheeses). We are far better off to drastically limit our intake of all animal protein, and eat only low-fat foods, for example egg white, fresh

fish, and chicken. Most people do not need more than 20 percent of their daily caloric intake to consist of protein, and no more than 20 percent of fats.

2. *Increase intake of complex carbohydrates.*

Most people do not get enough complex (unrefined) carbohydrates. Our diet ideally consists of about 60 percent complex carbohydrates, such as grains, vegetables, fruit, seeds, and sprouts. This will insure a steady flow of necessary glucose in our bloodstream, provide the bowel with essential fiber, and reduce the risk of various diseases, including heart disease, cancer, and diabetes. It could also reduce the incidence of bone loss (osteoporosis), which is especially important for increased energy and longer life span. For people who suffer from depression, it is especially important to increase their intake of complex carbohydrates and eliminate refined carbohydrates.

3. *Eliminate refined carbohydrates.*

Perhaps the most important dietary step to take for those who suffer from anxiety, uncontrolled anger, and/or depression, is the elimination of *all* refined carbohydrates. Ironically, this is the step that is most disliked, disregarded, and scorned. It is unfortunate that we foolishly continue to insist that food that tastes good must be good for us as well, or because most people do it, therefore, it must be right. For years, misinformed people have been scorning the idea of any relationship between food and mood. Therefore it's difficult to teach the suffering millions that their thinking is often out of control simply because their brain is out of control due to a self-destructive diet.

To reduce stress in general and to promote overall health, it is necessary to eliminate refined carbohydrates. Without question refined carbohydrates are the source of much illness in this country, the primary source behind obesity, and a major contributing factor (if not the cause) of several serious diseases.

Refined carbohydrates such as white flour, white rice, macaroni, spaghetti, refined sugar products (white or brown), and all the products derived therefrom such as pies, cakes, ice cream, and scores of other products are to be shunned by those who are suffering from any kind of depression, and especially depressions of an endogenous nature.

4. *Increase the supply of polyunsaturated fats.*

Whereas it is essential to reduce the intake of saturated fats, it is important to get an adequate supply of polyunsaturated fats, such as safflower and sunflower oils. The total fat intake from all sources should be no more than about 20 percent of our daily caloric intake.

5. *Drink plenty of water.*

Water is the *most* important nutrient in the body, and one of the more overlooked ones. Water helps to cleanse and detoxify our bodies and helps perform a host of functions such as digestion, circulation, and excretion. Although it is essential to drink plenty of water, it is important that it is sufficiently pure. Many drinking-water supplies are polluted and alternative sources might have to be considered. To aid the proper digestion of food it is generally not recommended to drink water or other fluids less than half an hour before we eat a meal.

6. *Decrease intake of salt.*

Millions of people have become addicted to the excessive use of salt (sodium chloride). Salt is a major cause of high blood pressure, damages the kidneys, retains water in the body, and reduces the potassium level in the blood stream. A good decision is to reduce or eliminate the use of the salt shaker. If you are going to use salt, as mentioned earlier, it is advisable to do so in the form of a mixture of sodium and potassium chloride, which is available in most food stores. Better yet use a salt mixture consisting of sodium chloride, potassium chloride, and magnesium. Such a mixture has been reported helpful as an "improvement in blood-sugar levels and glucose tolerance," something that is of importance to many people who suffer from endogenous depression.

7. *Eliminate addictive substances.*

Addictive substances such as alcohol, chocolate, coffee, and tea have already been described and will again be mentioned later in this chapter. These substances are not only stressful to our bodies but they are particularly harmful to people who suffer from various forms of depression.

These seven dietary guidelines, properly followed, will be a great help in overcoming certain forms of depression, and may help change your life and extend it as well. The Wellness Diet, however, is not something to be followed grudgingly. For complete success, it requires commitment and enthusiasm. Tackle it with joy, and see it as a fun project that can be shared with family and friends. Do not, however, consider the Wellness Diet as the final solution. It is a major step, but still only one step in a series of steps. *Remember that the solution to depression is not to be found in a single approach but in a wholistic, multiple approach.*

We don't have to go on the Wellness Diet all by ourselves or give up so many things that our body and mind seem to crave. We don't have to break all those self-defeating habits all by ourselves. God wants to help us with this. He wants to be part of our struggles and lead us to victory. Let's go for a happy, joyful, as well as reasonable lifestyle, and cling to that prescription for health found in Proverbs (4:20–22), which tells us, "My son, attend to my words; incline thine ear unto my sayings. Let them not depart from thine eyes; keep them in the midst of thine heart. For they are life unto those that find them, and health to all their flesh." The healing power of God is evident in so many ways.

Three scriptures in Proverbs complement the Wellness Diet:

1. "A merry heart maketh a cheerful countenance: but by sorrow of the heart the spirit is broken" (15:13).
2. "Pleasant words are like an honeycomb, sweet to the soul and health to the bones" (16:24).
3. "A merry heart doeth good like a medicine, but a broken spirit drieth the bones" (17:22).

As is clearly implied in these verses, happy thoughts give us happy feelings, a happy appearance, and a healthy spirit and body. The third verse declares that happy thoughts are *medicine* for our bodies. The opposite is also true. Whining, crying, complaining, bitterness, envy, jealousy, odious comparisons, and negative thinking poison our bodies and minds, and could undo every bit of good that we could attain with the Wellness Diet. Don't take on a Wellness Diet and be bitter, spiteful, or unforgiving. All gained could all be lost. Just as junk food is dangerous for our health, so are junk thoughts. Junk thoughts can be even worse. Although this diet is an important part of any wellness lifestyle, it has to be just a part of a balanced approach to body, mind, and spirit.

Choosing it over a diet that can lead to ill health and mental-emotional problems is very much like the basic commitment of choosing "blessing over cursing" and "life over death." This must be done wholeheartedly and with a great desire to do what is necessary. Depression is both a stress disorder and a thinking disorder. Reducing stress is essential and one of the most effective steps is through a stress-reducing Wellness Diet. Stick as closely as possible to the basic guidelines already discussed and use as much as possible only the recommended dietary items.

The Wellness Diet will not only produce a healthier and happier physical and emotional life, but it will also help to make you look and feel younger. Look forward to being more energetic, to having a trimmer and slimmer figure, and to improving your emotional control, judgment, memory, and ability to reason. It is a marvellous fact that a wholesome diet can actually slow down the aging process, restore youthfulness, and help prevent (as well as heal) many illnesses of the body and *mind.* The Wellness Diet must be part of the normal lifestyle of anyone who has difficulties with depression and of anyone who wants to live happier and healthier.

Because some well-meaning (but misinformed) peple oppose what has been just described, it should be emphasized that the people who have come up with many of the recommendations I have shared are experts in their fields. They are not faddists. They are not out to hinder but to help and heal. For example, Dr. Alex Forbes, author of *The Bristol Diet,* is a Fellow of the Royal College of Physicians. He served for twenty-eight years as Consultant Physician in Plymouth Hospital, England. In 1979, he was appointed as an advisor to the World Health Organization. In 1983, H.R.H. Prince Charles opened Dr. Forbes' new residential Cancer Help Center in Bristol, which has since received wide acclaim as a beacon of hope for many.

Also, there is a proven relationship between excessive physical, psychological, and spiritual stress and serious disorders such as cancer. Depression, not as a passing symptom but as a full-blown disorder—just like chronic worry, sorrow, and anxiety—must also be considered a potential stressor in the development of cancer (Padus 1986; Pearce 1983).

Like chain reactions, excessive physical, psychological, and spiritual stress will eventually affect the limbic system adversely,

4. Wellness Diet

(See Comments for further explanation.)

	Recommended	*Not Recommended*
Beverages	Fresh spring water, distilled water, herb teas, such as camomile, and fresh diluted fruit juices (in small quantities only).	Artificial fruit beverages, alcohol, cocoa, coffee, carbonated, canned, bottled, pouched, and/or pasteurized beverages.
Dairy Products*	Butter (very little), white cheese (little), yogurt (unsweetened, uncolored), low-fat and skimmed milk**.	Imitation and processed butter, ice cream, sour cream, whipped cream, and so forth. Colored, pasteurized cheeses, dips, cream cheese.
Eggs* *	Not more than one poached or boiled egg per day, and no more than a total of four per week.	All fried eggs. (Do not eat fried food of any kind).
Food Supplements	To rely solely on food products is not sufficient nowadays for good health. See Chart on pages 264–268 for further guidelines.	It is not recommended to use food supplements in lieu of food, nor to overindulge in them. Read guidelines in this book.
Fish* *	Only broiled or baked, fresh white fish in limited quantities.	Nonwhite, breaded and fried, or nonfresh fish.
Fruit* * *	Eat only fresh fruit in small quantities at a time.	All canned, processed and/or sweetened fruits.
Grains and Seeds* * *	Whole grain or wholewheat—use in moderation. Look for plenty of fiber in whole grain products. Use variety of grains: rye, bran, oats, wheat, buckwheat, millet, brown rice, and so forth. Use whole seeds (pumpkin, flaxseed, sunflower).	Experts universally agree that white flour products are bad for our health. Do not use white flour, hull-less grains and seeds, or crackers, macaroni, spaghetti, processed cereals, white rice, or cakes, pies, cookies made with white flour.
Meat Products* *	Use very little meat; instead, use chicken, turkey. Use very small quantities of lean meat only.	Red meat is not recommended. Bacon, sausages, are especially cautioned against.
Nuts* * *	Preferably fresh and raw. The exception is for cashews which must be cooked before eating, otherwise they are toxic.	Roasted, salted, and otherwise processed with additives, colorings. Do not use coconut.
Oils*	Use only cold-processed oils, such as safflower, sunflower, corn oils. Look for polyunsaturated products.	All shortening-refined fat and oils, saturated and unsaturated hydrogenated margarine. Do not use coconut oil.

Seasonings and Spices	Chives, garlic, herbs, onions, nutmeg, marjoram. Use spices *with caution.*	Do not use *hot* spices, pepper, or salt. Get your iodine from kelp. If you "must" use salt, use a mixture of potassium, sodium chloride, and magnesium. Do not use mustard or mayonnaise.
Soups	Homemade soups only, using products from the recommended listing.	Canned, bottled, pouched, processed, packaged soups, boullions.
Sprouts***	All sprouts such as alfalfa, lentils, peas.	
Sweets	Recommended only in very *small* quantities are carob, fructose, raw honey, and unsulphured molasses. The less, even of these sweets, the better. Best is to use none!	All artificial sweeteners, and all artificially sweetened products. All refined sugars (including turbinado, brown, and white sugar), candies, chocolates. Do not use maple syrup.
Vegetables***	Recommended in large quantities, especially eaten in a fresh and raw state. Include in particular dark green, leafy vegetables. Also included are potatoes, and frozen vegetables.	All canned, bottled, pouched, and preserved vegetables.

Comments on the Wellness Diet

1. Follow basic seven guidelines provided earlier.
2. About 60 percent of the diet is to consist of complex carbohydrates, marked ***.
3. About 20 percent of the diet is to consist of protein, marked **.
4. About 20 percent of the diet is to consist of fat, marked *.
5. No additive substances are to be part of the diet.
6. To obtain roughly sufficient calories for your age, sex, height, and to maintain, increase, or reduce your weight, it is important to understand recommended caloric intake, and the caloric values of the recommended foods listed on the Wellness Diet (*See* Appendix 5).
7. Milk, even low-fat, and skimmed milk, must be used with some caution. The milk issue has not been settled. There are worldwide reports that warn against the use of milk. The main reason why we use milk is because it has such a high content of calcium and phosphorus. However, bone

meal has a higher content, and we can obtain phosphorus and calcium from whole grains and vegetables. Some of the problems with milk are high cholesterol content, the transmission of diseases of the cow to humans, and hormones, DDT, Strontium 90, penicillin, and other residues in milk. The fact that cows are artificially bred to produce abnormally large amounts of milk through an overactive pituitary gland should be warning in itself to all who are concerned with normal metabolism. Last, but not least, any depressed person who uses a lot of milk needs to find out if he or she is perhaps allergic to this product in the first place.

8. The Wellness Diet is not only designed to strengthen our bodies, reduce stress, improve our overall well-being, and so forth, but actually is an anti-illness diet. For example, eating certain foods may reduce the risk of cancer. In order to reduce the risk of cancer of the esophagus, larynx, or lungs it may be helpful to eat apricots, carrots, peaches, spinach, cantaloupes, and tomatoes. To reduce cancer risk for the esophagus and stomach it may be helpful to eat berries, cabbage, citrus fruits, mango, and papaya. To reduce cancer risk for the gastrointestinal and respiratory tracts it may be helpful to eat broccoli, brussels sprouts, cauliflower, kohlrabi; and to reduce colon cancer risk it may be helpful to eat fresh fruits, vegetables, and whole-grain breads and cereals.

9. The dietary recommendations of the Wellness Diet are generally in agreement with the present philosophy of the U.S. Government which through the Department of Agriculture and Health and Human services, issued seven dietary guidelines in 1980 to help Americans achieve better health. These seven guidelines are all included in the Wellness Diet, and in other sections of this book.

A well-publicized report by the U.S. Senate in 1977, entitled "Dietary Goals for the United States" stressed that millions of Americans are suffering from health problems because of poor eating habits and inadequate diets. This includes such serious health problems as diabetes, heart disease, cancer, overweight, and early aging.

Not only the U.S. Government, but every modern health

organization is concerned with the present destructive dietary habits of the nation. All of these organizations have made recommendations for the restriction of salt, sugar, fat, dairy products, caffeine, nicotine, alcohol, and to reduce our total caloric intake. The American Heart Association (USA Today, August 27, 1986) advised to cut back on foods high in saturated fats, sodium, cholesterol, etc., and stressed the importance of fruits and vegetables, low-fat milk, lean meats in small quantities, and nonprocessed foods.

10. Please note that poor nutrition is only one of many reasons for our poor physical and/or mental health. It would be misleading to think that poor nutrition is the sole culprit behind our demise. In the case of depression we must not lose sight of the fact that it is a multifaceted body-mind-spirit stress disorder that is the final outcome of loss of physical balance, psychological integrity, and/or spiritual direction.

---

in particular the hypothalamus. This, in turn, leads to excessive pituitary responses, upsetting the entire endocrine system and increasing the possibility of abnormal cell growth. In addition, the hypothalamus and the endocrine system will impair the immune system by suppressing immune activity. This, combined with an increase in abnormal cells, might lead to cancer growth. If we add known dietary stressors that have already been implicated in the onset of certain cancers, then we have to be foolish indeed to eat and do as we please (White 1984). To help fight off many mental stressors, and provide some very important food for thought, I wholeheartedly recommend an excellent book by Dr. Donald E. Demaray. This book, *Laughter, Joy, and Healing* (Baker Book House, 1986), provides sound advice on the importance of laughter and joy in our lives.

Diet is such a major source of stress that it plays a vital part in all states of health and disease. The National Academy of Sciences published reports in 1982 and 1984 that many cancers are directly related to dietary factors. Therefore, many cancers are preventable. Furthermore, it is now common knowledge that dietary management (or treatment) improves the survival rate of most cancer patients. Unfortunately we are still treating many cancer patients just like arthritis and depressed patients, often without even mentioning the word *diet*.

Appendices 6 and 7 describe in detail why specific foods and food supplements are so important in the treatment of depression. The tables provide insights into the interrelationship of food and food supplements, with the various physiological actions in the body that have a direct or indirect bearing on our overall mental health and such specific problems as depression.

Food Supplements for Depression

Along with well-meaning but misinformed people who sincerely believe that nutrition plays little, if any, part in such disorders as depression, there are those who exert even stronger opposition to food supplements.

Food supplements are important additions to the Wellness Diet. The best proof of its importance is gained from a survey of registered dieticians in the State of Washington. This survey indicated that nearly 60 percent said they use some form of nutritional supplementation with their *own* diets (Worthington-Roberts and Breskin, 1984). If most dieticians in the State of Washington use food supplements, might it be possible that we can find a few in other states as well?

In recent decades, tremendous strides have been made by health practitioners, in this country and abroad, in the treatment of depression and other mental/emotional disorders with nutrition and food-supplement therapy. Unquestionably, what we eat or do not eat affects the way we feel—physically, mentally, and emotionally. Many such studies have been reported in professional journals. For example, on depression caused by B_6 deficiency in the *Lancet* (Adams, et al., April 28, 1973 and August 31, 1974), on endogenous depression caused by B_{12} deficiency in the *American Journal of Psychiatry* (Evans, et al, February, 1983); on depression caused by folic acid deficiency in *Psychosomatics: Journal of the Academy of Psychosomatic Medicine* (Ghadirian, et al., November, 1980). Not only vitamins but also minerals play a major role in our mental/emotional health. Minerals well known for their stress-reductive qualities are calcium, chromium, magnesium, manganese, and zinc (Faelton 1981; Kunin 1980; Mindel 1985). Also, three amino acids have been found helpful in the treatment of depression, namely tryptophan (Cheraskin and Ringsdorf 1974), tyrosine (Gelenberg, et al., 1980), and DL-Phenylalanine (*Nutrition News,* December 1983).

Outstanding physicians and other health practitioners have written excellent books on nutrition and health. These authors include Airola (1971, 1972, 1974, 1977), Brennan (1977), Fredericks and Goodman (1974), Hausman (1987), Kirschmann and Dunne (1984), Langer (1984), Lesser (1981), Mackarness (1976, 1980), Mandell (1980), Mindell (1985), Newbold (1975), Sheinkin and Schachter (1980), Wright (1979, 1984), and scores of others.

Although it is beyond the scope of this book to discuss at length the subject of vitamins, minerals, and amino acids, a few observations should be made. Vitamins, as the name implies, are vital for our health. We cannot exist without them. When one or more vitamins is deficient in our bodies we become ill, and sometimes even fatally so. God created this world with an abundant food supply for all of us, and as long as we treat that food supply correctly and use it properly, we will be healthier. Unfortunately we have treated neither the earth nor our bodies very wisely.

To a great extent our lands, waterways, and the air we breathe are polluted. Our soil has all too frequently become depleted of essential nutrients, and what we obtain from the soil is altered and processed to such an extent that many essential vitamins as well as minerals are lost. *Let me sum up a few reasons why we need the Wellness Diet and food supplements:*

Eating habits have drastically changed over the past decades, and we do not eat enough fresh fruit, vegetables, and whole foods.

Polluted environments not only affect the soil, but also the air we breathe, which increases the need for such supplements as vitamin C.

Overfarming and destruction of micro-organisms with pesticides leads to soil depletion.

Indulgence in junk food robs our bodies of essential nutrients, such as B-vitamins.

The use of processed (refined) foods and food additives.

Excessive environmental stresses, illness, and trauma.

Whole foods are often picked before they are ripe, and sprayed with chemicals. They are rarely fresh when bought.

Cooking, and especially overcooking, destroys vitamins.

Drug use, for example, birth-control pills, may deplete the body of B_6, B_{12}, folic acid, and vitamin C.

Addictive substances, such as alcohol, caffeine, nicotine, all greatly increase the need for vitamin supplements. Smoking seriously depletes vitamin C levels. Alcohol users need extra A, D, E, B_1, B_6, B_{12}, folic acid, C, K, zinc, magnesium, and potassium.

The irradiation of many food products with Cobalt-60, Cesium-137, and X rays, which diminishes the natural contents of vitamins A, B_6, B_{12}, C, and E, and alters the essential amino acids tryptophan, cystine, and methionine, and creates dozens of so-called URP's (Unique Radiolytic Products). It is not yet known what they may eventually do to the human organism. (People's Medical Society, 1986).

For these and other reasons, food supplements are becoming increasingly popular. Specific disorders have also been treated with large doses of food supplements. Appendix 7 lists the specific vitamins, minerals, and amino acids that have been found helpful in the "overall" treatment of depression. Food supplements, however, must not and cannot take the place of a healthy diet, such as the Wellness Diet described earlier. Food supplements are indeed only *supplements* and must be used with caution and discretion, as described in Appendix 7.

The Bible and the Wellness Diet

The Bible should never be considered as a handbook on nutrition or dieting; however, it would be foolish if we did not look to God for wisdom in all areas of our lives. The Bible provides general guidelines for a healthy and sensible lifestyle. We find advice on how to be good stewards, use our talents, and seek wisdom, knowledge, and understanding. Any thinking person quickly discovers that God indeed wants our "whole spirit and soul and body be preserved blameless unto the coming of our LORD Jesus Christ" (1 Thess. 5:23).

There is more than general advice in the Bible, however. For starters, we learn that we are created in God's image (Gen. 1:26, 27), that our body is the temple of the Holy Spirit (1 Cor. 6:19), and that it is to be presented a "living sacrifice" (Rom. 12:1), in which Christ shall be magnified . . ." (Phil. 1:20).

God created the earth to be inhabited by his children, and did not leave out the creation of food sources to optimally sustain their life. Not only did God create the food sources, but he also told what they were. "And God said, Behold, I have given you every herb bearing seed, which is upon the face of all the earth, and every tree, in which is the fruit of a tree yielding seed; to you it shall be for [food]" (Gen. 1:29). Clearly our original diet was vegetarian (Gen. 3:18), and this did not change until after the flood had destroyed the earth's vegetation. It was only then that God gave permission to use flesh foods, as we can read in Genesis 9:3, "Every *moving thing* that liveth shall be [meat] for you; even as the green herb have I given you all things" (*italics added*).

Another reason to allow flesh foods was the murmuring of the children of Israel, "I have heard the murmurings of the children of Israel: speak unto them, saying, At even ye shall eat flesh and in the morning ye shall be filled with bread; and ye shall know that I am the LORD your God" (Exod. 16:12, 13). However, it remained forbidden to eat blood and fat as described in Leviticus 3:17; 7:23, 25. The Bible is up-to-date, for we are increasingly learning that meat is not good for us and that animal fat is very unhealthy. Green vegetables (herbs) and fruit, on the other hand, are among the healthiest foods on earth.

Even if the Bible did not say one word about food, there would still be every reason to pay close attention to what, when, and how we eat, for God has given us minds to use wisely. The Bible is a book of faith and reason. First Timothy 4:3–5 tells us not to put people in bondage over food. My advice is to search the Scriptures and always combine faith and reason!

Some Additional Steps

Eating the right kinds of foods and taking appropriate food supplements are only two out of seven important steps we best take for stress reduction and overcoming depression. The other five steps are *the elimination of harmful substances, weight control, exercise, rest and relaxation,* and *recreation.*

Eliminate Harmful Substances for Stress Reduction

We have looked at the importance of changing our diet because poor diet is all too frequently involved in many cases of depression. It has been well established that allergies, depression, hypoglycemia, hyperactivity, learning disabilities, and juvenile delinquency frequently are influenced by nutritional factors. It is not only of the greatest importance to have proper nutrition in the treatment of depression, but also in its *prevention.* This is especially important for children and young people.

Changing our diet and taking food supplements is not enough unless we also eliminate addictive and other harmful substances. A healthy diet is stress reductive, but if we continue to indulge in alcohol, caffeine, and nicotine, we gain little.

Anyone serious about overcoming depression or the prevention of depression, should eliminate alcohol, caffeine, and nicotine from his or her lifestyle. Too many health practitioners downplay the importance of addictive substances. There are many reasons for this. One big reason is that our modern form of allopathic medicine holds that diseases originate outside of the body and are to be treated with certain agents (for example, drugs) to counteract these invasions. It is unfortunate that this theory of medicine is carried all the way over into the treatment of mental/emotional disorders, although frequently it is not applicable at all.

Medical schools until recently included little instruction on nutrition for the treatment and prevention of disease, mostly because allopathy (*see* Glossary) holds that disease is primarily exogenous rather than endogenous. Fortunately, even modern medicine is now discovering that the allopathic view of medicine is not always the best. The *AMA Family Medical Guide* (1982) frankly states: "... we discovered that non-infectious diseases such as cancer, heart and blood vessel disorders, congenital problems, and environmentally triggered diseases were quickly replacing infectious diseases as a major source of human suffering. These non-infectious diseases do not respond to 'standard treatment.' This tends to lead our thinking toward the vitalist view of health and illness."

Unfortunately, meanwhile most health professionals are carrying on business as usual, dispensing drugs for any and every conceivable ailment. The question is why do we have such a misplaced faith in drugs and excessively tolerant attitude toward the use of addictive substances?

The biggest reason for the *laissez-faire* approach is most likely the consumer. As a rule the consumer does not want any interference with the so-called pleasures of life. There is a stubborn unwillingness to give up smoking, drinking alcohol, using caffeine, and indulging in sweets. This unwillingness is perhaps based on the misbelief that it is impossible to give these habits up.

Christians, however, are increasingly aware that the Bible teaches what common sense also tells us: that we cannot separate the body from the mind, and that whatever negative practice we do to our bodies will be reflected in our minds and vice versa (Prov. 16:24; 17:22).

People who are set free from mood-control substances, such as alcohol, caffeine, dextrose, nicotine, sucrose, theobromine, and theophylline, greatly reduce unnecessary stress in their lives.

Maintain Correct Weight for Stress Reduction

It is essential for good physical and mental health to maintain correct weight. Having worked with scores of overweight people, I discovered that many of them suffer from a great number of mental and emotional difficulties.

Although most of these difficulties are the result of self-defeating beliefs, I also found that many of the seriously overweight and obese people were suffering from hypoglycemia as well as depression. Often there is a belief that these depressions are strictly the result of perceptual-cognitive factors. Nothing, however, could be further from the truth. Many overweight people suffer from endogenous depressions, and it is not until they start on a combination of the proper diet, regular exercise, and rational thinking that they begin to get well.

The evidence is overwhelming that many overweight people are suffering from a number of disturbances (not necessarily diseases) of the endocrine system. They have created these disorders as the result of self-defeating and even self-destructive lifestyles. On the other hand, it is also true that being overweight is far less acceptable to the overweight person than is often thought.

In classes where I have asked overweight people to write down, anonymously, their thoughts on being overweight, I have been struck by the fact that even the happiest, most smiling overweight person will admit to being unhappy, if not depressed. If we want to find some people with smiling depression then we should look at those who are grossly overweight.

It is important to maintain the kind of weight that is good for our physical, mental, and spiritual health. God warns about excesses of all kinds, and warns specifically against drunkenness and gluttony (Prov. 23:20, 21). We are told that the glutton shall come to poverty, and while this may be true sometimes in the economic sense, this is more true in a physical, mental, and spiritual sense. Many explanations and even more excuses are offered why so many overweight people populate our modern society. Why search for excuses when we have so many obvious ways of solving the problem?

In most cases, people become overweight because they eat too much of the wrong kind of foods and do not exercise enough to burn up the excess calories. Overweight produces excessive stress on both our physical and psychological systems, and directly contributes to depression. Proper weight reduces stress, increases self-esteem, and gives a sense of physical and psychological well-being. Appendix 5 has additional information for permanent weight control.

Get Regular Exercise for Stress Reduction

Exercise helps us to be healthier, more productive, energetic, live longer, and reduce stress. It can do so, however, only as long as we make it fun and not make it hard work, a compulsion, an obsession, an escape from reality, or all we live for. Exercise, of course, consists of some kind of bodily or mental exertion. We cannot exercise without a certain amount of effort, willpower, and motivation.

God created our bodies in such a way that they require regular exercise, and if we fail to do so then we will age prematurely, lose resistance to a variety of diseases, be more prone to emotional difficulties, and have less energy.

Exercise immediately benefits the depressed person in helping with blood-sugar stabilization and increasing the flow of oxygen to the brain. The long-range benefit is a decrease in anxiety and depression. For several years some therapists have been prescribing jogging for moderate depression. One study conducted by the University of Wisconsin Medical School has found that jogging worked as well as talk therapy for moderately depressed people (Jogging for the Mind, *Time,* July 24, 1978).

While objective data presently is inconclusive, many authorities believe that vigorous and regular exercise changes the chemical composition of our bodies in a powerful therapeutic way. Robert S. Brown, M.D., Ph. D. (1978) is one of the experts who has worked hard to spread the word on the importance of exercise for the treatment of depression.

Writes Dr. Brown, ". . . we are impressed by the benefits many depressed patients have derived from extended, systematic periods of regular physical exercise such as jogging, swimming, walking, tennis, and the like. Exercise is also effective in fending off the depressed and pessimistic moods that mentally healthy people have from time to time."

Dr. Brown's work at the University of Virginia involved about seven hundred subjects, including those with recognized clinical depression. On the basis of his studies he and his co-workers make the following observations:

1. Physical fitness is often associated with a feeling of well-being and reduces depression and anxiety.
2. Fitness appears to be associated with physical and psychological benefits regardless of the subject's age.
3. Although training may include a variety of exercise pro-

grams ranging from jogging to judo, competition may be minimized for maximum psychological gains.

4. Although physical exertion on the job may be physically beneficial, recreational or voluntary programs yield more psychologically useful exercise.
5. The biological benefits of exercise may be associated in part with changes produced among brain amines, salt metabolism, muscle neuronal activity, and striatal function.
6. A comprehensive history of the depressed patient's motor activity is useful in prescribing an exercise regimen of maximum benefit.
7. The role model of physicians who regard a physical fitness program as an important part of their own lives cannot be overlooked.

Reports from all over the world have, for a number of years, stressed the importance of exercise. Here are some of the beneficial effects. Exercise:

1. increases blood volume.
2. retards the aging process.
3. helps fight off heart attacks.
4. gives a better chance to live through a heart attack.
5. keeps energy levels high.
6. restores energy levels quickly when stricken with illness.
7. helps make daily tasks easier.
8. helps burn excess calories.
9. improves physical movement and posture.
10. reduces fatty substances (cholesterol and triglycerides) in our blood.
11. protects against some back problems.
12. is important for weight control.
13. opens new capillaries in muscles.
14. strengthens the heart muscle.
15. gives a more efficient heart and body.
16. increases muscle flexibility.
17. may help protect against accidents.
18. provides the brain with increased oxygen supply.
19. provides the brain with increased nutrients.
20. improves brain function and allows for clearer thinking.
21. stimulates absorption, elimination, and metabolism.

22. provides for deeper and sounder sleep.
23. serves as a safe and natural tranquilizer (endorphins).
24. helps prevent degenerative diseases.
25. improves circulation.
26. helps to build a sense of achievement and personal worth.
27. improves poise and grace and enhances self-esteem.
28. reduces anger and anxiety.
29. reduces stress.
30. reduces depression.

There are more solid reasons why we should participate in a regular exercise program. Such a program can be inexpensive, and can be done with others or by ourselves. Do not, however, start an exercise program without first obtaining a thorough medical examination. Also, exercise must be done gradually. If exercise brings on pain, dizziness, or nausea, stop immediately and obtain new medical advice. Exercise must remain fun.

A major benefit of regular exercise for people who suffer from mild to moderate depression is that it takes their thoughts off their problems and leads them to concentrate on a pleasurable and self-enhancing activity. Consequently, exercise must not be overly competitive, hurried, or in any way stressful. The objective is to have stress reduction. One of the very best physical activities to undertake is *walking*.

To Reduce Stress,
Take Time for Rest and Relaxation

Along with sensible eating and drinking, relaxation is essential for good health. If we do not relax regularly, we will sooner or later become ill. Ideally, take time out every day to relax. Many people fail to do this, and are not even aware that they are under excessive stress. These *stress warning signs* will tell you quickly if you are in need of regular relaxation:

Accident proneness	Constant fatigue
Alcoholism	Crowding and other
Asthma	environmental pressures
Biting nails	Depression
Concern over trivialities	Dizziness

Dryness of throat and mouth

Easily startled

Excessive tenseness

Excessive sweating

Feelings of inferiority

Feelings of superiority

Feelings of unreality

Fiddling constantly

Financial difficulties

Floating anxiety

Frequent illnesses, common colds, and so forth

Frequent need to urinate (no organic cause)

Gastrointestinal difficulties

Great urge to cry, run, or hide

Grinding of the teeth

High blood pressure

High-pitched, nervous laughter

Hyperexcitability

Hyperkinetic behavior

Impulsiveness

Inability to concentrate

Increased appetite

Increased use of addictive substances

Insomnia

Irritability

Lack of energy

Laughing inappropriately

Loss of appetite

Marital difficulties

Migraine headaches

Nervous tics

Neurotic behavior

Nightmares

No joy in living

Overwork indulgence

Pain in neck or lower back

Picking skin constantly

Premenstrual tension

Psychotic behavior

Rigidity

School difficulties

Stuttering or other speech difficulties

Tachycardia

Trembling

Ulcers

Violations of the law

Waking too early

Waking up tired

These are but a few of the warning signs of stress. It is apparent that many warning signs of stress and the signs and symptoms of depression overlap. This only highlights my hypothesis that depression is a stress disorder. Any excessive stress can become a potential stressor and eventually cause physical, psychological and/or spiritual depression. For depressed people who are interested in good health, a satisfactory amount of rest and relaxation is essential.

Rest refers first of all to sleep, and second to other forms of physical and mental inactivity. Relaxation refers to the relief of physical and/or mental stress, regardless of its cause. Anything that leads to a natural and healthy reduction of stress may be considered relaxation.

Sleep. Although the body may be able to get by with as little as one hour of sleep, the brain cannot do that. The brain needs sleep far more than the body. Our hearts never stop working, and our bodies get better through use. Less body rest and more body use will insure a long and healthy life. However, the brain needs time for repair and this comes primarily through sleep.

Sleep is essential for our overall good health and longevity. Most people need from seven to eight hours of sleep every night. During the first years of our lives we need about eighteen hours of sleep. In old age this may taper off to only about six hours. The cardinal rule to remember is that if we get less sleep than we require, this will induce stress and physical and mental/emotional disorders. This is what sufficient sleep provides:

1. physical and mental regeneration
2. relaxation of muscles
3. reduction in heart rate
4. reduction in blood pressure
5. reduction in body temperature
6. mental exclusion of internal/external stressors
7. reduction in cortisone output

The above actions are the opposite of what takes place during periods of stress, where we find the following:

1. physical and mental degeneration
2. increased muscle tension
3. increased heart rate
4. increased blood pressure
5. increased body temperature
6. mental inclusion of internal/external stressors
7. increased cortisone output

Satisfactory sleep is essential for all of us. There are two main states of sleep. The first state is called Rapid Eye Movement Sleep (REM Sleep), where the eyes move rapidly and most dreaming takes place. The functions of body and mind remain active, and it is during this phase that the mind is restored. The second state is called the Non-Rapid Eye Movement Sleep (Non-REM Sleep), which is about 90 percent dream-free. The functions of the body slow down during this phase and the body is rested and restored.

Factors that disrupt good sleep patterns include alcohol, caffeine, nicotine, age, types of food eaten before bedtime, sleep medication, and other drugs.

People suffering from depression should observe the following rules to sleep better:

1. Do not take heavy evening meals. Include high-protein and high-carbohydrate.
2. Do not use caffeine, and certainly not in the afternoon or evening hours.
3. Use tryptophan as described earlier and in Appendix 7. See *Glossary*, carbohydrate connection.
4. Exercise in the afternoon, or do only light exercises in the early evening.
5. Use only high-protein and high-carbohydrate combination snacks in the evening.
6. Establish a regular bedtime and stick to the routine.
7. Set a comfortable temperature for the bedroom. When the bedroom is either too hot or too cold, this may affect your dream patterns negatively.
8. Do not spend excessive amounts of time in bed.
9. Stick to a regular wake-up schedule.
10. Do not go to bed hungry. Remedy this by a high-protein with high carbohydrate snack.
11. Do not force sleep. It is better to read and have a light on until you are ready to fall asleep.

Relaxation. It is wise to come to a point where for short periods of time during the day (and at least one day a week), we stop our regular activities and simply concentrate on something that requires very little physical or mental exertion and relaxes us thoroughly.

Restful experiences range from relaxing healing imagery to actually going on the beach for walking, swimming, or sunning. Reading light literature, scanning through magazines, or visiting with friends can be relaxing. Any one of hundreds of events, as long as they are not stressful and involve enjoyment without exertion, are suitable for periods of relative physical and mental inactivity. The main point to remember is that there should be no activity of any kind that requires stressful effort.

Imagery is an excellent way to achieve relaxation. Of course, this holds true only for healing imagery. Imagery must be well constructed and based on a well-done, objective self-analysis, or fit in the category of rational and positive daydreaming, where we may see ourselves on a peaceful, deserted beach, reading one of our favorite novels.

If we are suffering from anxiety, anger, depression, or any other stress-related condition, we can practice relaxation imagery. Any script that enables us to relax our muscles, breathe slowly and deeply, and empty our minds of all thoughts is suitable. Further application of healing imagery is included in chapter 8. Here is a sample script that can be committed to memory for regular practice in relaxation:

> As I lie here quietly on my bed with my eyes closed, I am slowly relaxing my entire body. The muscles of my feet are now loose, and my feet are becoming weightless. There is a very pleasant feeling associated with this weightlessness. My leg muscles are relaxed, my legs are warm and weightless. This feeling is now also affecting my stomach and my chest. My lungs are slowly filling with air. I am breathing slowly and easily. The muscles of my neck and back are becoming loose and relaxed. I am seeing a large word that reads **RELAX.** I am spelling the letters one by one, *R-E-L-A-X.* I am breathing in deeply and holding my breath. I spell the letters *RELAX* before I slowly breathe out. I will get up in fifteen minutes and will feel completely refreshed.

Use Recreation for Stress Reduction

Apathy, dullness, and boredom are great enemies of good mental health. These mental states are especially bad if we are undergoing other forms of stress as well. Most of this unhappiness is of our own making, but it is a universal practice to blame it on others. Most negative mental states have little to do with colorless environments and much to do with colorless attitudes. We control our choices!

Nevertheless, a lot of lethargy is related to the lack of stimulation found in many environments. A majority of our work force is dissatisfied with their jobs. Dissatisfaction is more related to a need for interesting work and independence than wages. People need varied stimulation for optimum functioning. Many people who are confined to institutions, tied to dull work tasks, or living alone, are in need of stimulation.

Many lesser forms of depression (for example, the blues), can be eliminated through a good program of recreation and *any* form of depression may be helped by it.

Our brains are involved in the recreation process, and they require proper electrical and chemical stimulation. The latter depends on the *foods* we eat to produce amino acids, neurotransmitter, and glucose levels, and for proper functioning of the interconnected endocrine system.

Too much stress will upset this chemical system. Too much stimulation is so stressful that it may eventually lead to depression. But there is another side to the coin. Not enough stimulation is also very stressful and might also lead to depression. That is why the proper balance of recreation and nutrition is so important to good mental health.

A positive attitude is not enough to provide for the necessary electrical stimulation of our brain, for we also need change and newness. Research on chimpanzees, monkeys, and rats has shown that these animals engage in more than mere physical activities. They will engage in activity for the sake of activity. They seek the reward of mental stimulation, which is inherent in finding solutions to difficult problems. And how much more this pertains to people!

The optimum functioning of our brain depends on the continuous stimulation found in our environment. Recreation, rest, and relaxation are important in both the prevention and successful treatment of depression. However, to participate or not, remains your choice.

Conclusion

This chapter on the physical treatment of depression offers several insights on reducing stress for our bodies and minds. The proper application of these principles can bring increased health and happiness, especially if we closely follow the *progress chart* at the end of this chapter, and monitor ourselves carefully. Discerning and deciding is not enough. In the final instance it is the doing that counts. *We control our doing.*

The problem of depression is a multifaceted one. Victory over depression requires more than restoring the physical balance. We also need—among other goals—right thinking, and speaking. The next chapter provides us with necessary information to do just that.

5. Progress Chart for the Physical Treatment of Depression

1. Physical Examination   Date _____
Tentative diagnosis_____
Instructions/Referrals _____
Medications, if any _____

2. Laboratory Examinations   Date _____
Findings _____
Retests scheduled_____
Other actions planned _____

3. Wellness Diet   Starting Date _____
Foods eliminated_____
Addictive substances eliminated_____
New foods added _____

4. Food Supplements   Starting Date _____
Which products used? How much _____
Comments _____

_____

5. Weight Control   Starting Date _____
Present weight_____   Desired weight_____
Comments _____

6. Exercise   Starting Date _____
Type of exercise _____
When/Where _____
Comments _____

_____

7. Rest and Relaxation   Starting Date _____
Date regular bedtimes established_____
Date new rules to insure better sleep established_____
Date relaxation times established_____
Date relaxation script implemented _____
Comments _____

_____

8. Recreation   Starting Date _____
Type of recreation _____
Stimulating projects planned _____
Comments _____

_____

Note: To appreciate the importance of these treatment steps, it is worthwhile to review chart 1 "Physical Sources and Aspects of Depression," following chapter 4.

The Psychological Treatment of Depression

Most depressed people (about 75 percent) suffer from various forms of self-induced depression. These self-induced depressions are usually the result of misperceptions, misbeliefs, and misinterpretations.

How Do We Change?

How do we change? In only one way, and that is *voluntarily*. It is a fact of life (and well described in the Bible) that people change only if they want to. In spite of all the protestations of "I want to but I can't," there is no question about this at all. We change only if we choose to do so. Any change in our thinking, feeling, and actions, is directly related to our will and all the dynamics that go with this process, such as opportunity and perseverance. Even in the most horrendous situations, in sickness, or in poverty, some people have demonstrated that—however difficult—it is possible to learn to control thoughts and feelings.

Because our thinking is greatly influenced by the things we eat and by other physical factors it is especially difficult to think properly if our bodies are out of control. To rectify this usually requires a change in our diet or in some other aspect of our lifestyle. Unfortunately, most people fall short of their potential because they refuse to investigate this. By a choice of their will, they exclude themselves from positive change.

About 26 million people suffer from self-induced depression in this country, mainly because they have gotten into wrong thinking habits. How can they change? By changing their way of thinking. No one can do this for them, but they are able to do so themselves, if they really want to.

The most obvious requirement is *motivation*. If we are suffering from self-induced depression, we can change if we have a sincere desire to do so. No one makes us change against our will. God has given us a free will to choose. The only person who can make you change is you, and the only person who can make me change is me. Consequently, self-counseling is really the last and most important stage in all forms of counseling. We can be counseled by other people most of our lives without any results. It is self-counseling that will make us change or not change.

Perceptions, cognitions, and decisions lead to behavioral changes in our lives. We have been given an opportunity by God, and it is one for which he holds us accountable. It is the opportunity to choose life or death, blessing or cursing, gladness or sadness. It is *not* our environment, past, or present, that makes us do bad things, have bad thoughts, or become depressed. Although we have vulnerabilities, related to our genetic makeup, training, education, and other life experiences, including illness, we still have the final choice for a renewed mind. Obviously excluded are the mentally handicapped who cannot think or choose for themselves, or those who have drugged brains that hinder their ability to think and choose wisely.

What is needed for change is a wholehearted desire to do so. This requires a willingness to listen, learn, investigate, and do the required work. Once our minds are made up, we only need to master five sequential steps:

1. Create the emotions we want.
2. Make sound decisions.

3. Analyze our behavior.
4. Practice wholesome self-talk.
5. Practice healing imagery.

These are not difficult to learn. The process is uncomplicated. *God did not make the world so complex that ordinary people could barely function in it.* To change from unhappiness to happiness is a manageable process, but it does require work. Some simple guidelines based on scriptural truth can be followed. Before we start learning these guidelines, don't forget that positive change is not only a matter of our will but also a willingness to apply the guidelines. Only the doer succeeds. Let us now look at these five steps:

How to Create the Emotions We Want

Thoughts Become Feelings. Although other factors influence our lives, we are *ultimately* the outcome of our thinking. Our emotions, too, are the final outcome of our thinking. If we think negatively, we shall have negative feelings. If we think positively, we shall have positive feelings. If we think depressed thoughts, we shall have depressed feelings. Our thinking can make or break us.

Is this too simple? You mean that all I have to do is change the way I think, and I will also feel differently? Yes! That is what the Bible teaches and also what we have learned from studying the brain.

Unless we change our self-defeating thinking, our self-defeating feelings will remain. The reason for this can be found in the way our brain works. We think with our cerebral cortex. Our feelings, however, depend on another portion of the brain, the so-called limbic system, and corresponding physiological changes in our body. Some of these changes will feel good, others will feel bad.

Depression thoughts, such as "I am ugly; I am no good; I am hopeless; I am a loser; I am a failure; I am worthless; I cannot change"—all will lead to the corresponding feeling we don't want, namely depression! Merely changing these words, we can start to feel better; however, we make more lasting progress if we go back to the origin of our depressive self-talk. Depressive thoughts are actually erroneous —they are misbeliefs, based on misperceptions and misunderstandings.

Our thinking depends on various inputs from our sense organs, as well as previous learning, conditioning, and other life experiences. For example, there is little or no actual truth in depression thoughts. They are based on perceptual and cognitive errors. If you say you are ugly, then this implies that you are "totally" ugly and that no one in the entire world would think differently of you. For starters, God would think differently. If you say that you are hopeless, you are implying that you are hopeless in everything that concerns you.

Misperceptions and misbeliefs lead to negative interpretations, exaggerations, self-defeating attitudes and beliefs, and all manner of distortions that can be summed up as misinterpretations. Examples of such misinterpretations may be found in "allness" thinking which cannot meet the test of objective reality, such as:

I am "always" left out.

I am "never" appreciated.

"Everybody" is smarter than I am.

I mess up "every time."

I am "forever" stuck with my past.

I am being picked on "all the time."

Understating and Overstating. If we understate or overstate we are not telling the truth. It is essential to become *scrupulously* honest in everything we say. If our self-talk is not correct, then our feelings will not be correct either. Incidentally, some "allness" statements are true. For example, all of us make mistakes and are fallible. The Bible is explicit, "For all have sinned, and come short of the glory of God" (Rom. 3:23).

The Bible is also clear that all can be forgiven (John 3:16), and that there is "no condemnation to them which are in Christ Jesus, which walk not after the flesh, but after the Spirit." (Rom. 8:1).

The Need for Objectivity. Habits that lead to misinterpretations include jumping to conclusions, labeling, hasty generalizations, judgments, categorizing people, and various forms of arrogance, intolerance, bias, and prejudice, as well as insisting on feeling rather than fact. These habits prevent us from speaking the truth. Whether we are dealing with allness thinking, or any other type of thinking or beliefs, attitudes, opinions, wishes, dreams, or desires, we need to get into the habit of asking that all important question, "Am I speaking the truth?"

What is the objective basis for my thinking? What does the Bible teach? Where is the objective evidence? Am I merely using the common vocabulary peculiar to my particular circle, group, organization, fellowship, church, family, school, college, or political party? People quickly pick up the various forms of speech (and therefore, thoughts, feelings, and actions) of the people that they are closely associated with. After a while, each individual's self-talk is, to a great extent, a reflection of the self-talk of the group and not necessarily based on objective reality.

The self-talk of even one person can eventually become group-talk, and in turn the unchallenged self-talk of individuals. It is important to check out what we hear, and verify the information and test for validity and consistency in our perceptions and thinking. Get into the habit of logically evaluating, verifying, and searching for the truth. God wants us to be truthful.

Only when we are scrupulously honest can we begin to master the art and science of creating our own freely chosen emotions. In the next paragraphs you will see how this is done.

First, we need to know that a complete emotion consists of three parts: namely, *perceptions, self-talk,* and *feelings.* Our perceptions, self-talk, and feelings can be objective, subjective, or a combination thereof. Remember that our emotions are the result of our self-talk.

Anyone who seriously questions any form of depressive self-talk (which is negative, subjective, and self-defeating) quickly discovers that the truth will indeed set us free. First, Jesus who is the truth will set us free from our sinful past, remove all of our burdens, and give us eternal life.

The truth in the form of objective thinking will definitely liberate us from the bondage of depression. We may think that we are worthless; however, it is a lie and contrary to God's Word and love for us.

We might believe that we cannot change; however, that belief goes 100 percent against God's Word, which tells us that, through God's grace, we can change from sinner to saint. We might think that our talents are insignificant, but this, too, contradicts God's Word. God wants us to do something worthwhile with the talent(s) that he has given us.

Sometimes even committed Christians think or feel that they cannot be sure that they are saved from their sins. However, it is precisely the purpose of Jesus' death and resurrection to redeem them from their sins. Or, we might think that we are totally helpless or hopeless, just mere accidents in a long chain of events. Again, this feeling goes directly against the Word of God which says we are "fearfully and wonderfully made." David and Jeremiah were sure that God knew them while they were still in their mother's womb.

It is not only possible to create our own emotions, it is also the will of God that we do so. God does not take this choice away from us, and no one can take it away from us. We can give it up only voluntarily. The truth remains that we have a choice. To feel good we need to think good. Look at two examples in the case of the expired passport.

Depressed Thoughts Lead to Depressed Feelings

1. *Perception.* This morning I discovered that my passport is expired, and I will be unable to go on a planned trip to Europe tomorrow.
2. *Self-talk.* I am really stupid. No one could have made that mistake. I always do the wrong things. This is terrible. I don't know what to do. Everybody is going to laugh at me. I must be losing my mind. I hate myself. I am worthless.
3. *Emotive feeling.* I feel very depressed.

Calm and Happy Thoughts Lead to Happy Feelings

1. *Perception.* This morning I discovered that my passport is expired, and I will be unable to go on a planned trip to Europe tomorrow.
2. *Self-talk.* I am sorry that I made this mistake, especially since this will also inconvenience my wife and family. It is

very unfortunate that I have allowed myself to be so busy as to overlook checking on the expiration date of my passport. There is certainly a valuable lesson to be learned from this as it is a reflection of my busy life.

I am so grateful that God loves me in spite of all my fallibilities. I am sure that he can use this disappointment, and turn it into an opportunity for all of us. I am thankful that this mistake was discovered this morning rather than at the airport tomorrow. That would have meant driving another four hours, and additional suffering for my family. I am going to reschedule the trip and also slow down and be more careful. I will make this up to my family. Rather than lose by this event, we can all gain by it.

3. *Emotive feeling.* I feel calm and happy.

The event in the examples is the same; however, the self-talk is obviously quite different. The *first example* reflects self-defeating thinking. This person's thinking is filled with misinterpretations and misstatements. Making a mistake, even a serious one, does not make a person stupid. To say that no one could have made that mistake means 5 billion people on earth have never made that kind of error. Always messing up means never doing anything right, which is, of course, impossible. "Everybody" laughing at you would include the whole world, while in reality most likely not a single person would laugh at all. "Losing one's mind" is impossible to do at any rate.

The *second example* reflects self-enhancing thinking. This person is appropriately sorry for inconveniencing others and wants to make restitution. He searches for the good that may be found in any situation. He reminds himself of God's love and God's willingness to turn negative things around. This person, rather than losing by his mistake, is gaining by it. He is learning new self-enhancing behavior, creating his own emotions, and doing precisely what the Scriptures teach us, that is, to praise God in all of our circumstances. It is no surprise that a same event can produce such different emotions in different people. *The difference lies in the way we talk to ourselves.*

Our emotions are self-made. We can choose how we feel, but only after we have the necessary discernment that all people are imperfect, make mistakes, and sometimes suffer. Our fallibility does not determine our value to God. We are *free, redeemed—purchased with the blood of Jesus.* We are *conquerors, children of God, fellow heirs with Jesus Christ, overcomers,* and *members of the household of God.* Remind yourself of this every time you are tempted to think anything else or anything less.

How to Make Sound Decisions

Daily we find ourselves in situations where we need to make sound decisions. This process can be tiresome, and we often make wrong decisions unless we follow some specific rules. Christians need to ask at least these three questions:

Is it the Truth? Is my decision based on the truth, that is, on objective reality? Can I base my decision directly on Scripture? Is my decision in harmony with the will of God? Can my statement, behavior, or decision be objectively verified by others?

Is it Goal Achieving? Does my decision help me achieve my goals? Some of these goals involve my family life, my career, and general well-being, but no goal is more important than that of spiritual achievement. I want to use my talents not just to enhance my life here on earth but to serve God in the best way I know how. This could be through witnessing to others what God has done in my life; it could be through working for his kingdom through the church; it could be in serving the less fortunate by actively participating in social programs that further the Christian message.

Is it Good for Others? Is my decision good for others? Will it avoid harm to them or significant conflict with them?

Our decisions should be based on at least two out of three of these factors. The first one, however, must always be included. It is senseless to do anything that is not based on the truth. Ideally all three factors apply, but for any decision at least the first and second, or first and third must apply. Sometimes we are unable to make good decisions because we are imperfect and live in a very subjective and imperfect world. Yet we must strive to make the best possible decisions at all times. It is a good idea to get into the habit of asking yourself: "Is this thought (feeling, behavior) based on the truth? Is it goal achieving? Is it good for others?" In fact, those questions could well be memorized.

How to Analyze Our Behavior

Can Christians Be Objective? Jesus said, "And ye shall know the truth, and the truth shall make you free" (John 8:32). First, we need to understand the truth about ourselves, namely that we are sinners without direction, lost without God. Once we recognize that Jesus is the truth (God's answer to all our needs), we are ready to decide for him, turn to him, rely on him, and follow him. Throughout the Scriptures we find a constant emphasis on the truth—truth based on everlasting objective reality. Or if you will, truth based on eternal facts rather than subjective assumptions. Belief in the God revealed in the Scriptures has brought joy, compassion, wisdom, understanding patience, knowledge, unending faith, hope, and love to the hearts of people everywhere. Nothing is more objective than the reality of God.

Learning to Analyze Ourselves. When we speak in a materialistic sense of objective reality, we simply mean that an event, a fact, finding, or whatever, can be duplicated elsewhere under the same circumstances and that it will produce the same results. Objective self-analysis helps us to achieve more truth in our lives. It helps us to make decisions based on rules for sound-decision making, which produce the feelings and actions we truly desire. The more experienced we become in objectively analyzing our thoughts, feelings, and behaviors, the more we grow in qualities such as self-understanding, responsibility, tolerance, humility, self-direction, and courage.

Objective self-analysis will free you from the bondage of negative emotions (anxiety, depression, fear). It will also help you to be free from the destructiveness of addictions, self-defeating habits, and other behaviors that stand in the way of a renewed mind and transformed life. And certainly it will help you to see whether or not your behavior lines up with the Word of God. (Review the example of the expired passport.)

How to Practice Wholesome Self-Talk

More and more it has become obvious that our lives need to be filled with *more than* objective thinking. First of all, they must include the positive power of Jesus Christ, which will be reflected in our faith and in the gifts and fruit of the Spirit.

Wholesome self-talk is based on love—that powerful gift of God through which we can reach out to others with understanding, acceptance, and respect, as well as understand, accept, and respect ourselves. Wholesome self-talk goes far beyond objective thinking as it includes both faith and reason, and a humble acknowledgement of our limitations.

Certainly we need to recognize that we see and speak only from a limited vantage point. We know in part and "look through a glass darkly." Wholesome self-talk includes the power of God's Word and appreciates the fact that our self-talk makes or breaks, justifies or condemns, lifts up or tears down. It is the most available, yet most overlooked ability that we all have.

Practicing wholesome self-talk is essential for new self-enhancing behaviors to overcome addictions, and bad habits. It is amazing how some people try to teach how to overcome bad habits without making it clear that "as he thinketh in his heart so is he . . ." (Prov. 23:7), and that "all things proceed from within the heart of man" (see Matt. 15:19). Both the Bible and modern science show *that the way we think needs to be changed before we change.*

It is also amazing how some people teach at great length about such things as motivation (the desire to get something or to get away from something), opportunity, skills, parenting, and scores of such topics, without making it clear that it is not complicated to change.

All people with average intelligence and undrugged brains can learn new self-enhancing behaviors. They *can* change; they *can* overcome negative emotions and even addictions. They can do so, however, only with wholesome self-talk. It is not an easy undertaking.

So many people are their own worst enemies. They speak words of dislike, self-hatred, self-rejection, self-denunciation and self-condemnation, and indulge in misbeliefs, misperceptions, and misinterpretations. More often than not, their *own* thoughts and words are at the heart of their depression problem.

The less truthful we are about ourselves, the greater the chances for depression. It is a lie to say that we are losers, worthless, or failures. God tells us that we can do "all" things through Christ (Phil. 4:13).

How foolish are those who spend hours and dollars in so-called therapy, or taking drugs for the elevation of moods when their real problem is the wrong use of the tongue. The Bible tells us that "Death and life are in the power of the tongue, and they that love it shall eat the fruit thereof" (Prov. 18:21).

God created the world by the power of his word. Jesus is the incarnate Word. We have access to that Word. God is ready to heal us and set us free.

There is awesome power in the spoken word. It can kill, and it can heal. The spoken word—the one we believe—can set us free, or keep us firmly in chains. Those who say that they can't, can't. Those who say that they can, can. We *can* change because God tells us, shows us, helps us, and leads us. Nothing else is required. Jesus promised; "If ye abide in me, and my words abide in you, ye shall ask what ye will, and it shall be done unto you" (John 15:7). Let God's words of love, hope, and faith abide in you and let us abide in Him who is the vine, as we are the branches (John 15:5).

How to Practice Healing Imagery

This skill requires little else than a basic understanding and lots of practice. Healing imagery consists of vicariously practicing a future desired behavior. This is done through memorizing a mental scenario called the "healing-imagery script." The imagery is best practiced for about twenty minutes, three times a day. It is important to be in a comfortable position and as relaxed as possible. Close your eyes and concentrate on "seeing" the desired behavior.

It is only through practice and more practice that we shall overcome old habits and behaviors and learn new ones. Actual practice, however, is time consuming and sometimes difficult. Without this practice, however, we will not learn new behaviors, and therefore practice (actual or vicarious) is of the utmost importance. For best results in healing imagery we first do an objective self-analysis, as described in table 6 on page 149 and base our script on the *F* section of that analysis.

Actual Versus Vicarious Practice

There are two ways in which we can practice the new feelings and behaviors we desire. We can go through some theoretical steps and then go out and actually do the steps we have learned. For example, if we are learning to drive a car, we can read a booklet and learn some basic essentials—such as making sure that the brake is on and the gearshift is in neutral—before we place the key in the ignition and start the car.

Of course, we still have to learn other steps before actually driving the car. There are many steps involved in driving a car, and the best way to learn is to actually do it. We can, however, also learn many of the necessary steps vicariously by forming a picture in our mind. We mention the steps to ourselves and see ourselves do them.

We can close our eyes and vicariously practice pulling the brake, putting the gear in neutral, and placing the key in the ignition and turning the key. After we do this many times in our imagination, then it becomes easier to do this in actuality. The reason why it becomes so easy is that our brain has formed a rather permanent picture of what to do once we get behind the wheel of a car.

People everywhere use both "pretend" and actual practice whenever they learn something. Most people, however, do not give this any thought. If we are interested in learning new behaviors quickly and effectively, it is important to take time out to practice our desired future behaviors.

The very best way to do this is through *"healing" imagery*. I stress "healing" so that we will base our imagery on our wholesome self-talk. Too many people practice pathological imagery. They see themselves defeated, sick, failing, or lost. They do this so much that when they are in actual situations their negative self-talk becomes self-fulfilling prophecy.

Thus people who have a fear of flying continue to vicariously practice their fear. As soon as they are in actual flying situations, they will normally, logically, and naturally be fearful. The same holds true for other situations in life. If a person tells himself that he cannot refuse an alcoholic drink, that it tastes so good, that he has to have it, that he cannot overcome the habit, and that he is stuck with it, then this person will naturally, nor-

and logically act in accordance with these vicariously reinforced behaviors. He will drink.

6. The Objective Self-Analysis

A. Facts and Events (Perceptions)	Da. Objective Verification and Correction of Perceptions	Fa. Future Facts and Events (Anticipated Perceptions)
UNDISPUTED	**DISPUTED**	**PROGRAMMED**
B. Self-Talk (Thoughts, Beliefs, Attitudes, Opinions, and so forth.)	Db. Objective Challenges	Fb. Future Desired Self-Talk (Objective Alternatives to B and Db)
1 2 3 4	1 2 3 4	1 2 3 4

C. 1 Feelings
    2 Actions
       (Behavior)
	E. 1 New Feelings
	    2 New Actions
	       (Behavior)
		Fc. 1 Future Desired Feelings
		    2 Future Desired Actions (Behavior)

PAST	**PRESENT**	**FUTURE**
Objectification		Vicarious Practice

Instructions

1. Copy this chart on a blank piece of paper.
2. Under A, fill in the facts and or events as best you remember and as concisely as possible.
3. Go to section C and list how you feel (or felt) and what you are doing (or did) as a result. Note: *Complete C before going to section B.*
4. Fill in the B section and list your present thoughts, especially attitudes and beliefs about the facts/events.
5. Under Da, challenge the A section by asking if the statements under A are really true. Ask if an audio-video recorder would have recorded the identical facts or events. You need to be scrupulously honest to succeed in this analysis.

6. Now comes perhaps the most important step. You need to challenge every statement in the B section. List those challenges in the Db section. To make sure that you do this correctly, follow the three questions (rules) for sound decision making: (1) Is it the truth? (2) Is it goal achieving? (3) Is it good for others? Remember that, as a minimum, rules (1) and (2), or (1) and (3) must apply. Again, the purpose of the objective self-analysis is to become more objective, that is, more truthful.
7. List under E your new feelings. A correctly done objective self-analysis usually reveals either happy or calm feelings, and results in life-enhancing behaviors.
8. In the F section, describe your future desired thoughts, feelings, and actions to anticipated facts or events. You can use this section to learn healing imagery scripts.
9. The objective self-analysis is an extremely powerful device which not only will help you to learn from the past, but also to help insure a healthier and happier future.
10. If you wish to get some practice in writing these self-analyses, transcribe the details of the self-analyses described on the following pages (angry, anxious, guilty, and depressed employee). After writing these four self-analyses, you will be ready to write one pertaining to yourself. Remember that you need to do this in writing, not just in your imagination.

The Bible makes it clear, and it has been shown for thousands of years, that what we tell ourselves creates our feelings. *Words* are the main ingredients. Whenever we practice words of self-defeat, we are going to feel self-defeated. Whenever we practice depressive thinking, we are going to have depressive feelings. Consequently it is essential to practice specific thoughts in specific circumstances.

For example, if you are working for a difficult employer who daily harasses his employees, has no kind words for them, frequently threatens them with dismissal—if he is also sarcastic and critical of even the slightest errors—then it is more than likely that the employees are fearful, depressed, angry or anxious. Their *specific emotions* will depend on their perceptions and cognitions. In other words, how they see the situation and what they tell themselves produces their feelings. But the choice remains theirs.

These employees, however, can overcome any emotive feeling by vicariously practicing healing imagery.

Let us look at a few examples of self-analyses, followed by healing-imagery scripts.

The Angry Employee

Objective Self-Analysis

1. My boss criticizes me constantly, by calling me stupid.
2. He is a real jerk. He should not do what he is doing. He should be polite to people. I hate him.
3. I feel angry.
4. He does call me stupid, but I know that he calls the other employees names too, and that his calling me stupid does not make me stupid, anymore than his calling me a camel would make me a camel. He is not a jerk, but an unhappy person, and he "should" do what he is doing for it is the natural, logical, and normal outcome of his thinking. Unless he changes his thinking, he will continue to act the way he does. I feel sorry for him.
5. I feel calm.

Healing Imagery Script

I am sitting at my desk and my boss walks over and looks at my work. He calls me stupid, and I immediately forgive him, feel sorry for him, and say a silent prayer for God to bless him. I also remind myself that while I do make mistakes, I am an experienced employee and highly valued by the company. As my boss calls me names, I can direct my own thoughts and I feel very happy inside.

The Anxious Employee

Objective Self-Analysis

1. My boss criticizes me constantly by calling me stupid.
2. I am afraid of him. Every time he comes to my desk I feel my heart just race. I think that I may be dismissed soon.
3. I feel anxious.
4. My boss does criticize me, as he does the other employees. Things are not upsetting me, but I am upsetting myself. Nothing is going to get worse, unless I allow it to happen. I am not really afraid of him, for he has not done and would not do any physical harm to me. I am perfectly safe working in the office, probably more so than outside the office. My heart does not race every time he comes to my desk although I have palpitations sometimes. I will not be dismissed. The situation has gone on for several years. Even if I were dismissed, this would not be the end of the world. I would not starve. My boss is not a tyrant; he is imperfect like everyone else. He has some self-defeating habits. He is actually a very lonely man, and probably more anxious than I have been.
5. I feel calm.

Healing Imagery Script

I have made an error, and my boss calls me into his office. As I am walking to his office I think about the wonderful opportunity I will have to bless my boss by my willingness to act rather than react. I can hear myself say, "I am sorry about the error, and I will correct it immediately. Thank you for finding it, and I am grateful for all your help." I feel calm and good while I am doing this. I notice that I am speaking slowly, while looking directly at his face. It is a good feeling to know that there are no inferior or superior people, but only imperfect ones. I remind myself that the Bible teaches me that we have all sinned, and that "every man's way is right in his own eyes." I am happy each time when I have an opportunity to grow and I praise God for this. I feel calm and happy.

The Guilty Employee

Objective Self-Analysis

1. My boss criticizes me constantly, by calling me stupid.
2. I realize that I need to shape up. I make far too many errors, and I don't seem to be able to learn from my mistakes. I am not taking things seriously enough. I ought to be grateful for my job and work harder at pleasing my boss. Also, I shouldn't have talked back last time. I had no right to do that. It's my fault that no one likes me. I am pretty bad and hard to get along with.
3. I feel guilty.
4. It is not true that my boss criticizes me constantly. This would mean that he does it all the time. Actually it only happens a few times a week. He is in the habit of calling anyone stupid who makes a mistake. I think it is just a habit that he has picked up somewhere. He may not even be aware that he has it, and no one has bothered to point this out to him. I can do my best to make fewer errors, but in this kind of work it is common to make some mistakes. We are all working under tremendous pressures, with deadlines to meet every day. I do learn from my mistakes, and rarely make the same mistake twice. Also, I take things seriously and I am happy to have a job. If I talked back, then I should have, for the world is an orderly place, and our actions are the result of our thoughts. This means that they are the logical outcome of my beliefs, attitudes, and opinions. Only if I change my self-talk, will my feelings and actions change. It is nonsense that no one likes me; for one thing, my wife and children love me, and I have many friends. I am not bad because I make some mistakes, and I would not be human if I did not make any mistakes at all.
5. I feel calm.

Healing Imagery Script

I am listening to my boss calling me stupid and I am thinking that words cannot hurt. Only what I tell myself can inflict harm upon myself. Thus I concentrate not on words but the overall situation. Did I really make an error? In what way can I do a better job and help my boss? The more he screams, the more convinced I become that self-control is all important. I remind myself of the Scripture in Proverbs 25:28, that says: "He that hath no rule over his own spirit is like a city that is broken down, and without walls." I just feel good and happy doing that.

I am taking the opportunity to learn from the lack of emotional control of my boss, so that I can strengthen mine, and set a good example. Each incident now becomes a blessing rather than a curse.

The Depressed Employee

Objective Self-Analysis

1. My boss criticizes me constantly, by calling me stupid.
2. I continue to make all kinds of mistakes. It is no wonder that no one likes me. I should be far more qualified than I am, but I cannot learn very well. I should be more careful, but I cannot change. I see no purpose in staying on that job for I never do anything right anyway. I am a real failure. A born loser. I lack willpower to stick to things. I hate myself for it. When I get up in the morning, I feel depressed just thinking about getting to work. I have more and more difficulties in getting to sleep or staying asleep. I dislike my job and I dislike myself. I am physically and mentally tired. I have started to lose weight. I feel really sorry for myself being in this terrible situation. I doubt that it will change. I am sorry that I am so stupid. I should be more qualified and intelligent. Life is a real bummer.
3. I feel depressed.
4. It is true that my boss sometimes calls me stupid. However, it does not happen every day. I do make mistakes, but I have learned to make fewer mistakes. I have checked on the error rates of the other employees and they are about the same as mine. This means that I am just as qualified as anyone else in my department. I have a number of very good friends, and obviously I can only be as qualified as I am now.

Saying that I should be more qualified, without additional training and experience, is pure nonsense. In addition, I have all the qualifications the job calls for. I have received four promotions since I started this job five years ago. All my effectiveness reports show that I am a qualified and respected employee. I believe that I have gotten in a worse habit than my boss. He calls me stupid, and probably does not mean it. I call myself stupid—knowing that I am not— and have begun to believe it. It makes no difference what my boss calls me, but it makes all the difference what I call myself. I am a child of God. I am respected, accepted and understood by God. God loves me. I know that my physical symptoms are directly related to my thinking about the job, because during weekends and vacations I feel so much better. I have changed in many ways, and I can, with the help of God, change completely. I am mindful of the Scripture that says, "I can do all things through Christ, who strengthens me" (Phil. 4:13).

5. I feel calm.

Healing Imagery Script

My boss walks up to me and calls me stupid. I immediately have a wonderful sense of tranquility come over me. In my mind I am silently saying, *Thank you, Lord, for the peace you bring into my heart,* and as I listen to my boss I do not react negatively, but correct the things that he wants to correct. I also see myself looking at him with the love of God, and I hear myself saying, "I will be happy to correct these errors. Thank you for bringing them to my attention." I praise and thank God for every opportunity that comes my way to increase my faith in him and to share his love in a practical way. I feel happy.

Feelings Flow from Thinking

Here we have four employees, all working in the same office, for the same employer, all being harassed by their boss in the same way. It is obvious, however, that they do not respond and feel the same. It is not a situation or incident that makes us depressed, but rather we make ourselves depressed. Depression is a thinking disorder as well as a stress disorder.

The varied reactions of anger, anxiety, guilt, and depression were directly related to the self-talk. The physical, mental, and spiritual conditions, of these individuals, however, played important parts. Both vulnerability and choice are involved.

For example, a person who becomes angry quickly might, in addition to a thinking disorder, also suffer from allergies or glucose problems. I usually find a more rapid response and more permanent change in self-talk when people obtain satisfactory diets, exercise, sleep, relaxation, and recreation. To treat a thinking disorder strictly with new ways of thinking is not always effective and certainly not efficient.

Healing Imagery Expedites Positive Change

Healing imagery is an important part of the psychological treatment of depression. We are going to change only if we have discernment and have wholeheartedly decided to change. It is the doing, however, that is the most important and difficult part. This doing can be greatly advanced by vicarious practice in the form of healing imagery. Don't forget these points:

1. *Vicarious practice is not pretending.*

Healing imagery is real and must be taken seriously. Whatever we think, see, and believe, we might become.

2. *Practice regularly.*

Ideally we practice healing imagery every day at the same times and in the same location. It is best to be as relaxed as possible, perhaps utilizing some relaxation exercise. It is helpful to have a comfortable and quiet place. It is best to close the eyes, and to have no outside noise or interferences, such as the telephone.

3. *The script must be objective.*

The script is ideally based on the third column of the Objective Self-Analysis. The more objective this analysis, the better the script will be.

4. *Memorize the script.*

Memorize the script as much as possible. One helpful way to start is by using a tape-recorded script. Listen to this over and over until it is committed to memory. A taped message can also be used while driving your car or taking a walk.

5. *Consider these additional incentives.*

To make the vicarious practice more powerful it is possible to do this before breakfast and lunch. Lunch may be refused until such time that the healing imagery has been completed. Also do the imagery just before going to sleep.

6. *Amount of time differs.*

The amount of time necessary differs from individual to individual. About fifteen or twenty minutes is ample for most people.

7. *How long will it take?*

Many people are successfully changing their emotive feelings in days or weeks, and certainly over a period of several months. For some people, however, a longer period is required.

8. *Actual practice is important.*

Healing imagery is a vicarious practice. Complete success comes only when we begin to practice. The sooner actual practice is begun, the more quickly we shall learn the behaviors we desire. There is nothing to worry about, for sooner or later every person who wholeheartedly practices vicariously will eventually do so in actuality.

9. *Is it safe?*

It is the safest, sanest, and most effective, efficient way of overcoming phobias, fears, negative emotions, habits, and other forms of self-defeating behavior.

10. *Is it scriptural?*

It is scriptural. In 2 Corinthians 5:17 we read that if we are in Christ, we are to be new creatures. We can greatly help this process along by applying God's Word in faith. We need to believe God's promise that we *can* change.

God tells us to be renewed in our minds (*see* Rom. 12:2), and this means that we must update our minds.

It is important for us "to put on the new man" (Eph. 4:24; Col. 3:10). God is not going to do this, for he clearly tells *us* to do this—if we want to. If we are going to change, we need to change our thoughts. In Ephesians 4:22, we are told " ... put off concerning the former [manner of life] the old man ..." How do we do this? According to the Scriptures, first of all by becoming more honest (objective). Therefore, we are told to "speak every man truth with his neighbour" (Eph. 4:25).

Summary

The psychological *sources* of depression are many. They include loss of acceptance, achievement, challenge, confidence, ego, employment, energy, faith, familiarity, goals, health, hope, independence, loved ones, memory, opportunity, respect, self-esteem, self-sufficiency, security, stimulation, trust, and many other real or imagined losses. All of them reflect loss of control.

Yet there is only one primary psychological *cause*, and that is the disintegration that takes place in our value system. Influenced by a myriad of negative factors, as explained in chapter 5, our value system's protective shield begins to crumble, and we start to process potential stressors. This is quickly followed by misperceptions, misbeliefs, and misinterpretations, and soon we are entertaining actual stressors. We become engaged in wrong thinking, and begin to experience depression and/or other negative emotive feelings.

Since wrong thinking leads to wrong feelings, it is obvious that only right thinking can set things straight for us. Unfortunately, the problem of depression involves a self-feeding ever-growing closed circular system. As we can see from table #2 following chapter 5, our body, via the limbic system of the brain, has also become involved. Our endocrine system is by this time sending negative signals back to our limbic system (the feeling portion of our brain), and this in turn influences the neocortex (thinking portion of our brain).

The solution is, therefore, ideally seen as a multiple one—treating our psychological depression with wholesome self-talk and healing imagery and taking important physical steps such as the Wellness Diet, exercise, additional sleep, rest, and recreation. By positively stimulating our physical wellness, we are accelerating our ability to perceive, think, and feel more appropriately. Man lives neither by bread nor by thinking alone, as can be seen in the next chapter on the spiritual treatment of depression.

Before going on to the next chapter, review the progress chart for the Psychological Treatment of Depression, which follows this chapter, and make some concrete plans to follow these steps closely. Learning to do all of the five steps is crucial to overcoming self-induced depressions.

7. Progress Chart for the Psychological Treatment of Depression

1. The Complete Emotion Formula   Date Memorized _____

Three parts of a complete emotion are _____

_____

_____

_____

_____

2. The Sound Decision-Making Formula Date Memorized _____

The three questions we need to ask ourselves are_____

_____

_____

_____

3. The Self-Analysis Formula   Date Memorized _____

Date of first self-analysis _____

The six parts of the formula are _____

_____

_____

_____

_____

_____

_____

4. The Wholesome Self-Talk Formula   Date Memorized _____

Three characteristics are _____

_____

_____

_____

_____

5. The Healing Imagery Formula   Date of First Script _____

Healing imagery consists of_____practicing a future desired
behavior. This is done through memorizing a mental scenario, called the
_____ script.

The Spiritual Treatment
of Depression

Whatever the causes of one's depression, be they physical, emotional, or spiritual, human beings, who are created in God's image, need to look to God for help and reorientation. They need to take the promises of God seriously and believe that he will "give good things to them that ask him" (Matt. 7:11).

Depression Is Not in God's Plan for His Children

One of the more common misunderstandings among Christians is the belief that somehow depression is in the will of God for them. Do they think perhaps that whatever happens to them happens because God wants it to happen (since, after all, no event lies outside his control)? It is true that nothing in human life falls outside the sphere of God's will, but that is not the same as saying that God is equally the cause of good and evil in human life. Such a statement would be blasphemous. It would confuse God the Father with Satan the father of lies. No: God is the fountainhead of all that is good!

161

There are many players in the field of human experience. The all-important and all-powerful one is God. In the end all other powers must bow down before him. An opposing power called Satan, or "adversary," in Scripture sometimes appears as "an angel of light" to seduce human beings and at other times assaults them as "a roaring lion" to intimidate them. Satan also is a player—a dirty one—on the field of human experience. It greatly pleases him to see human beings, especially if they are believers, confused, disoriented, and generally unable to function with joy in their hearts.

It is the privilege of Christians to know that God is different. At the heart of Christian experience is the knowledge that God is the agent of good things in human life. " . . . let him that glorieth glory in this, that he understandeth and knoweth me, that I am the Lord which exerciseth loving kindness, judgment, and righteousness, in the earth; for in these things I delight, saith the Lord" (Jer. 9:24).

Human beings are a third category of players in human experience—a category that includes parents, spouses, children, friends, police, lawyers, doctors, ministers, neighbors, and business people. They all affect us in different ways. To be human is to have to decide at all times how they shall affect us. To that end God equipped us with mental faculties of discernment, emotional faculties of response, and a will with which to make choices.

As we have seen, depression is very often the result of bad choices we have made, the outcome of a fundamentally mistaken lifestyle. But if that is true, how can we blame either God or Satan?

The Scriptures throughout picture human life as an arena in which a choice for good has to be made. God the Father, God the Son, and God the Spirit all confront us with this necessity. Listen to Moses as God's spokesman: "I call heaven and earth to record this day against you that I have set before you life and death, blessing and cursing: therefore choose life that both thou and thy seed may live . . ." (Deut. 30:19). Listen to Jesus: "A good man out of the good treasure of his heart bringeth forth good things: and an evil man out of the evil treasure bringeth forth evil things. But I say unto you, that every idle word that man shall speak, they shall give account thereof in the day of judgment. For by thy words thou shalt be justified, and by thy words thou shalt be condemned" (Matt. 12: 35–37). Listen to Paul speaking of the Holy Spirit: "For ye have not received the spirit of bondage again to fear, but you have received the Spirit of adoption, whereby we cry, Abba, Father. The Spirit himself beareth witness with our spirit, that we are the children of God: And if children, then heirs, heirs of God, and joint-heirs with Christ . . ." (Rom. 8:15–17). The Spirit of adoption is the spirit of freedom from bondage, the privilege of a member of God's household who can make the right choices.

God Our Ally in Overcoming Depression

Actually, it is the will of God that his children not be depressed. Just consider some of the blessings God wants people to enjoy:

Victory over the world (1 John 4:4).

Joy in various trials (1 Peter 1:6).

Freedom from despair in the midst of perplexity (2 Cor. 4:8).

Rest from our burdens (Matt. 11:28)

The privilege of casting our anxieties on God (1 Peter 5:7).

Courage in the face of opposition (Ps. 56:3, 4).

Renewal of the mind and a transformed life (Rom. 12:1, 2).

Freedom from unwholesome emotions and the enjoyment of wholesome emotions (Eph. 4:31, 32).

Control over our spirit (Prov. 25:28); (Gal. 5:23).

Good health (3 John 2).

Soundness of body, mind, and spirit (1 Thess. 5:23).

Peace (John 14:27).

In each of these passages—and many more could be added—the message that comes through is that God allies himself with believers in the battle against depression. In each instance the assumption is that believers are not robots or victims of forces beyond their control. Believers have been graced with responsibility. They are players in the field. They are participants in the arena of life. They have choices to make and commitments to pursue. They have a large say in the kind of emotions, good or bad, that will fill their hearts and minds.

Look at Psalm 43:5 and see the spectacle of a man battling for emotional health: "Why art thou cast down, O my soul? And why art thou disquieted within me?" Challenging self-talk! "Hope in God; for I shall yet praise him, who is the health of my countenance, and my God." Not blaming others but preaching to himself, the psalmist gets to the point when he can again sing in the night hours.

The chapter discussing the spiritual sources and aspects of depression, described three of the more common forms of spiritual depression: God-void, God-neglect, and God-confusion. The Scriptures bring home to us the necessary treatment: "Believe in Jesus Christ and follow him with all your heart!" These are not just words. They are a power package which, if allowed to function, can change our lives forever.

Since depression is not a part of God's will for us, and since God wants us to have victory over depression, there must somehow be a way in which we learn to overcome it and to live a life filled with the joy of God.

Healing the God-Void Depression

God-void depression results from the loss of an illusion—a misplaced confidence in the meaning and purpose of the material world. Sadly, some people have sought peace and gratification through other spiritual worlds or "religious" groups, such as cults, transcendental meditation, New Age, even satanism. Once a person has discovered this void and realizes that life without God is meaningless, the motive for wanting to find him has been established and the process of finding him may actually be underway. It is then that a person in a variety of ways—recalling fragments of earlier instruction, reading the Bible, or meeting a Christian— may be confronted by the claims and promises of the gospel and feel the power of the call of God to leave that world of empty promises behind. There is no question as to what God then wants a person to do: to yield to that call. He wants "self" to move over and to let him sit on the throne of one's heart. But he will not crash the gates to the throne room. He wants that place freely offered by his willing servant.

To make a choice in line with God's intent, we need discernment. This may be obtained by looking again at our situation, by evaluating what this world has to offer, and how the followers of the trends of this world fare. Then we turn around to look at the claims God makes in the gospel and what happens in the lives of those who trust and follow Jesus. Really to know God one has to hear his call through his Word. Faith comes from what is heard (Rom. 10:17). To believe is to say *Amen* to the story of salvation as it catches up with the story of our lives.

Once we become acquainted with the Word of God we learn that God truly calls us out of the darkness of a self-centered existence and into the light of community. We discover that God is the original chooser; that he chooses his followers (John 15:16) just as surely as he chose Abraham (Neh. 9:7); and that he wants us believingly to accept that choice rather than to rebel against it. God calls us to choose in his favor that we may live an abundant life.

The Scriptures tell us that God is love (1 John 4), and being love, he naturally wants his children to be well. He wants his sons and daughters to be free from anxieties, fears, depressions, bad habits, loneliness, boredom, anger, frustration, or whatever else may trouble them. God wants his children to be healed spiritually, mentally, and physically (Exod. 15:26; Ps. 103:3). This is how I explained it in *The Way to Wholeness* (Crossway Books, 1984):

> The Scriptures tell us something that is very important for us if we want to investigate the claims made by God. In 1 John 4:6 we read: "We are of God: he that knoweth God heareth us; he that is not of God heareth not us. . . ." But then we might say it would be impossible for all of us who do not believe in God ever to hear him. Not so, for God goes on to tell us that by loving him and others he will dwell in us *and* will give us his Spirit (1 John 4:13).
>
> God has made it easy for us to know him. We are the ones who are making it difficult to know him, because of our lack of faith, our doubts, fears, greed, and selfishness.
>
> God has shown us that he loves us by means of a plan. This is the plan of salvation. He has provided a simple plan, whereby

we may have salvation, learn to speak with God, receive the Holy Spirit, and receive answers to our questions. We may test whether or not he will do all the things that he promises us in the Scriptures. Here are the simple steps to salvation and ultimate fulfillment. . . .

Then I went on to summarize these simple steps to salvation. Simple, yes, but Christians ought to review them from time to time—a reminder of when each one of us reached out to embrace our Lord Jesus Christ.

First, we must acknowledge our sins. Not one of us is perfect and the Bible reminds us, "For all have sinned, and come short of the glory of God" (Rom. 3:23). Knowing we are sinners is not enough, however. We must admit this to God and ask for his mercy.

Second, we must repent of our sins. The admission of our sins is just the beginning. We must have true remorse for these transgressions. The Bible tells us " . . . except ye repent, ye shall all likewise perish" (Luke 13:3). Only after we do repent can we start a new life in Christ.

Third, we must confess our sins. It is all-important to success or failure that we speak of our sins. In 1 John 1:9, the Bible says, "If we confess our sins, he is faithful and just to forgive our sins, and to cleanse us from all unrighteousness." Only when we actually confess can we receive the great reward.

Fourth, we must forsake our sins. All good and evil things come out of our heart, and we must accept the good before we can reject the evil. Isaiah 55:7 expresses it this way: Let the wicked forsake his way, and the unrighteous man his thoughts; and let him return unto the Lord . . . for he will abundantly pardon."

Fifth, we must believe in Jesus. We can act only on the thoughts we believe. Only if we believe in Jesus Christ as the Son of God, as the promised Savior, can we have the benefits of his sacrifice of love. "For God so loved the world that he gave his only begotten Son, that whosoever believeth in him should not perish, but have everlasting life."

Sixth, we must receive Jesus into our hearts. Only when Jesus becomes the center of our lives do we receive his power. John 1:12, 13: " . . . As many as received him, to them he gave power to become the sons of God, even to them that believe on his name."

And finally, do not overlook baptism. Although we are saved "by grace . . . through faith" (Eph. 2:8), outward symbolic actions such as baptism should not be downplayed. Jesus himself said in Mark 16:16: "He who believes and is baptized will be saved, but he who does not believe will be condemned." It is through baptism that we are incorporated into the fellowship of believers (1 Cor. 12:13).

Christians should remind themselves that God wants to make us his children, regardless of what we have done. Too often Christians forget the basic steps to salvation that they took perhaps many years earlier. We sometimes forget that in order to receive the numerous powerful blessings from the Lord, we need to follow his instructions for everything in our lives.

Healing the God-Neglect Depression

Human beings, including Christians, are fallible. They have their down seasons as well as their up seasons. Most Christians will admit that occasionally they neglect God.

Many persons who confess Jesus Christ as Savior and Lord have at some time returned to some sinful ways. Unhappy consequences inevitably follow. One cannot possibly know God and then turn away from him without experiencing the consequences of walking on two roads at the same time. Some believe that a person can love both God and materialism but it is a mistake. Jesus said: "No one can serve two masters: Either he will hate the one and love the other, or he will be devoted to the one and despise the other. You cannot serve God and money" (Matt. 6:24 NIV). To attempt it is utterly self-defeating.

Becoming absorbed in the merry-go-round of moneymaking and spending is a great obstacle to faithful Christian service. The so-called "good" life seems to enthrall many Christians as though they did not know it was godlessly humanistic and hedonistic. It is the old illusion of security through money, possessions, connections, and privileges. Sooner or later the truth comes out and so-called needs are revealed as destructive wants and desires.

God-neglect is the outcome of a loss of closeness with God and other believers, and refusing to obey his Word for guidance. Sooner or later such persons come to grief. They become disoriented, unsure of their priorities; they have all sorts of inappropriate excuses—for instance, that they are too busy. Meanwhile their *real* needs—the need for righteousness, goodness, faithfulness, divine direction, and, above all, forgiveness—go begging for attention. A great burden of unconfessed sin and feelings of guilt steadily increases. One cannot neglect God and not pay the terrible price of a loss of direction and self-esteem.

For a person who has begun to neglect God one step is needed: reconciliation with God. Unless this takes place, there is little that can be done for this type of spiritual depression. For at the root of the depression is a need for restoration to fellowship. The person who neglects fellowship with God is bound to suffer from a depression that requires the confession of sin (1 John 1:9), acceptance of forgiveness (1 John 2:12), and the willingness to forgive others. This last point is essential: "For if you forgive men their trespasses, your heavenly Father also will forgive you; but if you do not forgive men their trespasses, neither will your Father forgive your trespasses" (Matt. 6:14, 15).

Love, as noted earlier, is the highest form of right thinking, leading to health in mind and body. Fear, hatred, and bitterness are examples of the worst possible kind of thinking. Our nation is full of people suffering from serious physical, mental-emotional, and spiritual problems because they fail to love. They do not pray for others, share with others, or give to others. Worst of all, they refuse to forgive. Said a well-known British general to John Wesley: "I never forgive anybody." John Wesley replied: "Then I hope you never sin."

Some people may go to church, work hard, read the Bible, and even give donations to worthy causes—but little happens. The Scripture is clear: if they do not lovingly forgive others, they themselves are not forgiven. If they give their bodies to be burned but have not love, they are nothing (1 Cor. 13:3).

Whenever people fail to forgive, the inevitable personal breakdown occurs. To forgive means "to let go"—to let go of negative thoughts and feelings pertaining to certain people, events, or situations. Only when one gets into the forgiving habit does that person regain peace of mind. Even if one cannot remember all the specifics of a grievance, it is still a good idea to start forgiving and speak words of love. It is a law of healing.

It is essential, therefore, to cleanse our minds, from anger, bitterness, resentment, condemnations, odious comparisons, and all other sorts of negative thinking toward others—and to forgive all who hate, despise, or dislike us. We need to be willing to forgive others unilaterally, to ask God to forgive us, and then to accept that forgiveness even to the point of forgiving ourselves too. That may seem almost impossible; "Therefore, as God's chosen people, holy and dearly loved, clothe yourselves with compassion, kindness, humility, gentleness and patience. Bear with each other and forgive whatever grievances you may have against one another. Forgive as the LORD forgave you" (Col. 3:12–14 NIV).

Healing the God-Confusion Depression

Wrong thinking is responsible for one's loss of vision and leads to depression. If a person can no longer see what life's foundation and goals are, that person is in trouble.

The only way to overcome loss of clarity, vision, peace, or conviction is to rely on the Scriptures. This means that we stop taking our cues from the harshness of our circumstances or from the voice of defeat in our own heart. It means that we take our position in the grand assurances of the gospel. It means that we seek to recapture a sense of awe and delight over the fact that God's love embraces us (John 3:16), that we are "joint-heirs with Jesus" (Rom. 8:17), and that we are God's workmanship (God's *poems*) created "in Christ Jesus unto good works which God has before ordained that we should walk in them" (Eph. 2:10).

We can tell ourselves all sorts of contrary nonsense. It often comes down to calling ourselves rotten, hopeless, or useless—a burden to others and a horror to ourselves. But God will not hear of it. He says in his Word that he cares, loves, forgives, heals, restores; and then goes on to prove it with numerous stories. God is the most available contemporary friend we have.

The world is full of trouble. Every home has its cross to bear. Every person has some problems. But this does not mean a person is helpless or has no choice but to resign to defeat. As long as we are not brain-dead there are things to do and steps to take. Here is a list of definite acts we can undertake to overcome depression resulting from God-confusion:

Confess and forsake sins (Prov. 28:13).

Forgive and be forgiven (Matt. 6:14, 15).

Seek the kingdom of God (Matt. 6:31–34).

Pray and praise (Phil. 4:4–7).

Give thanks (1 Cor. 15:57).

Present body a living sacrifice (Rom. 12:1).

Trust in God (Prov. 3:5, 6).

Speak right (Eph. 4:29).

Think right (Prov. 23:7).

Do things wholeheartedly (Eccles. 9:10).

Summary and Conclusion

The bottom line is that most spiritual depression is the outcome of sin. At the root of it, in many cases, is that our greed, self-centeredness, and self-will leads us into believing in the power of material things and ignoring the call of God. Whether the subject is God-void depression or God-neglect depression the basic problem is the futility of our self-defeating thinking—our alienation from the life of God, ignorance, and hardness of heart (*see* Eph. 4:17, 18).

In both God-void and God-neglect depression we are dealing with the "fruit of darkness." A willful choice—the adoption of a self-serving perspective on life—brought on unwanted depression. The arrogance and selfishness of King Saul made him lose God's Holy Spirit and fall prey to an evil spirit (1 Sam. 16:14, 15). His depression clearly resulted from God-neglect; the basic issue was sin. Spiritual depression calls for spiritual regeneration, the work of the Holy Spirit.

Remember:

1. *God-void* disappears as people repent of their sins and call
   on the name of Jesus (John 3:16; 3:36; 5:24; 6:47; 20:31;
   Rom. 10:13–17).
2. *God-neglect* is removed as people return to God. God wel-
   comes and pardons all who do. The well-known story of the
   prodigal son makes clear that God rejoices when backsliders
   and rebels come home (Luke 15:3–32).
3. *God-confusion* is healed when we allow the Holy Spirit to
   remind us that we are the children of God and are justified
   by Jesus (1 Cor. 6:11). We must steadfastly refuse to be placed
   into any form of bondage, be it fear, doubt or confusion. "For
   you have not received the spirit of bondage again to fear,
   but you have received the spirit of adoption, whereby we
   cry, Abba Father. The Spirit itself beareth witness with our
   spirit that we are the children of God . . ." (Rom. 8:15, 16).
   God-confusion is not necessarily the result of conscious sin.
   Ignorance and stupidity, however, when permitted to control
   our physical, mental, and spiritual life, can be just as
   destructive.

The good news is that whatever the type of *spiritual* depression
we have incurred we can be healed by looking to God and following his instructions—not only for our spiritual, but also for our
physical and mental/emotional life. We are promised spiritual
regeneration. He saved us,

Not by works of righteousness which we have done, but according
to his mercy he saved us, by the washing of regeneration, and
renewing of the Holy Ghost; Which he shed on us abundantly
through Jesus Christ our Savior; That being justified by his grace,
we should be made heirs in the hope of eternal life (Titus 3:5–7).

8. Progress Chart for the Spiritual Treatment of Depression

1. Decide for Eternal Life   Date _____

God-void depression results from not knowing the will of God that we are to be saved by the blood of Christ. Following our own imperfect will, and believing in godless materialistic humanism inevitably leads to disillusionment.

The answer to God-void depression is the yielding of our own imperfect will to the perfect will of God. We must repent of our sins, and believe in, and call on the name of Jesus.

Discern: Read Deuteronomy 30:19; John 3:16, 36: 5:24; 6:47; Matthew 6:10; Romans 10:9; 1 John 2:17.

Decide: For eternal life.

Do: Practice the decision.

2. Decide for Reconciliation   Date _____

God-neglect depression results from turning our backs on fellowship with God and the multiple other losses associated with it. The following of our own imperfect will in disobedience to God's perfect will inevitably leads to guilt.

The answer to God-neglect depression is repentance and deciding wholeheartedly to walk with God. This includes to love him, to love others as ourselves, and to be forgiving as we are forgiven, to be witnesses for Christ, bear good fruit, and increase in knowledge, understanding, and wisdom.

Discern: Read Psalm 24:3–4; Matthew 5:48; 18:11; Luke 15:3–32; Romans 6:1; 1 Thessalonians 4:3–7; Hebrews 12:14; 1 John 3:3–10; 5:18.

Decide: To wholeheartedly walk with God in complete surrender to his perfect will.

Do: Practice the decision.

3. Decide for Victory   Date _____

God-confusion results from loss of discernment which is reflected in anxiety, doubt, fear, and worry. Following our own imperfect will, manifested in believing negative human emotions, inevitably leads to loss of clarity and vision.

The answer to God-confusion depression is to steadfastly claim victory by holding to—that is claiming—the Word of God, which promises total victory over all of our troubles.

Discern: Read Psalm 18:28–32; Isaiah 54:17; John 14:1; Romans 8:15, 16, 37; 1 Corinthians 6:11; 2 Corinthians 4:8–10; 2 Timothy 4:18; Titus 3:5; 2 Peter 5:7.

Decide: Remove all confusion by concentrating on right thinking, based on the Word of God, while paying proper attention to body and mind.

Do: Start to practice the decision.

Part **4**

A Summary

Depression is a multifaceted disorder of body, mind, and/or spirit. It is caused by excessive stress, which results in loss of physical balance, psychological integrity, and/or spiritual direction.

It is not stress itself or stressful situations that get us into trouble, but the way in which we react to them. What causes depression in one person might not cause depression in another, and what heals one person might not heal another. That is why singular approaches and universal claims are ineffective, inappropriate, and often dangerous.

We do not become depressed because of external lack, and/or loss, but very specific, individually determined, internal lack and/or loss. We become depressed as a result of ways in which each uniquely different body, mind, and/or spirit reacts to potential stressors. It is strictly our inability and/or unwillingness to successfully deal with potential stress that converts it into actual stress.

Human beings are basically geared for survival, health, and healing. God has provided us with built-in physical and mental protective systems that enable us to live in an often hostile and unaccommodating world. The question to consider in dealing with the cause of depression is to what extent are we talking about vulnerability (ability versus inability) and choice (willingness versus unwillingness)? It will then become evident that indeed excessive stress is the real culprit behind our national epidemic of depression. Yet it is important to remember that we ultimately choose to control or not to control our stress levels. *We have the final word.*

In the case of *physical* stress, it is primarily our physical condition that determines whether or not we are going to suffer loss of physical balance. The better our health, the greater the amount of stress we will be able to endure.

In the case of *psychological* stress, it is primarily our perceptual-cognitive field that turns potential stressors into actual ones. The more rationally, realistically, and positively integrated we are, the less likely will potential stressors become actual stressors. The greater our ability and willingness to reason, and the greater our desire for realism and optimism, the more able we are to deal with psychological stress, and thus prevent loss of psychological integration.

In the case of *spiritual* stress, it is primarily our willingness to yield our imperfect will to the perfect will of God. The depth of our relationship with him will determine the strength of spiritual direction. The greater our obedience to God, the smaller the chances for spiritual distress.

Although we speak of the necessity for physical restoration, emotional reeducation, and/or spiritual regeneration, every disorder—whatever its origin—is a disorder of the whole person. Depression is not only a multifaceted and complex disorder, but it is an interactional and self-sustaining disorder. Physical, psychological, and spiritual factors act and feed on one another. In every case of depression, both in origin and expression, there is involvement of the entire person.

The wholistic approach to depression utilizes many tools of modern medicine, such as physical examinations and laboratory tests, and less frequently, medications. In general, however, the modern medical approach, based on the germ theory model, is largely inadequate to deal with the problem of depression, which is not primarily a medical problem in any case. For example, 75 percent of the depressed population suffers from self-induced perceptual-cognitive (thinking) disorders, which are best treated with emotional re-education.

Most important, however, the wholistic approach deals with the evaluation and treatment of the total person, while simultaneously providing identification and treatment of primary causes. Through the logical application of tried and proven sequential steps, no part of the person is overlooked.

The three-step approach, as discussed in this book, emphasizes the importance of making an appropriate diagnosis before deciding and executing a specific plan of action. This three-step approach of (1) *discerning,* (2) *deciding,* and (3) *doing,* is again sequentially applied to (1) *body,* (2) *mind,* and (3) *spirit.*

Singular approaches dealing with any type of depression as an entirely physical, mental/emotional, or spiritual problem are less effective and efficient. They are also fraught with potential trouble. The common practice of treating every conceivable type of depression in the same manner, for example, only with drugs or only with psychotherapy, is archaic, irresponsible, and often dangerous.

As the Bible teaches, human beings are body, mind, and spirit. Once we begin to understand that inescapable interrelationship, we will gain a better understanding of health and disease and various forms of healthy and unhealthy behavior.

Singular approaches have achieved various degrees of success. Those who have specialized in medical approaches (and successfully used several drugs) should realize, however, that many of the people they find at their offices are those who are in need of medical treatment in the first place. Many of these people had already gone through a seemingly endless search for an answer to their pressing problems; very often they had already tried various other means, such as psychotherapy. If their problems were not primarily of a mental/emotional or spiritual nature, then logically they would respond more readily to medical treatment.

We find similar success stories at some of the specialized clinics at major universities in this country, where primarily cognitive psychological means are employed. For example, at the University of Pennsylvania Mood Clinic or the University of Kentucky RBT Center, most people—whose problems were such that they met the suitability criteria for cognitive therapy—were restored to health. If there are no primary physical or spiritual causative factors involved, then emotional re-education is an effective treatment for depression.

Success stories also come from the offices of pastors and pastoral counselors. Depressed people who had earlier sought help from other sources found their depressions lifted, once they decided for eternal life and reconciliation with God, or began to claim victory on the Word of God.

Unfortunately it is seldom recognized that physicians, psychologists, and pastors, more often than not see each other's failures. By a process of elimination and often extensive suffering, many depressed people finally wind up at the right places to receive the appropriate resolution to their problems. If each professional would consider the wholistic approach and be willing to treat the whole person rather than some fragmented part, what needless suffering could be prevented and what precious time (and money, in many cases) conserved.

Another reason, however, why various professionals erroneously claim that their methods are superior is that many depressions disappear spontaneously. These are depressions that are primarily caused by self-defeating thinking. Although there is usually some organic involvement, the primary reason for these depressions was faulty thinking. Because many depressions of this type disappear while the client is undergoing "treatment," confusion has resulted as many practitioners assumed that their methods were responsible for healing. Unless they have a success rate that, at the very minimum, exceeds the 75 percent mark, they are proving very little. Truly wholistic clinics ought to question anything less than a 90 percent success rate.

Also, some depressed people get better regardless of the treatment method employed because of the placebo effect. This phenomenon with drugs (inert or otherwise) is well known. Among all kinds of placebo effects, some are even derived from the aura surrounding outlandish and often spectacularly unscientific methods. At other times great benefits are obtained merely through the personality of the therapist. Of course, when the therapist has a genuine and unconditional positive regard for the client, this is definitely a plus. When a person is genuinely loved or feels accepted, respected, and understood, part of the battle has already been won.

Depressed people are bombarded with erroneous information—to shape up, take a vacation, look for another job, or talk things out. What many depressed people need before they can do any so-called shaping up is a compassionate friend, a decent diet, and a healthier lifestyle.

It is time that we finally acknowledge that many disorders are indeed caused by chemical imbalances. We must also understand, however, that the needed chemical substances (with the exception of air and water) are manufactured in our bodies with the food we eat. Some people can be brought out of their depressions by diet alone, and many others can greatly speed their recovery by adding a proper diet to other treatment programs, which include psychotherapy, pastoral counseling and/or drug therapy.

The majority of depressed people, however, are primarily suffering from self-induced and self-maintained depressions. To treat such people, who are suffering from self-defeating attitudes and beliefs only with diet or only with drugs, or only with food supplements, is unscientific, dangerous, and unjustifiable.

The wholistic treatment approach to depression is safer and saner than any other treatment method because it relies on the skills of several helpers in several disciplines, who jointly focus on the proper identification and treatment of depression. Wholistic treatment, more often than not, will succeed where singular treatment methods had to fail. Frequently, dramatic results are obtained in depressions of the longest standing.

It is common sense to treat the whole person instead of only some fragmented part. Yet it is important to find the primary sources of depression and to start treatment as quickly as possible. For example, if a person is suffering from self-defeating attitudes and beliefs—and physical sources are ruled out—we best start a program of emotional re-education and explain how healthy emotions can be created.

Emotional re-education must be enhanced, however, by doing whatever is necessary for the physical and spiritual life of that person. By providing the Wellness Diet, food supplements, exercise, recreation, and relaxation, we enable the depressed person to have a physiologically better functioning brain—a brain that can now more readily absorb a program of emotional re-education! The more wholistic the program, the faster and more permanent the recovery, and the greater the spillover in all areas of positive living.

Sometimes it is not even possible to start dealing with a mental/emotional problem until the strength of the person's body has been built up. When a person is in an exhaustion stage, it is difficult to engage in psychotherapy. The priority here is to strengthen the body through wholesome eating methods, rest, exercise, and fresh air. At times, some medications might also be helpful, and hospitalization might be advisable or necessary.

As quickly as possible, add the process of emotional re-education, for this will not only help in the elimination of the primary causative factors, but it will also intensify the healing process of the entire body. A human being owns, operates, and works within a closed system. Whatever happens in any part of that system affects all other parts.

The far-reaching effect of the spirit on the mind, and of the mind on the body and vice versa has been known for thousands of years. We can find examples of it on a daily basis by closely observing our own lives. The Bible also tells us that our thinking is directly responsible for the happiness of our mind and the health of our body (Prov. 14:30; 15:13; 16:24; 17:22; 23:7).

Every part of our body is subject to our mind, and every part of our mind is in some way influenced by and dependent on our body. In turn, both body and mind are subject to the power of God, who can heal instantaneously or gradually, with or without using health specialists.

We cannot do anything to any part of our body, mind, or spirit that will not affect all three in some way. Because our mental/emotional, and even spiritual wellness intimately depends on a well-functioning body, there is every reason to pay special attention to proper nutrition and all other aspects of a healthy, well-balanced lifestyle. If the body is in bad shape, if vitamin or other deficiencies are serious, if toxic problems dominate, if low blood sugar leads to irrational thinking and behavior, or if the neurotransmitters are depleted, then all the psychotherapy will fall on unresponsive minds.

From time to time the wholistic approach is resisted, and this is understandable. Those who have been trained in exclusively singular methods—who belong to specialized professional societies, and who have spent time, money, and effort in learning their skills—are not usually thrilled to discover that exclusiveness is not necessarily the best.

Obviously, therapists trained in only one modality need to learn additional skills. Those trained only in behavior therapy might be shocked to discover that depression is not all a matter of the mind. Others trained only in the medical sciences might find it disheartening that the very medications that are supposed to help, often actually hinder the permanent healing of depression—in spite of pharmaceutical advertisements. It may be troublesome for others to discover that it may take many hours of repeated visits to diagnose properly a certain type of depression, and that it might also involve a number of tests and even referrals.

Those trained to think that depressions merely reflect sin in a person's life might be amazed that millions of cases of depression have nothing to do with personal sin at all. Indeed, many are born-again Christians who have gone from prayer meeting to prayer meeting, minister to minister, retreat after retreat, only to discover that a change in diet or sometimes a simple medication settled the matter. Even ministers have found themselves in this position and were grateful that God led them into the revelation that we are physical, mental, and spiritual beings. God hears our cry and answers if we but listen and believe that he can graciously heal us through a variety of procedures.

Can we agree that God does not want his children to have depression? The biblical characters who became depressed were shown how they could overcome it—not to mention that as a rule they gave the depression to themselves. God teaches us how not to become depressed, and even if we suffer from afflictions permitted by God, they do not include depressions. The Bible teaches us not to accept but to reject depression. For those who sneer at God and his love for us or his healing power, I would like to state unequivocally that I have seen his miraculous healing power at work in seemingly hopeless cases. I thank God for opening my eyes wide to the fact that indeed nothing is impossible with him.

Unfortunately, some professionals and nonprofessionals alike are so entrenched in one particular professional or spiritual method that their eyes remain closed to the obvious—a truly wholistic approach. To all who scoff at the integration of healing modalities my advice has been, is, and will remain the same—don't reject without investigating.

I have never failed to see positive results in anyone who faithfully and wholeheartedly participated in a program of physical restoration, emotional re-education, and spiritual regeneration. It is superior to any singular approach for the treatment of depression, and indeed of any other mental or emotional disorder.

A prayer of the apostle Paul concludes this book effectively: "And the very God of peace sanctify you wholly; and I pray God your whole spirit and soul and body be preserved blameless unto the coming of our LORD Jesus Christ" (1 Thess. 5:23).

Appendices

Appendix 1

The Various Types of Depression

Chapter 2 on the Classification of Depression emphasized that depression and other mood disturbances are difficult to classify. Nevertheless, considering such factors as the age of onset, signs and symptoms, origin, and severity, are all helpful in distinguishing various types of depression.

Reviewing different types of depression—most of which have an endogenous basis—might serve to reinforce a widely held myth that most depressed people are in need of medications. Nothing is further from the truth!

In a recent discussion with a distinguished psychiatrist friend of mine, we both agreed that only a minority of depressed persons are good candidates for medications. My friend believed that no more than 25 percent are good candidates. I think that it is probably closer to 15 percent. Some sources believe that 15 percent of the depressed population have psychotic symptoms (and might therefore warrant medication). The exact figure, however, is not so important. But it is important to know that the overwhelming majority (about 75 percent) of depressed people suffer from self-induced and self-maintained exogenous (external) depressions.

Most of the depressions discussed in this Appendix are of a physical nature. Yet, it is necessary to remember that they involve a minority (25 percent) of depressed persons. And even in this group many suffer from self-induced physical problems that are related to self-defeating lifestyles. This does not diminish the perplexing problems associated with genetically based depressions, such as bipolar and unipolar depression (*see* Glossary— depressive illness).

It also does not diminish the vulnerability of an unhappy childhood, impoverished environment, lack of education, and other factors. Throughout the text and the Glossary these factors are mentioned without giving them undue credit. It is my finding that most people, can be victorious over depression, and that *all* can be helped to live healthier and happier lives.

The following types of depression and other mood disorders are briefly described in alphabetical order: (This Appendix does not necessarily follow the *Diagnostic and Statistical Manual of Mental Disorders,* commonly known as the DSM-III. However, DSM-III categories are included in the Glossary under *DSM-III.*)

Agitated depression

Bipolar depression:
   manic phase
   depressive phase
   mixed type

Brain allergy depression

Childhood depression

Climacteric depression

Involutional depression

Metabolic depression

Narcissistic depression

Nutrient deficiency depression

Postnatal depression

Premenstrual syndrome depression

Psychosocial depression

Reactive depression

Schizophrenic depression

Secondary depression

Senile depression

Spiritual depression

Unipolar depression

Agitated Depression

In agitated depression—which can be moderate (neurotic) or severe (psychotic)—we find anxiety, sadness, and self-defeating thinking (such as self-pity, self-blame, other-blame). A person with agitated depression has depressive symptoms as well as agitation (severe restlessness, increased activity, sleep disturbances, fear, and inability to concentrate). The main characteristics are moderate-to-severe depression with moderate-to-severe anxiety. If thinking is distorted (delusions and hallucinations), the depression is considered of a psychotic nature. Major tranquilizers such as Thorazine (Chlorpromazine) might be included in the treatment of agitated depression.

Bipolar Depression

Bipolar depression is a serious endogenous disorder with major up and down mood swings. An individual might be in one phase (manic or depressive) or both phases (mixed) at a given time.

It is believed that a dominant defective gene is responsible for some forms of bipolar depression. Since not all bipolar depression can be linked to this defective gene, it seems that bipolar illness consists of a group of related disorders, rather than a single entity. Nevertheless, heredity is an important factor in bipolar depression.

A diagnosis of bipolar depression is made when there is a documented history of an episode (or episodes) of *both* depression and mania. This diagnosis is made regardless of the number of "opposite" episodes, or the amount of time that has elapsed between the opposite episodes. It is sufficient to have only one episode of each opposite pole in an entire lifetime to eventually receive a diagnosis of bipolar depression.

If currently suffering from a manic episode (with a history of at least one serious depressive episode) a person is diagnosed as *bipolar depression, manic phase.* If currently suffering from a serious depression (with a history of at least one manic episode) a person is diagnosed as *bipolar depression, depressive phase.*

Bipolar depression usually benefits from medications, such as lithium for the manic phase, and tricyclic antidepressants (*see* Glossary) for the depressive phase. The disorder may or may not be of a psychotic nature. The latter is true when hallucinations or delusions are present.

Persons suffering from *bipolar depression, manic phase,* are euphoric, convinced they can do anything, and they may engage in hopeless business or social ventures, or sexual exploits. They also have excessive talkativeness, sleeplessness, irritability, easy distractions, racing thoughts, rapid movements, and incoherent thought patterns. Delusions of grandeur are sometimes present.

A person suffering from *bipolar depression, depressive phase* has a deep depression manifested in sadness, despair, hopelessness, self-criticism, slow movements, and sometimes delusions of unworthiness and persecution. Suicide is often a real danger. Although long periods of symptom-free behavior may prevail, it is possible for a person with bipolar depression to be manic and depressed virtually at the same time, or to experience an elation and depressive phase all in one day. This kind of depression is called *bipolar depression, mixed type.*

Another form of depression called *atypical bipolar depression* shows some features of either elation or depression in a person who has experienced an episode of the opposite form in the past (see Glossary *DSM-III*).

Brain-Allergy Depression

Some people suffer from depressions due to food allergies. These are acquired by exposure to specific foods or chemical substances that have been added to the food. Others suffer from brain allergy depressions due to chemical substances in the air such as fluorocarbons, natural gas, lead, and so forth. There is also a tendency for allergies to be inherited, yet this tendency may remain dormant until other variables interact.

Dr. Mackarnness (1976) lists criteria to recognize food allergies: (1) a fluctuating illness: (2) evidence of food addiction; (3) repetitive menus; (4) conventional allergies such as hayfever, rashes, headaches, asthma, and such symptoms as swelling of different parts of the body; (5) heavy sweating not related to exercise; (6) fatigue not relieved by rest; (7) a racing pulse; and (8) marked weight gain or weight loss.

Allergies may lead to physical ailments and mental emotional problems such as panic attacks, chronic anxiety, depression, and hypomania (mild). According to Mackarnness (1980) various chemicals "enter the blood stream and reach the brain where they may set up allergic and/or toxic reactions which manifest as depressions or abnormal behavior in susceptible people."

William H. Philpott, M.D., and Dwight K. Kalita, Ph.D. (1980) emphasize that "an individual's ability to handle toxins, pollens, foods and chemicals contracted from the environment differs considerably according to his unique chemical make-up (*Health & News Review,* May/June 1987)." Yet, this does not mean that bizarre reactions to common substances are rare. *Chronic physical or emotional stress leads* to *chronic physical or emotional illness.* Allergic and addiction reactions are more and more common because more and more people are unable to properly deal with toxins, pollens, various foods, and chemical fumes. This is mainly due to nutritionally deficient junk-food diets and other stresses which have increased defective tissue states in the human body.

Many people live under "chronic stress" with bodies that are addicted to a variety of substances, ranging from food and various chemicals to alcohol, coffee, and tobacco. As long as these addictive substances are regularly used the person stays in a "relief" state. This precarious condition can change at any time.

According to Philpott and Kalita (*Health & News Review,* May/June 1987), an acute illness *will* take place when additional stress is introduced, such as: "(1) an overload of the allergen; (2) the addition of seasonal allergens such as pollens or other environmental stresses; (3) physical stresses such as excessive cold, heat, or fatigue; (4) harbored infections; and (5) emotional stress."

Allergy addiction to foods and chemicals is a serious metabolic problem and a major source of physical and mental/emotional disorders, including depression.

Brain-allergy depression is a very real condition that must be considered in any differential diagnosis of depression. The connection between diet and disease is a well-established fact. To better understand this connection, a spring-water fast—under appropriate professional supervision—might be considered. If a person is suffering from a physical or mental-emotional illness caused by allergic reactions then the illness will be greatly reduced in severity or disappear completely on a four-day fast! After the fast, foods are reintroduced one at a time so that specific offending substances may be identified. When an offending food is introduced, there will be an acute (severe) reaction to that food. All addictions, regardless of their source, display the same pattern. After a four-day fast reintroduced substances will evoke an acute re-emergence of symptoms. These may range from mild disturbances to psychosis.

Until more information becomes available, and the wholistic approach more widespread, the diagnosis of brain-allergy depression will be used infrequently.

Childhood Depression

Depressions of *infancy* (sometimes referred to as anaclitic depression), *childhood,* and *adolescence* are not uncommon. Depression is seen even in young infants. The symptoms of *infant depression* include screaming, panic reactions, serious physical deterioration (marasmus), and severe introversion. Years ago this form of depression was seen mainly in institutionalized infants. In recent times we are experiencing an increasing incidence of depressed babies that are not maternally deprived or institutionalized.

Infants born to loving parents may yet suffer from depression. The sources of these depressions might be found in prenatal, natal, and postnatal conditions, including poor parental health, inefficient nutrition, psychosocial problems—affecting the biochemical makeup of the parents—genetics, addictive substances used by the parents, and other factors. Even the unborn infant is all too often exposed to poisoning, malnutrition, and other sources of stress.

Many symptoms of depression found in adults are also found in children. Some of the more common symptoms in *childhood depression* include: anxiety, apathy, behavioral problems, chronic fatigue, unhappiness, crying, difficulty in concentration, feelings of inferiority and unworthiness, self-accusations, loss of interest in pleasurable activities, marked weight gain or loss, talk of suicide, overwhelming sadness, and withdrawal from friends, family, and peers. Any one of these symptoms is ample reason to investigate the possibility of depression.

In *adolescents* we might find the addition of substance abuse and sexual promiscuity. Thorough physical and laboratory examinations are also likely to reveal allergies and such hormonal disturbances as erratic glucose, low-growth hormone, or high cortisone levels. The dexamethasone-suppression test described in Appendix 3 might be helpful in identifying potentially suicidal children.

Excessive stress is behind every form of depression, regardless of the age at which it occurs. There is also no depression without loss, regardless of age. In infants the primary loss is one of physical balance, and the same holds true—to a lesser extent—in children. For adolescents, however, irrational choices might be the primary factor, rather than biological vulnerability. In any case, professional help must be obtained whenever symptoms of depression are seen in infants, children, or adolescents.

Climacteric Depression

Climacteric (menopausal) depression is found in women who are usually fifty years of age or older. In addition to such symptoms as dizziness, headaches, insomnia, irritability, and anxiety, we might find sadness, self-defeating thinking, psychomotor retardation (including reduced sexual desire), fatigue, and insomnia.

Treatment with hormones and/or antidepressants is often helpful. A consultation with a gynecologist is very important. Once the climacteric is over the woman recovers spontaneously and usually feels better than she did before the menopause. Specialists do not always make a distinction between climacteric depression and involutional depression which is described below.

Involutional Depression

Persons who suffer from involutional (age-related) depression ordinarily do *not* show a history of previous depressions. Involutional depression is found in women aged forty-five to fifty-five and in men aged fifty-five to sixty-five.

Involutional depression is usually severe and characterized by anxiety, agitation, chronic insomnia, guilt, worry, many physical complaints, and psychotic symptoms. The precipitating sources may be difficult to identify. Involutional depression is distinguished from *unipolar depression* by the absence of prior depressive episodes, and from *schizophrenic depression* because difficulties with objective reality are primarily related to the mood disturbance, rather than any inherited mental disturbance. Involutional depression is further distinguished from other types of *depressive reactions* by its gradual onset at the change of life, and because there are usually no exogenous factors involved.

Involutional depressions are of a psychotic nature when there are clear-cut psychotic symptoms, such as hallucinations and delusions. Specific symptoms of involutional depression include withdrawal, agitation, self-blame, lack of interest, apprehension, restlessness, insomnia, excessive worry, preoccupation with real or imagined sins, errors, and mistakes. The person often believes that no forgiveness can be obtained for any of these.

Metabolic Depression

Endocrine disturbances often result in both physical and psychological disorders, including depression. Some people suffer from mild to moderate depression for which no exogenous or endogenous sources are readily identified. A thorough investigation might reveal metabolic

190

problems as the source of trouble. Thyroid, adrenal, and pancreas dysfunctions are among the chief sources of metabolic depressions.

(a) *Thyroid Dysfunction*

When the thyroid gland oversecretes (hyperthyroidism) there is an increase in metabolism, loss of weight, insomnia, tremors, tenseness, and emotional excitability. Oversecretion might also result in neurotic and psychotic symptoms. Treatment for hyperthyroidism involves surgery and/or medications.

More frequently the thyroid gland undersecretes (hypothyroidism), resulting in the opposite physical symptoms of oversecretion. Included are weight gain, listlessness, sleepiness, and generalized fatigue. Many of the psychological symptoms, however, are similar to those in oversecretion, such as restlessness, nervousness, and irritability. Undersecretion of the thyroid gland is a source of depression for many people. Conservative tests used for measuring thyroid function do not always show up low thyroid.

A simple home test for low thyroid function is the Barnes Basal Temperature Test. This test consists of measuring temperature under the armpit on two consecutive mornings before getting out of bed. To prepare for this test, shake down a thermometer the night before and leave it next to the bed. Immediately upon awakening, place the thermometer under the armpit for ten minutes while lying down. According to Stephen Langer, M.D. (1984) the temperature should be 97.8 to 98.2 degrees Fahrenheit. If it is lower, the thyroid gland is probably underfunctioning. It is best not to test during menstruation or ovulation as temperature will fluctuate at these times.

This test is said to be fairly accurate for thyroid functioning. However test results need to be evaluated by a physician and seen in light of all other available data pertaining to that person.

(b) *Adrenal Dysfunction*

The adrenal glands, located on top of the kidneys, are known as the stress glands. In every stressful condition these glands are directly involved. The glands' inner portion—the medulla—secretes epinephrine and norepinephrine, and an outer layer—the cortex—releases several hormones—cortisone, cortisol, corticosterone—that regulate the rate by which we use sugar in our bodies, and exert an anti-inflammatory effect.

The adrenal glands are supremely important for physical, and mental-emotional health. They maintain the sodium and electrolyte balance, and play a major part in the manufacture of glycogen in the liver. Dysfunction of the adrenal glands underlies many depressions.

(c) *Pancreas Dysfunction*

The pancreas plays a major role in the raising and lowering of blood sugar. When the pancreas secretes too much insulin, hypoglycemia results.

When a depressed person suffers from hypoglycemia, it is essential that the cause for this condition be investigated without delay. Treatment of depressed persons with reactive hypoglycemia is often dramatic: frequently showing positive changes in a matter of days or weeks on the proper diet.

Hypoglycemia has been well documented. One of the more scientific books is by Dr. T. I. Cleave, British Royal College of Physicians, entitled *The Saccharin Disease* (1974). Hypoglycemics may have a long list of depressive symptoms, as well as headaches, dizziness, sweating, insomnia, heart palpitations, irritability, and cravings for sweets, caffeine, nicotine, or alcohol.

Until more information becomes available and the wholistic approach more widespread, the diagnosis of metabolic depression will be used infrequently.

Narcissistic Depression

Narcissistic depression is manifested by a tremendous amount of self-centeredness. It can be observed in people who are overly concerned with their egos, personal well-being, and personal interest. Because of frail egos and extreme self-centeredness, they are hypersensitive to any criticism, however well meant.

Narcissistically depressed persons will not accept responsibility for their behavior. They constantly blame others and often lack a social conscience. Narcissistic depression diminishes in those who bask in unlimited attention. This is bestowed on them by the people they control and who must cater to their every wish, feel sorry for them, and admire them.

The depression will come and go under these circumstances. In narcissistic depression we may find sadness and self-defeating thinking which centers primarily on the "lost self."

Narcissistically depressed persons often have many blessings: prosperity, home, family, money, and good health. They mourn because they are not what they believe they "should" be or should have been. (*See* Glossary under *Personality Disorders*.)

Nutrient Deficiency Depression

Many people suffer from depressions due to a lack of essential nutrients, such as vitamins, minerals and/or amino acids. Several authors have described how depression may result from vitamin deficiency, (Lesser, 1981; Mandell, 1980; Wright, 1979).

Ideally, laboratory tests are used to identify a specific deficiency. It is often difficult, however, to get these tests, and most people resort to the use of multiple vitamins and minerals. In most cases, this means megadoses. Appendix 7, Food Supplements for Depression, discusses this at length.

A nutrient deficiency might contribute to psychological depression, but a psychological depression might also contribute to a nutrient deficiency. Emotional distress seriously interferes with the proper absorption of vitamins, minerals, and amino acids in our bodies, and consequently with the proper functioning of neurotransmitters. Until more information becomes available and the wholistic approach more widespread, the diagnosis of nutrient deficiency depression will be used infrequently.

Postnatal Depression

Postnatal depression (also known as postpartum depression) probably dates back to the days of Eve. Yet many people continue to overlook this type of depression. Postnatal depression is found in mothers following childbirth. From 50 to 80 percent of all women are said to suffer from mood disturbances following childbirth. Fortunately this lasts only one to two days. About 20 percent may suffer from depression that may last from two to twelve months.

Postnatal depression may have a gradual or sudden onset, with mild to severe mood changes. Postnatal depression might be of a physical, psychological, or even spiritual nature.

Major hormonal changes are taking place within the female body at this time. Fatigue and the mental/emotional stress of childbirth, as well as biochemical changes, are involved in postnatal depression. During pregnancy "gradual" changes within the mother's body were made to take care of her child. Following the birth of the baby, however, major hormonal changes are made abruptly.

Psychological factors are also at work. Many women feel elated after childbirth, while others suffer from excessive worries. They cry without reason and appear unhappy with their newborn baby or new status as mothers. The reasons for this may center in anxiety about responsibilities or feelings of guilt. Some women worry about the new relationship with their husbands.

Most postnatal depressions are resolved with professional reassurance or minor medication, and the help of a supporting husband. Some cases of postnatal depression need psychotherapy as well as medication.

Premenstrual Syndrome Depression

Before, during, and—sometimes—after menstruation many women suffer from depression. In addition to many physical complaints there are often difficulties in interpersonal relations.

Irritability, tiredness, and sudden changes in mood seem primarily related to lowered levels of circulating sex hormones.

Various studies, (*Psychology Today,* February 1972), have shown that the levels of female hormones do affect mood. Anxiety, hostility, and depression are frequently found when estrogen and progesterone are at a low peak. Conversely—during midcycle—when these hormones are at a high peak, happier moods usually prevail.

Although the levels of female hormones do affect the moods of many women, there are also psychological, social, and cultural factors which might have led to negative attitudes about menstruation, such as seeing menstruating women as "unclean."

The *physical* symptoms of PMS include water retention, weight gain, headaches, cramps, bloated or distended abdomen, sensitive swollen breasts, constipation, insomnia, backache, low blood sugar, tiredness, restlessness, skin eruptions, accident proneness, thirst, and joint pains. The *psychological* symptoms of PMS include anxiety, restlessness, aggressiveness, tenseness, irritability, lethargy, and depression.

Dr. Lloyd (1973) stated "in those patients [of a women's prison] who reported premenstrual tension, we found that some time before menstruation the progesterone fell while the estrogen remained elevated, so that the ratio was radically altered. As soon as this ratio changed, the tension appeared; as the progesterone dropped relative to the estrogen, the women began to feel uncomfortable." The administration of progesterone for a week premenstrually was found effective in cases of an aberrant estrogen-progesterone ratio.

Other sources for PMS have been found in vitamin B_6 and magnesium deficiencies, prostaglandin imbalance, and central nervous system malfunctions. PMS is a multifaceted stress disorder. Medical treatment with progesterone has brought relief to many women. Yet a new lifestyle might be a better choice. Such a lifestyle should include: (1) *proper nutrition;* (2) *food supplements:* A, C, B_6, E, folic acid; (3) *evening primrose oil;* (4) *rest;* (5) *relaxation* and *recreation,* (6) *exercise;* (7) *emotional re-education.* Most PMS sufferers will succeed with this program! The nutrients most frequently suggested are evening primrose oil (six to eight 500 mg. capsules per day); B$_6$ (50 to 100 mg. per day); and E (100 to 200 I.U. per day). (*See* Glossary under *Premenstrual Syndrome,* and also see *Appendices 2, 5,* and *6.*

Psychosocial Depression

Many psychological depressions have a social origin. People often allow themselves to be negatively influenced by the social setting in which they find themselves. Blue collar, single parent, unemployment, college, and housewife blues, are all psychosocial depressions, but the terms can be misleading and prevent the diagnosis of other depressions that might be involved, such as narcissistic or spiritual depression.

Psychosocial depressions are primarily the result of erroneous perceptions and appraisals and are successfully treated with environmental changes, or emotional re-education as described in chapter 8 of this book.

Reactive Depression

Reactive depression is often used as a general diagnosis for various exogenous depressions, especially the moderate depressions that result from self-defeating perceptions and appraisals.

The majority of depressed people have reactive depression rather than depressive illness. Reactive depression is often the outcome of self-defeating responses to losses, separations, and reversals in life. An example of reactive depression is *grief* that lasts more than a year.

Reactive depression is found in people who are in touch with reality, have normal mental abilities, and who can refer to some actual, or perhaps imagined loss in their lives. While sadness, self-defeating thinking, and slowness of movement are common symptoms of reactive depression, there is no gross personality disorganization, or loss of contact with reality, as found in psychotic depressions.

Reactive depression is sometimes the result of a neurosis—a mild functional personality disorder—rather than an actual loss. Most of these exogenous depressions usually do not require drug treatment or hospitalization, are self-limiting, and are sometimes described as moderate depressions.

The overwhelming majority of depressed people suffer from self-induced and self-maintained exogenous depressions. The good news is that they can all be helped to overcome these depressions.

Schizophrenic Depression

Schizophrenic depression is an integral part of schizophrenia. Schizophrenia is primarily of a biochemical nature. There are certain similarities in both manic depressives and schizophrenics. Both seem to suffer from inherited disorders—or at least an inherited tendency to these disorders. Both, more often than not, suffer from hypoglycemia (Newbold 1975). Brain scans of schizophrenics and manic depressives show abnormalities of glucose consumption in the brain. *Decreased* glucose consumption is found in some areas of the brains of schizophrenics and *increased* consumption of glucose in manic depressives during the manic phase (Diagram Group 1982).

Schizophrenia and schizophrenic depression are sometimes misdiagnosed by Christians in deliverance ministries. Extreme care and absolute discernment is required here. Schizophrenia involves perceptual disorders such as disturbed thinking, feelings, and actions. Sensory distortions might include hearing, smell, sight, touch, taste, time, and position. Tactile hallucinations might also be found, such as pressure in body areas, "things" crawling under the skin, and nerves moving all over the body. Food may seem spoiled, the ground to move, time to pass extremely slow or fast. All this leads to feelings of isolation and withdrawal in the schizophrenic person.

Following an acute phase of schizophrenia, there might be sadness, hopelessness, self-pity, and/or self-blame. These are probably exogenous rather than endogenous symptoms and require psychotherapeutic as well as biochemical intervention. On the other hand, the depression may be the result of high doses of depressant neuroleptics. These drugs produce an altered state of consciousness—making the patient indifferent to the surroundings.

There are also disorders with serious thought *and* mood disturbances, known as *schizoaffective disorders*. These disorders include manic, depressed, or mixed episodes. (*See* Glossary under *Psychosis,* and *Schizophrenia.*

Secondary Depression

Secondary depression might result from such diverse problems as the flu, malignant disease, or organic brain disorders. *General paresis* (an inflammation of the brain caused by syphilitic infection), *Huntington's chorea* (an inherited disorder), and *Parkinson's disease* (a neurologic disorder) are examples of organic brain disorders which include depression.

Some people suffer from depressions caused by illegal or legal drugs. The following illegally used drugs might produce symptoms of depression: (1) marijuana, (2) Lysergic Acid Diethylamide (LSD), (3) Psilocybin (STP), and (4) Diethyl Tryptamine (DMT).

Many legal drugs also can cause depression. For example, Reserpine—used for the treatment of high blood pressure—sometimes lowers norepinephrine levels in the bloodstream and this consequently leads to depression. The physical sources that might induce depression are mind boggling and include allergies to food, food additives, and other chemicals. Some people become depressed because of excessive amounts of minerals, such as, copper, or from elevated levels of histamine (Lesser 1981). Illegal drugs must never be taken for the treatment of depression, and legal drugs *only* under close supervision by a physician. (*See* Glossary under *Iatrogenic Depression.*)

Senile Depression

Senile *dementia* refers to the serious mental impairment found in older people—usually after age sixty-five. This dementia is caused by physical atrophy and degeneration of the brain. In senile dementia there are no signs of cerebrovascular disease. Senile dementia is characterized by memory loss for recent events, agitation, lack of interest, and major personality changes (coupled with temporary returns of more normal behavior). Senile *depression* can be a reaction to senile dementia, or might be related to infections, anemia, electrolyte imbalance, endocrine dysfunction, toxic conditions, arteriosclerosis, nutritional deficiencies, drugs, physical injuries to the head, and systemic illnesses, resulting in a decreased oxygen supply to the brain. It is important to distinguish senile depression from Alzheimer's disease. Senile depression is *not* always an organic brain disorder.

In Alzheimer's disease, on the other hand, we are always dealing with an organic brain disorder. In the earlier stages of Alzheimer's disease—early confusional, delayed confusional, and early dementia phase—the patients may suffer from depression related to their inability to remember recent events, or to perform satisfactorily in the world of work, at home, or interpersonal relationships. Alzheimer's disease is primarily a *genetic disorder* leading to destruction of brain tissue. Difficulty with memory, concentration, and disorientation to time and place, all take their toll. The patient is likely to manifest such symptoms as denial, withdrawal, sadness, and restless wandering. Alteration of several neural transmitters—acetycholine, somatostatin, Substance-P, and norepinephrine—affects the mental, physical and emotional behavior of the Alzheimer patient.

How do we know if a person is suffering primarily from depression or Alzheimer's disease? Powell and Courtice (1983) explain that depressed persons *admit*, while Alzheimer's patients *deny* a decrease in intellectual areas and memory. Likewise, depressed persons are more likely to exaggerate their sense of distress, and Alzheimer patients are more likely to show little emotional reaction.

Older people suffering from pernicious anemia—caused by vitamin B_{12} deficiency—can be misdiagnosed as suffering from Alzheimer's disease. Early blood tests and urine tests for a rise in methylmalonic acid might be helpful.

Depression and Alzheimer's disease can, of course, exist side by side. In that case treatment for the depression will not improve memory and intellectual functioning. In the advanced stages of Alzheimer's disease—the middle and late dementia phase—there is a corresponding and eventual complete decrease in all emotive experiences.

In *senile psychosis* we find symptoms of severe depression, in addition to defective memory, disorientation, and delusions which alternate with periods of relatively normal behavior. There usually is degeneration of cerebrum, basal ganglia, and dark cells in the *substantia nigra* of the brain stem. (*See* Glossary, *Senile Dementia*.)

Spiritual Depression

Spiritual depression is characterized by an awareness of loss. One form of spiritual depression is based on the loss of an illusion. It is found in people who have come to realize that humanism, hedonism, or materialism cannot give true fulfillment. A *void* remains that can only be filled by God.

Another form of spiritual depression results from the loss of a sense of fellowship with God. It is the final outcome of *God-neglect*. It is possible to experience the love of God and yet, through neglect, lose the awareness of that love. Failure to practice the presence of God, willful disobedience to his commandments, and wrong thinking easily leads to unresolved guilt and other negative emotions, including depression. A break in one's awareness of God's presence is often compounded by the loss of fellowship with other believers, family, and friends.

Yet another type of spiritual depression results from the loss of peace. It is the result of *God-confusion*. Here we might find people believing things that are quite contrary to the nature of God. God-confusion often results when people lose sight of the totality of their personhood. Not being aware that mind and spirit are interwoven with the body leads to the misunderstanding that our peace (with God) is disturbed by some action on the part of God. In reality physical and mental/emotional problems cause the confusion which prevents us from taking corrective steps.

Spiritual depression ultimately is the result of a general loss of spiritual direction. Not all depressions are of a spiritual nature. Yet, most depressions benefit from spiritual treatment administered in conjunction with physical and psychological treatments.

Unipolar Depression

This major endogenous (internal) depression is characterized by feelings of sadness, helplessness, and hopelessness. Psychomotor retardation to the point of complete apathy may occur. Thinking is sometimes so retarded that the person cannot finalize one thought. Slow movements, slow talk, and physical tiredness are some of the major symptoms. The diagnosis of unipolar depression is reserved for those people who have no history of ever having been manic. It is estimated that about half of all the people who suffer from unipolar depression will not have more than one such episode in their lifetime. Most of these people recover completely within a matter of months. Others, who have recurrent episodes, may have years without an episode of unipolar depression.

Most of the symptoms found in unipolar depression are the opposite of those found in the manic person. We find a lack of interest, no hope in the future, bad memories of the past, little or no contact with people, a conviction of guilt and sinfulness, insomnia, lack of appetite, tiredness, absence of sexual desire, hypochondriasis, and daytime variations in mood. The sufferer usually feels worse in the morning and better at night. There is often no true desire to live. The skin is usually dry because there is little perspiration going on. Constipation is frequently a problem. With this major depressive disorder there is always the danger of suicide. However, there is good news. With medications (especially the tricyclic antidepressants), psychotherapy, and some common sense lifestyle changes (a healthy diet and well-thought-out program of regular exercise), a great deal of success may be achieved.

Other Types of Depression

More than twenty different types of depression have been described in this Appendix. Yet, there are many more types of depression. Some are rare, others are part of specific mental/emotional conditions. Most of these depressions are listed in the Glossary under *DSM-III*. Also see the following glossary entries: Adjustment Reaction, Atypical Depression, Characterologic Neurotic Depression, Cyclothymia, Depressive Illness, Dysthymia, Grief Reaction, and Neurosis.

A brief review of different depressions highlights the fact that depression is a multifaceted disorder, and the ultimate outcome of endogenous *and* exogenous factors. Depression is clearly a question of choice *and* vulnerability as can be seen in table 9, *Approximate Age Incidence of Certain Depressions*.

9. Approximate Age Incidence of Certain Depressions

Senile Depression	Involutional Depression	Unipolar* Depression	Bipolar** Depression	Premenstrual, Postnatal, Schizophrenic Depression
65-99	45-64 (Men 55-65 Women 45-55)	41-55	31-40	18-30

*Unipolar—(abrupt or insidious)
**Bipolar—(often abrupt)

Appendix 2

Specific Physical Sources of Depression

The physical sources of depression are numerous and varied. Included are maladaptive (toxic, allergic) reactions to common substances such as foods, pollens, and chemicals contracted from the environment, disease, drugs, and hormonal dysfunctions.

Depression and happiness are ultimately based on choices. These choices, however, are far from simple. Unless there is up-to-date information and knowledge about the many sources of depression, a choice for happiness might be extremely limited and difficult.

Since it is not possible to describe all the physical sources of depression in detail, I will discuss only some of the more common physical sources. These include metabolic disorders caused by adrenal, pancreas, pituitary, or thyroid dysfunction, and vitamin, mineral, amino acid, and neurotransmitter deficiencies, as well as allergic reactions. These and many other physical sources might result in loss of physical balance and play a key part in the formation of depression.

Pancreas Dysfunction

The pancreas—a long thin gland that lies crosswise behind the stomach—has many functions, including the production of digestive

201

enzymes, and the blood-sugar level regulating hormones glucagon and insulin. When blood-sugar levels are too high, insulin will lower them. When too low, glucagon will raise them. The pancreas helps to insure that a steady amount of sugar is available in the blood. Of course, it is essential for good physical *and* mental/emotional health that an adequate and steady amount of sugar is available in the blood at all times. Whenever the pancreas becomes hypersensitive—usually because of dietary and/or emotional stress—it will secrete too much insulin. This in turn causes an excessive drop of glucose levels resulting in hypoglycemia (low blood sugar).

There are many reasons for hypoglycemia, including alcoholism, enzyme defects of sugar metabolism, liver disease, malabsorption of food, and malignant tumors outside the pancreas. The most common cause, however is a reaction (reactive hypoglycemia) to refined carbohydrates. Poor dietary habits are the main reason behind most glucose disturbances (see chapter 4 and this Appendix).

Depression is one of the more common symptoms of hypoglycemia. Other symptoms include anger, headaches, heart palpitations, hunger, gastrointestinal problems such as peptic ulcer, excessive perspiration, and nervousness. Convulsions, especially in children, do also occur. These convulsions are sometimes misdiagnosed and the child is placed on anticonvulsive medications such as Dilantin or Phenobarbitol.

That hypoglycemia is *low* blood sugar confuses some people. They take sugar to raise blood sugar levels, but only to discover that this results in even more frequent and more serious bouts of low blood sugar. Taking sugar for the *emergency treatment* of a very serious attack of hypoglycemia is one thing. However, it is a dangerous and self-defeating practice to treat hypoglycemia with refined carbohydrates and in particular with refined sugar or sugar products. The proper treatment for hypoglycemia is discussed in chapter 7.

To diagnose hypoglycemia, pay close attention to subjective symptoms, for which primary stressors cannot be identified and obtain a thorough physical examination and laboratory tests as quickly as possible. The test that is most important for proper diagnosis of hypoglycemia is the Six-Hour-Oral-Glucose-Tolerance Test (6 hr OGTT). Additional tests are sometimes obtained if there are abnormalities on the OGTT. These might include adrenal, thyroid, pituitary, and liver function tests. Other available tests include (1) observing the response to intravenously injected Tolbutamid (Orinase); or (2) the physical and mental responses to a 72-hour diet of 1,200 calories, consisting of low protein and carbohydrates; or (3) the effects of a 48-hour fast. Additional tests are described in Appendix 3.

In summary, pancreatic dysfunction often leads to hypoglycemia and depression. Hypoglycemia, however, is only one of several conditions that come under the heading of glucose disturbances, and the latter is only one of many physical sources that might lead to loss of physical balance and depression.

It is sometimes difficult to make accurate distinctions between hypoglycemia related to pancreatic, adrenal, pituitary, or thyroid dysfunction. The experts are not always in agreement either. Abrahamson and Pezet (1977) stress pancreas dysfunction; Tintera (1955; 1966; 1967) stresses adrenal dysfunction; and Langer (1984) stresses thyroid dysfunction, as the primary source for hypoglycemia. It is best to consider pancreatic, adrenal, thyroid, as well as pituitary dysfunction, as possible sources for hypoglycemia and depression. *See* Glossary under *Hypoglycemia* and Appendix 3.

Adrenal Dysfunction

The adrenal glands, commonly known as the stress glands, are only the size of grapes—yet they are super powerful. One of these small glands is located on top of each kidney. They are involved in every stressful condition.

The inner portion of the adrenal glands, the *medulla,* secretes epinephrine and norepinephrine, and the outer layer, the *cortex,* releases several hormones—glycocorticoids—that control the rate by which we use sugar in our bodies.

It appears indisputable that the adrenal glands play a major part in depression. To understand the relationship between the adrenal glands, stress, and depression consider the following points:

1. *The adrenal glands play a definite part in both endogenous and exogenous depression.* The adrenal glands are involved with proprioceptive or perceptual-cognitive stressful stimuli.
2. *The extent of adrenal involvement depends on the amount and the duration of the stress.* During the *alarm* stage the adrenal medulla releases epinephrine and norepinephrine. During the *resistance* stage the adrenal cortex releases cortisone and cortisol.
3. *A great variety of stressors stimulate the release of adrenal hormones.* These stressors include: excessive work, lack of sleep, poor diet (junk food, such as sugar, salt, refined carbohydrates); illegal or legal drugs (including caffeine, nicotine, and alcohol); bacteria, viruses, physical and emotional trauma; worry, anxiety, fear, hatred, hostility, bitterness, extreme temperatures,

overeating, undereating, as well as positive experiences and emotions, such as love and joy.

4. *Stress reactions are hormonal chain reactions.* During the *alarm* stage various stressors stimulate the hypothalamus to send out nervous impulses to the adrenal medulla. This leads to the release of adrenaline and other stress responses. During the resistance stage, a message is received from the hypothalamus—in the form of the neurohumor CRF (corticotrophin-releasing factor)—which signals the anterior lobe of the pituitary gland and causes it to release ACTH (adrenocorticotrophic hormone). This in turn stimulates the adrenal cortex to release glucocorticoids (hydrocortisone), and mineralocorticoids (aldosterone), which leads to further stress responses. At this time the adrenal cortex has also been alerted by the stress reactions of the adrenal medulla. The increased heart rate and blood sugar levels additionally stimulate the adrenal cortex to release glucocorticoids.

5. *The adrenal stress responses during the alarm stage prepares for fight or flight.* The *alarm* state results from nervous impulses of the hypothalamus to the sympathetic division of the autonomic nervous system and the adrenal medulla. The responses are immediate and of short duration and include increased heart rate and dilatation of bronchial tubes. This enhances catabolism (for the production of energy) and restricts nonessential functions, such as, a decrease in urine production.

6. *The adrenal stress responses during the resistance stage prepare for survival.* It is during the *resistance* stage that a long-term battle is fought to return blood chemistry to normal levels. The *mineralocorticoids* increase sodium and water retention and the *glucocorticoids* provide the necessary energy to counteract stress.

7. *Adrenal exhaustion leads to hypoadrenocorticism.* If elevation of blood pressure, perspiration, heart rate, glucose, insulin, and sweating occurs too frequently—or is too prolonged and severe—the body enters into the *exhaustion* stage of the stress syndrome. The greater the stress (and the lower the resistance) the more physical and emotional illness results.

For example, excessive stress leads to adrenal exhaustion known as hypoadrenocorticism (subclinical Addison's disease). According to Tintera (1955), this may be congenital or acquired. In a study of 200 subjects with hypoadrenocorticism he found that 79 percent had symptoms of depression and 86 percent had nervousness and irritability, and many other physical symptoms.

Significant laboratory findings included (1) low blood sugar;

(2) low basal metabolism (−11 to −15); (3) low titer of 17-Ketosteroids (3-12mg in men, and 2-8 mg in women per 24 hours); as well as other significant laboratory and physical findings, including hypotension (Tintera 1955).

8. *Adrenal dysfunction causes electrolyte and fluid imbalance.* Under or overactivity of the adrenal cortex leads to disturbances in sodium and potassium levels and creates an electrolyte and fluid imbalance. Electrolyte disturbances are often found in people with depression. Electrolytes play a vital part in the proper functioning of the neurotransmitters.

9. *The adrenal glands play a major part in the manufacture of glycogen in the liver.* Liver disease is a frequent cause of hypoglycemia, and thus a possible source of depression. The liver has many metabolic functions and responds to calls from the adrenal glands to maintain proper blood-sugar levels.

10. *The production of low levels of glucocorticoids by the adrenal cortex stimulates the hypothalamus and pituitary glands.* Extreme stress or low levels of glucocorticoids results in the secretion of CRF, alerting the pituitary to secrete ACTH, which in turn alerts the adrenal cortex to secrete more glucocorticoids. As this negative feedback system becomes overworked, chronic hyposecretion occurs. This leads to subclinical Addison's disease, or more rarely to Addison's disease. (*See* Appendix 3 and Glossary, *Pituitary Gland.*)

Pituitary Dysfunction

Excessive stress of any kind can also lead to disturbances of the pituitary gland. Among many other functions, the pituitary regulates the activities of the thyroid gland and adrenal cortex. High levels of cortisol—which is the main glucocorticoid secreted by the adrenal glands—are found in many people who suffer from depression. Emotional stress increases cortisol levels, which decreases levels of tryptophan, and eventually the neurotransmitter serotonin.

The pituitary—a peanut-size gland, with a diameter of 0.5 inch and barely weighing 0.5 gram—is known as the master gland. The master, however, is controlled by the hypothalamus! The two lobes of the pituitary gland—the anterior (front) and posterior (rear) lobe—regulate the endocrine system. The anterior lobe—also known as adenophysis—releases six important hormones. Three of these are known as the *gonadotrophic hormones*: prolactin (lactogenic hormone), FSH (follicle stimulating hormone), and LH/ISCH (luteinizing hormones).

The other three hormones are: TSH (thyroid stimulating hormone), ACTH (adrenocorticotrophic hormone), and STH (somatotrophic or growth hormone).

Dysfunction of the pituitary gland causes many disorders including dwarfism, gigantism, acromegaly, sexual difficulties, and diabetes insipidus (due to hypersecretion of vasopressin-ADH by the hypothalamus). Important to our discussion is *pituitary fatigue* and *pituitary deficiency,* which could result in hypoadrenocorticism and depression.

The pituitary is a link between the central nervous and endocrine system, reminding us of the absolute interrelationship of mind and body. The pituitary is essential for general metabolism, that is, the physical and chemical changes occurring within the cells of our bodies. By this process food is built up (anabolism) into living protoplasm. In turn protoplasm is broken down (catabolism) into simpler compounds with the exchange of energy.

Pituitary tumors are the more common reason for the serious pituitary disorders which are readily diagnosed by physicians. Underfunctioning of the pituitary, however, also causes problems and may result from excessive adrenal demands and "unknown" sources.

Thyroid Dysfunctioning

More commonly found as a source of depression is underfunctioning of the thyroid gland. Underfunctioning does not necessarily imply disease. It only refers to the absence of normal functioning.

The thyroid gland's two lobes which form a butterfly shape are located on either side of the trachea. A mass of thyroid tissue joins the lobes that produce two hormones, namely *thyroxine,* and *thyrocalcitonin.*

Thyroxine is synthesized from iodine and the amino acid tyrosine and controls the rate of metabolism. Thyroxine is responsible for both *anabolism* (the energy building up processes), and *catabolism* (the energy releasing processes).

Thyrocalcitonin, on the other hand, is primarily concerned with maintaining the necessary blood calcium level. When blood calcium levels are too high then it is lowered through accelerating calcium absorption by the bones.

When blood calcium levels are too low, then the parathyroids—embedded on the posterior surfaces of the lateral thyroid lobes—get into action by releasing PTH (parathyroid hormone). This increases the blood calcium level and decreases the blood phosphate level. Both the thyroid gland (thyrocalcitonin) and the parathyroid glands (PTH) work together in a negative feedback control system to regulate our blood calcium level, which is essential for proper mental and physical health.

Unneeded thyroxine may unite with the protein thyroglobulin and be stored in the gelatinous substance (coloid) of the gland. Released into the blood when needed, the thyroxine unites with a protein called thyroxin-binding globulin (TBG). Both thyroxine and thyrocalcitonin contain iodine. Iodine bound to TBG is known as PBI (protein-bound iodine). The normal amount of PBI is 4-8 micrograms per 100 milliliters of blood. Underfunctioning of the thyroid gland can be diagnosed in several ways, including by measuring thyroxine, or PBI. A very simple temperature test is claimed to be even more accurate than a blood test for hypothyroidism and is described in Appendix 3.

Thyroid disorders may result in either over- or under-secretion. In this book the primary concern is with hypofunctioning of the thyroid gland as a source of depression. The thyroid gland affects carbohydrate metabolism and is frequently implicated in hypoglycemia. Underfunc-

Regulation of Thyroxine and Thyrocalcitonin

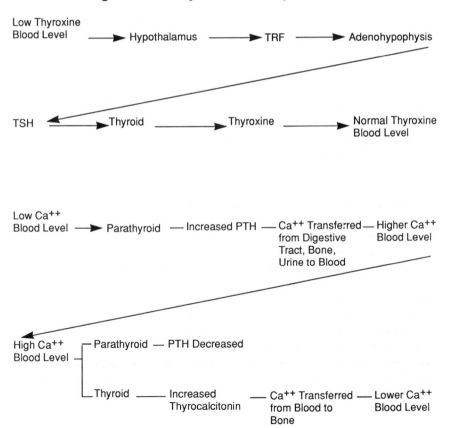

tioning of the thyroid gland lowers cellular metabolism and adequate brain functioning. The result is confusion, memory problems, and depression.

Overstimulation of the thyroid gland due to severe stresses, will eventually lead to understimulation, and to various physical and emotional problems, including depression.

Vitamin, Mineral, and Amino-Acid Deficiences

Dozens of different nutrients are present in our bloodstream. Included are the vitamins, minerals, and amino acids that enable us to function optimally. Even slight imbalances of vitamins, minerals, or amino acids are sufficient to negatively affect our thinking and emotive feelings. A serious deficiency, however, of vitamins such as B_1, B_6, B_{12}, Biotin, pantothenic acid, or vitamin C may cause mild, moderate or severe depressions (Brandt 1983).

Many vitamins, minerals, and amino acids depend on each other for proper functioning. Vitamin B_2 is necessary for tryptophan metabolism. Also a shortage of one vitamin may affect the proper utilization of other vitamins, or neurotransmitters. Vitamin B_6 (pyridoxine) is necessary for the production of the neurotransmitter serotonin. Lack of B_6 might cause a lack of serotonin, which in turn might cause depression. Women on a contraceptive pill often deplete their bodies of Vitamin B_6, folic acid, and Vitamin C. Their depressions might be related to this particular means of birth control.

Deficiencies of amino acids like tryptophan, tyrosine, and phenylalanine can also lead to depression. Tryptophan is necessary for the neurotransmitter, serotonin. It is known that low levels of norepinephrine or serotonin are sources of depression.

For adults dietary protein must provide eight essential amino acids, namely, isoleucine, leucine, lysine, methionine, phenylalanine, threonine, tryptophan, and valine. These amino acids are called essential because the human body cannot manufacture them. They must be obtained from animal protein. In early life two other amino acids are essential, namely histidine and anginine. Amino acids are essential for the manufacture and maintenance of cells, hormones, bones, and muscle.

Protein deficiencies often lead to amino-acid deficiencies and eventually to depression. The vitamins, minerals, and amino-acid deficiencies that have been implicated in some forms of depression include especially:

Vitamins: B_1, B_6, B_{12}, folic acid, niacin, pantothenic acid, vitamin C.

Minerals: calcium, chromium, manganese, magnesium, zinc.

Amino Acids: tryptophan, tyrosine, phenylalanine.

Neurotransmitter Deficiencies

Neurotransmitters are substances secreted by neurons and chemicals used in the transmission of messages between nerves, or nerves and muscles. A microscopic opening between the nerves—called neuroeffector junctions or synapses—must be crossed by neurotransmitters, which are released via an electrical impulse in the nerve fiber endings. The neurotransmitters act as "on" switches for the nerve cells. When nerve "A" releases its chemicals (via an electrical impulse) then this creates an electrical impulse in nerve "B" (the receiving nerve). In the process the chemical messengers are destroyed, and the waste products enter the bloodstream and are eventually eliminated in the urine.

The manufacture and breakdown of monoamines (brain chemicals) is part of brain metabolism. This could not take place without oxygen, which is added to the amines by the enzyme *monoamine oxidase,* which breaks down many monoamines, including epinephrine, norepinephrine, and serotonin.

Dopamine, norepinephrine, and serotonin are neurotransmitters produced by so-called adrenergic fibers (nerve endings), while acetylcholine is a neurotransmitter produced by so-called cholinergic (parasympathetic) fibers.

The neurotransmitters play a crucial role especially in the formation of endogenous depression. Van Praag (1977) reviewed a number of studies which show that monoamines can be positively influenced with tricyclic antidepressants and MAO inhibitors in the treatment of depression. Van Praag writes:

At least two types of "vital" depression exist: 5-hydroxytryptamine (serotonin) deficiency plays a role in the pathogenesis of one, while noradrenaline deficiency is important in the pathogenesis of the other. Both of these types of depression are indistinguishable in psychopathological terms. Patients of the first group seem to respond best to anti-depressants with a strong ability to potentiate 5-hydroxytryptamine (serotonin) and less to noradrenaline-potentiating compounds, while the reverse applies to the noradrenaline deficient patients.

MAO inhibitors and the tricyclic antidepressants are chemically unrelated, however, both increase neurotransmitter levels in the brain.

Monoamine oxidase breaks down norepinephrine, and it is the purpose of the (MAO) inhibitors to retard the oxidation process and slow down amine metabolism. As a result norepinephrine levels in the brain are increased.

Tricyclic antidepressants work somewhat differently. For example, Elavil increases serotonin levels in the brain, and Aventyl and Tofranil increase both serotonin and norepinephrine levels.

Diet and Depression

Depressions that result from chemical imbalances are common. They are usually not the result of heredity (exceptions include bipolar depression and schizophrenia) or disease, but rather of faulty living habits. The physical restoration by natural means rather than by drugs deserves the greater priority. There is most definitely a direct link between many forms of depression and poor nutrition. Please consider the following:

1. *Sound Eating for Sound Thinking.* Your ability to think rationally and control your emotions and behaviors is directly linked to the food you eat. It is also true that this ability depends on genetic inheritance, training, education, and general life experiences. You are what you think, "as a man thinketh in his heart so is he (Prov. 23:7)," but, the quality of your thinking depends greatly on the quality of your food. As early as 1966, J. I. Rodale stated that "there is a very definite connection between what one eats, and how the mind functions."

2. *Sound Eating for Sound Feelings.* Foods needed for the manufacture of brain chemicals include protein, carbohydrate, and fat. Three amino acids, when in short supply, have been implicated in depression.

   (a) *Tryptophan.* The amino acid tryptophan becomes the neurotransmitter serotonin. The latter is very important in the regulation of appetite and mood. A shortage of the neurotransmitter serotonin causes several disorders including depression. Serotonin also stimulates the female sex drive. Foods that are important for serotonin include both high-protein and high-carbohydrate foods. (Please see the *Glossary* for a more detailed description of serotonin, tryptophan, and the carbohydrate connection).

   (b) *Tyrosine.* The amino acid tyrosine is necessary for the manufacture of the neurotransmitter norepinephrine. Tyrosine is involved in the regulation of blood pressure and mood. A shortage of norepinephrine might cause—among other problems—

depression. The male sex drive is stimulated by norepinephrine, for which high protein food sources are important. *See* Glossary, *Tyrosine.*

(c) *Phenylalanine.* The amino acid phenylalanine is important for the manufacture of PEA (phenylethylamine), a neurotransmitterlike substance and a natural brain stimulant. The chemical structure of PEA is similar to that of amphetamine. Low levels of PEA have been found in depressed persons.

Phenylalanine is also involved in the regulation and control of pain thresholds and moods. This is probably because it inhibits enzymes that break down endorphin hormones in the brain. High levels of endorphins cause euphoria. Phenylalanine is also involved in the manufacture of the neurotransmitter norepinephrine. A shortage of phenylalanine, with its multiple influence on brain functions might result in depression. *See* Glossary, *Phenylalanine.*

3. *Sound Eating for Sound Memory.* The brain amine choline is necessary for the manufacture of the neurotransmitter acetylcholine. Choline ($C_5H_{15}O_2N$) is derived from ammonia. It is also classified as a vitamin and found primarily in the fat emulsifier lecithin. The latter is obtained from such foods as egg yolks, soybeans, and liver. Acetylcholine is the most prevalent neurotransmitter in the brain and particularly in the hippocampus, which is a very important functional component of the limbic system of the brain.

The hippocampus, septum pellucidum, and amygdala are the emotional centers located in the limbic system. These centers, together with inputs from, and outputs to the hypothalamus are primarily responsible for a person's emotional responses.

The neurotransmitter acetylcholine is of great importance not only for mood but also for perception and memory. Studies indicate that raising choline levels might even help with memory failure, for example, as found in senility. These studies are only in a beginning phase. There is no question, however, about the importance of choline in our diet.

Choline also raises phosphorus levels, and has been successfully used in the treatment of tardive dyskinesia. The latter is a neurological disorder which may result from a lack of acetylcholine in the brain, and is found as a side effect in patients treated with antipsychotic drugs. A shortage of the neurotransmitter acetylcholine might lead—among other problems—to depression.

In summary, there is a definite relationship between diet and depression. Not only physicians, but also behavioral scientists are increasingly aware of this relationship. At the annual meeting of the American Psychological Association held in August 1986 in Washington, D.C., several researchers presented their findings on the influence of food (in particular carbohydrates) on mood.

Malnutrition

The USA is one of the richest nations in the world, but paradoxically, we are not the best fed. It has been said that the *majority* of Americans suffer from malnutrition. We do get plenty to eat, and this is reflected in another fact. We are the most overweight nation in the world. Most of us are rich, overweight, and malnourished.

Junk food especially is a major source of stress and illness, including depression. Foods are overprocessed, laced with unhealthy preservatives, and all too often depleted of essential fiber, trace minerals, and vitamins.

More than forty different nutrients are needed to feed our cells. Unfortunately many people eat deficient diets and consequently cope with unnecessary ailments and disturbances. It is bad enough to live in toxic and otherwise stressful environments, but why add the stress of improper nutrition? Why indulge in refined carbohydrates, alcohol, caffeine, and excessive fat, or use vitamin-, mineral-, and fiber-depleted foods? Malnutrition is bad for our general health, and causes a number of specific disorders. One answer to the problem can be found in the Wellness Diet discussed earlier.

Food and Chemical Allergies

Much has been written during the past decade about the interrelationship of food, chemical allergies, and depression. Faelton (1983) states, "If you are depressed and have allergic problems—such as asthma, hayfever, hives, or eczema—there's a reasonably good chance your depression is at least partially related to allergy, especially if other causes have been ruled out."

Food and chemical allergies can be disastrous. Those allergic to food substances may thrive on them (feel good for a while, once they get their "fix"), or have violent reactions, and even engage in antisocial behavior (Philpott and Kalita 1980).

I have counseled many people who suffered from allergies, including youthful offenders, fatigued housewives, and others who often suffered from "uncontrolled" outbursts of anger. Many were suffering from allergies to sugar and chocolate. So frequently do I find a particular candy bar used by these people that I have dubbed their common symptoms, the "X Bar" syndrome.

Food allergies cause tremendous havoc in the lives of children, adolescents, and adults. Many suffer from depressions which are directly related to allergies. Sometimes allergies are one of the symptoms that fit in with a larger problem. Tintera (1955) found allergies present in 73 percent, and depression in 79 percent of the 200 cases of hypoadrenocorticism he described. In a paper presented to the American Society of Ophthalmologic and Otolaryngolic Allergy, in October 1969, Tintera stated "the allergic state is one of the constitutional manifestations of hypoadrenocorticism whether inherited or acquired" (Light 1980).

Arthur F. Coca (1979) has described a simple test for allergies in *The Pulse Test.* An increase in pulse rate often accompanies allergic reactions. Other excellent books to help with suspected allergies are by Mackarness (1976; 1980), Mandell and Scanlon (1979), and Sheinkin and Schacter (1980).

Dr. Marshall Mandell (1979), one of the leading bioecologic physicians in this country discovered (during testing for physical reactions to allergic substances) that his patients sometimes developed mental/emotional symptoms. He went on to investigate and produced in thousands of patients, symptoms such as depression, restlessness, irrational behavior, and violence.

In most cases allergies (including brain allergies) are caused by common everyday foods:

Coca (1979) lists allergic reactions to commonly eaten foods as follows:

Eggs	Oranges	Fish	Onions	Pork
Wheat	Beef	Tomatoes	Asparagus	Chocolate
Potatoes	Peas	Bananas	Cabbage	Lamb
Milk	Beans			

Mandell and Scanlon (1980) found the following foods prominent in starting allergic reactions:

Wheat	Eggs	Carrots	Peanuts
Corn	Beef	Tomatoes	Green Beans
Coffee	Potatoes	Yeast	Oats
Cane Sugar	Pork	Apples	Chocolate
Milk	Oranges	Soy Products	Lettuce
Chicken			

Berger (1985) found that *only seven foods* were responsible for about 85 percent of allergic reactions in thousands of patients, namely:

Cow's milk products	Corn
Wheat	Cane Sugar
Brewer's and Baker's Yeast	Soy Products
Eggs	

Most people have some allergies to foods. They need to check for allergies, however, only if they are not feeling well and cannot find satisfactory explanations for this.

Candidiasis

Sometimes *depression* and various chronic illnesses are related to the uncontrolled spread of a common yeast germ called Candida Albicans, which lives in all human beings. However, the uncontrolled growth of Candida Albicans weakens our immune system, toxifies our bodies, and creates havoc with our physical and mental health.

Treament for candidiasis consists of antifungal medications, such as Nystatin, as well as dietary and lifestyle changes discussed in this book. In addition, however, the diet must be free from all foods containing yeast. The body must also be kept free from all foods, medications, vitamins, and environmental conditions which *promote* the growth of yeast. Included here are certain antibiotics, birth-control pills, cortisone, cheese, all fruit, mushrooms, and vitamins made from yeast.

Also avoid yeast breads and pastries, milk and milk products, fruit juices, and *everything* listed on the "Not Recommended" section of the Wellness Diet, in chapter 7. In addition, house and work place must be free from mold and chemical irritants. Here are some of the symptoms that may be related to candidiasis:

Cravings for alcohol, bread, and sweets

Endometriosis or pelvic inflammatory disease

Extreme sensitivity to chemical irritants, such as fumes, perfumes, pollutants

Frequent spots before eyes

Gastrointestinal disturbances, as seen by bloating, distension, diarrhea, constipation

Lack of sexual desire

Mental disturbances, such as poor memory, feelings of unreality

Mood swings, depression, fatigue, lethargy

Recurrent cystitis, prostatitis, vaginitis, urethritis

Premenstrual depression and other premenstrual problems

Recurrent oral or vaginal thrush

Repeated fungal infections of hands, feet, nails

Unexplained aches and pains

Vaginal discharge, menstrual cramps

Numerous allergic problems

Persistent and recurrent upper respiratory infections, colds, sore
throats

Multiple Physical Sources—A Summary

Physical sources are commonly found in bipolar (together with apparent inherited factors), brain allergy, climacteric, unipolar, involutional, metabolic, nutrient deficiency, postnatal, and premenstrual depression. All are primarily endogenous depressions.

This does not mean, however, that most depressed people suffer from physical depressions. The opposite is true! About 75 percent of depressed people suffer from perceptual-cognitive disorders. A physically healthy Central Nervous System can translate faulty thought processes into exogenous depressions.

At times depressions are related to Central Nervous System (CNS) disorders caused by head injuries, intracranial tumors, strokes, and Parkinson's disease. The latter may have finally manifested itself as a result of an earlier encephalitis, metallic poisoning (for instance manganese), carbon monoxide poisoning, or hardening of the brain arteries.

Depression may be associated with *Parkinson's disease.* Here we find lesions that involve the basal ganglia (and thus the restricted movements), and the cerebral cortex (the thinking portion of the brain). In *Huntington's chorea,* we find physical problems and mental decline. Depression is usually associated with a concern over the disorder. Interference with rational thinking is due to the cerebral cortex involvement of this hereditary disease.

In *multiple sclerosis* (MS) patients we find demyelination of multiple areas of the Central Nervous System, without a severe decline of mental faculties. Consequently, there are not as many emotive difficulties such as depression in MS patients.

Epilepsy, a brain disorder manifested by paroxysmal transitory disturbances of brain functioning, may also lead to depression. Metabolic disturbances might produce seizures in both epileptics and nonepileptics. Increased stress leads to an increase in seizures, and decreased stress leads to a decrease in seizures—a reminder of the important role excessive stress plays in our lives.

It is also possible to experience depression as a result of taking legal drugs (iatrogenic depressions), or illegal drugs such as marijuana, LSD, STP, and DMT.

The physical sources for depression are many. This highlights the hypothesis that depression is a multifaceted stress disorder. *Physical stressors* include: (1) allergies; (2) amino-acid deficiencies; (3) disease; (4) drugs; (5) glandular dysfunction; (6) glucose disturbances; (7) heredity; (8) malnutrition; (9) mineral deficiencies; (10) neurotransmitter deficiencies; (11) overstimulation; (12) poisoning; (13) trauma; (14) understimulation; (15) vitamin deficiencies; (16) unfavorable weather conditions; and (17) yeast infections.

Appendix **3**

Laboratory Tests for Endogenous Depression

The Blood Profile

A battery of routine laboratory tests—often called a blood profile—is usually ordered as part of a standard physical examination for endogenous depression.

A helpful profile includes at least: *blood values* such as hematocrit, hemoglobin, and blood counts, and *blood chemistries* such as cortisol, glucose, albumin, calcium, phosphorus, sodium, potassium, chlorides, cholesterol, total lipids, serum alkaline phosphate, PBI, T3, and T4. All of these tests are listed either in this Appendix or the Glossary.

Some physicians also request a Six-Hour-Oral-Glucose-Tolerance Test (6-hr OGTT) at the same time. To take such a battery of tests is rather simple. It merely involves being in the fasting state and spending a morning at the waiting room of a hospital laboratory. This waiting period is only necessary if the 6-hr OGTT is ordered. For that test several hourly blood samples are required. These tests are usually the only ones needed to help make a firm distinction between endogenous and exogenous depression. For example, certain abnormal glucose

217

curves, as well as high levels of cortisol, are often found in endogenous depression.

In this Appendix a brief description is given of normal blood chemistry values, and the Glossary provides additional information if needed. A few special tests are also included. These special tests will *rarely* be ordered strictly for the investigation of endogenous depression. They are usually part of other clinical investigations.

Normal Blood Chemistry Values

The conditions listed below do sometimes play a role as "potential" stressors in various types of endogenous depression. However, none have to become "actual" stressors. A certain physical condition does not automatically lead to depression. Normal values are variable according to laboratory or methods used. In addition these values are for adults only. They might be different for children and for adults over age sixty. Sources: Bauer (1982), Burroughs Wellcome (1978), Flint & Cain (1975), The Merck Manual (1982), and Tintera (1955).

10. The Normal Range of Blood Chemistry

Blood Chemical	Possible Related Conditions	
	Below Normal	Above Normal
Cortisol (A.M.) 10-25 ug/dl (P.M.) 4-13 ug/dl	Addison's disease Orthostatic hypotension Insulin sensitivity Hypoglycemia Hypoadrenocorticism	Cushing's syndrome Adenoma of adrenal glands
Glucose 80-120 mb/dl	Addison's disease Adenoma or carcinoma of islands of Langerhans Hypoadrenocorticism Hypoglycemia Hyperinsulinism	Acromegaly Adrenal tumors Brain injury Diabetes mellitus Cushing's pituitary basophilism Hyperthyroidism Hemochromatosis Myasthenia gravis
Total serum protein 6.0-8 g/dl	Liver disease Malnutrition	
Albumin 4.0-5.5 g/dl	Liver disease Malnutrition	Dehydration
Albumin-Globulin ratio 1:00-3.1		Dehydration and chronic infectious diseases

Nonprotein nitrogen (NPN) 25-38 mg/dl		Metallic poisoning Various diseases
Urea Nitrogen (BUN) 10-18 mg/dl	Liver disease	Metallic poisoning Various diseases
Creatinine 0.6-1.2 mg/dl		Metallic poisoning
Calcium 8.5-10.5 mg/dl	Hypoparathyroidism Various disorders	Hyperparathyroidism
Phosphorus 2.5-4.8 mg/adults 3.5-6.0 mg/ children	Hyperparathyroidism, Loss of weight, appetite, and so forth	Hypoparathyroidism
Sodium 315-340 mg/dl 125-145 mEq/L	Addison's disease *Hypoadrenocorticism*	
Potassium 3.5-5.6 mEq/L	Hyperadrenocorticism	Addison's disease *Hypoadrenocorticism*
Chlorides 355-376 mg/dl 98-109 mEq/L	Gastrointestinal problems	
Cholesterol 150-220 mg/dl	Liver disease	Myxedema
Total lipids 400-850 mg/dl		Diabetes Hypothyroidism
Serum Alkaline phosphate 1.4-4.1 Bodansky, and 15-20 King-Armstrong units in adults		Hyperparathyroidism

The laboratory tests listed below are also briefly described in the Glossary:

Albumin
Aldosterone
Ascorbic acid
Blood count
Blood urea nitrogen (BUN)
Calcium
Chloride
Cortisol
Creatinine
Erythrocytes
Glucose tolerance test
Hematocrit
Hemoglobin
Immunoglobulins

Ketosteroids
Leucocytes
Leukocytosis
Lithium
Lymphocytes
Monocytes
Neutrophils
pH
Phosphorus
Potassium
Protein (-total)
Protein bound iodine (PBI)
Serotonin
Thyroid function

Specialized Laboratory Tests for Endogenous Depression

Several blood and urine tests are available to investigate sources of endogenous depression. Some of these tests investigate how well the endocrine system functions, or to investigate disease processes and toxic conditions that might be an indirect source of depression. Other helpful tests discover deficiencies of amino acids, glucose, hormones, minerals, neurotransmitters, and vitamins.

The Six-Hour-Glucose-Tolerance Test (OGTT) is especially helpful in the investigation of any kind of depression (including exogenous depression). Historically glucose was among the first substances determined in blood and consequently there are very many different laboratory methods to measure it. The most helpful, however, is the glucose-tolerance test.

The Oral Glucose-Tolerance Test (OGTT)

The oral glucose-tolerance test (OGTT) needs to be administered over a six-hour period. Shorter tests (two or three hours) may not be diagnostic and frequently result in taking the longer six-hour-test later. The results are perfect—which is a rarity—when the fasting blood-sugar level (FBS) is 100 mg, per dl (100 cc) of blood (Cannon 1960, Page 1972), and when it rises to approximately 150 mg per dl (100 cc) of blood within the first hour following the administration of 50, 75, or 100 grams of glucose. The glucose level also is to return to its fasting level (FBS) not later than three hours following the administration of the glucose, and remain there for the duration of the test.

Because perfection is hard to find, so called normal (average) glucose levels have been established. The OGTT is considered normal when the glucose levels do not fall below 80 mg/dl of blood, and do not rise above 165 mg/dl, within one hour following the administration of glucose and with a return to glucose levels of 80-120 mg/dl, within three hours. Individual differences do occur, and low or high glucose levels do not necessarily indicate serious trouble. It is important that physicians and other specialists draw the actual glucose curve, and verify this against all other objective and subjective data on the client.

Contraindications for the OGTT

There are certain contraindications for taking the OGTT. First of all, the test must not be repeated too quickly. If it is not absolutely necessary, do not repeat the test. Secondly, the test must not be taken by a person who is on adrenal steroids (cortisone), large doses of salicylates (aspirin), diuretics, birth-control pills, Dilantin, or L-Dopa. If possible the drugs should be discontinued for several days prior to testing.

In addition, the test is best performed in a hospital laboratory setting, especially for those who suffer from seizures or similar disorders. The test is best performed on ambulatory patients in any case as bed rest also affects the test.

Conditions and medications that increase or decrease blood glucose levels (Bauer 1982; Light 1980, 1981):

Increase	Decrease
Adrenocorticotrophic hormone (ACTH)	Addison's disease
Adrenal steroids	Alcohol
Advanced age	Aminobenzoic acid
Aldosteronism	Aspirin*
Anacidity	Barbiturates
Androgens	Bishydroxycoumarin
Arthritis	Chloramphenicol
Chlorpromazine	Chlorpromazine
Coffee	EDTA
Cortisol	Fever
Diuretics	Haldol
Emotional stress	Isoniazid
Epinephrine	Islet cell tumors of the pancreas
Estrogens	Manganese
Gastrectomy	MAO inhibitors
General anesthetics	Mebanzaine
Glucagon	Oxyphenbutazone
Growth hormone	Oxytetracycline
Hypertension	Para-Aminosalicylic acid
Indomethacin	Phenylbutazone
Infection	Phenylramidol
Jejunectomy	Probenecid
Liver disease	Propanolol HCL
Marijuana	Propylthiouracil
Miocardial infarction	Strenuous physical exercise
Nephritis	
Nicotinic acid	
Obesity	
Oral contraceptives	
Overfeeding	
Pheochromocytoma	
Pregnancy	
Prolonged inactivity	
Smoking	*Salicylate (aspirin) intoxication
Starvation followed by refeeding	may lead to a serious increase in
Thyroid hormone	glucose levels.

Other contraindications for the OGTT include sprue, celiac disease, hypothyroidism (slow absorption produces a flat curve), thyrotoxicosis (fast absorption produces a hyperglycemic curve), and in patients who have had all or part of the stomach removed (gastric resections).

Bauer (1982) also points out that infectious diseases and surgical or other trauma as well as pregnancy affect the glucose-tolerance test. Among drugs he lists oral contraceptives and other hormones, large doses of salicylates (aspirin) and thiazide diuretics. Insulin and oral antidiabetic medications need to be discontinued—if possible—for several days. Bauer (1982) further states that "in patients with heart disease there may be a decrease in serum potassium of as much as 0.4 mEq/L during a glucose-tolerance test or the ingestion of large amounts of glucose."

Preparing for the OGTT

For three days prior to taking the test it is important to include a minimum of 150 grams of carbohydrate in the daily diet. However, excessive use of sugar (sucrose, glucose) is to be avoided. An average diet (without loading up on sugar) is sufficient. Immediately prior to the test there should be a period of fasting of at least 8 but not more than 16 hours. There should be no smoking. The test is usually scheduled between 7:00 and 9:00 A.M. No food or drink is taken after midnight (water is the exception and may be taken freely). Alcohol is to be excluded during the previous evening. During the test no food or drink (except water) is to be taken. A frequent error found in some laboratories is to offer the patient coffee during the test! Do *not* smoke during the test.

Low Blood Glucose Levels (Hypoglycemia)

Low or rapidly rising and falling levels of glucose in the bloodstream lead to a variety of unpleasant signs, symptoms, and disorders ranging from hunger, nervousness, sweating, and tremulousness to serious depression. *Hypoglycemia* may be indicative of many conditions including Addison's disease, hypofunction of the anterior pituitary (Simmond's disease, pituitary myxedema), Von Gierke's disease (glycogen storage disease), and hypothyroidism.

The Importance of Glucose-Tolerance Curves

One of the many advantages of the Six-Hour-Glucose-Tolerance Test is that glucose-tolerance curves can be constructed out of the test results. These curves provide insights into a number of glucose-related conditions. For example, eight *specific* curves will point to the following conditions: (1) diabetes mellitus, myasthenia gravis, brain injury, Cushing's pituitary basophilism, and early acromegaly; (2) alimentary glycosuria, and infusions of glucose; (3) hypogonadism, hyperthyroidism, and emotional strain; (4) insulin shock, spontaneous hypoglycemia, and hypoadrenalism; (5) renal glycosuria; (6) pituitary fatigue; (7) pituitary deficiency and myxedema; (8) anorexia nervosa; Simmond's disease; hyperinsulinism; and Addison's disease (Bauer 1982). The importance of these curves is greatly increased once diabetes is ruled out.

The Interpretation of Normal Glucose-Tolerance Curves

The oral-glucose-tolerance-test curve is normal when fasting blood sugar is in the range of 80-120 mg/dl. Following the ingestion of glucose, a rise of approximately 50 percent is expected by the first hour, and a return to the fasting level by the second hour. Sugar levels are to remain normal throughout the remainder of the test period. Sub-

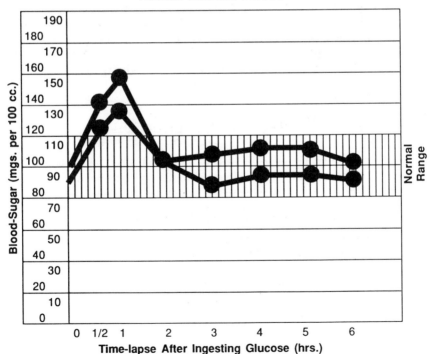

Normal Glucose Curves

jective symptoms are also absent during the test. Below is an illustration of normal glucose curves.

The Interpretation of Abnormal
Glucose-Tolerance Curves

Any deviation from the normal glucose-tolerance curves described earlier is abnormal. Abnormal curves, however, differ greatly in severity and cause. The abnormal glucose curves shown below could—among other conditions—point to the following:

Abnormal Glucose Curves

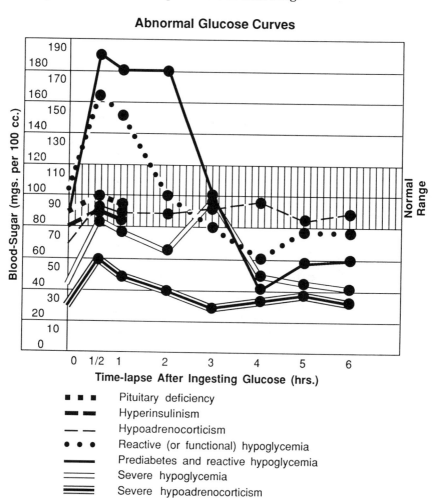

Blood-Sugar (mgs. per 100 cc.)

Normal Range

Time-lapse After Ingesting Glucose (hrs.)

■ ■ ■ Pituitary deficiency
▬ ▬ Hyperinsulinism
— — Hypoadrenocorticism
● ● ● Reactive (or functional) hypoglycemia
——— Prediabetes and reactive hypoglycemia
═══ Severe hypoglycemia
▬▬▬ Severe hypoadrenocorticism

Adrenal Hormones and Health

Hormones produced by the inner and outer portion of the adrenal glands—especially in response to stress—dramatically affect our physical and mental health. The outer portion of the adrenal glands—*the cortex*—produces the so-called *glucocorticoids* (cortisone, cortisol, and corticosterone), *mineralocorticoids* (such as, aldosterone, which regulates the salt-water balance) and *androgens* (the precursors of estrogen and testosterone).

The inner portion of the adrenal glands—*the medulla*—also secretes hormones in response to stress and plays a significant role in physical and mental health. The hormones of the medulla—dopamine, epinephrine, and norepinephrine—are known as the catecholamines.

Serious disorders, such as malignancies, can disturb the functioning of the adrenal glands. More frequently, however, nutritional deficiencies and mental/emotional stress create havoc with the adrenal glands. This is especially due to the functions of the hypothalamus. This important part of the brain controls both the endocrine and autonomic nervous system, making it a key player in the formation of depression.

The hypothalamus is sensitive to stress signals from both body and mind, with each one reinforcing the other. Even the very location of the hypothalamus emphasizes its importance as executive director. The hypothalamus lies above and is directly connected to the posterior pituitary gland and stimulates or directs the release of that gland's pituitary hormones.

To make sure that its power is absolute, the hypothalamus has its nerve endings connected to the cortex (thinking portion of the brain), midbrain, hindbrain, and spinal cord. The pituitary gland is considered the master gland, but it takes orders from the hypothalamus.

The hypothalamic-pituitary relationship, and its powerful coordination of physical and mental activities, emphasizes that body and mind are inseparable. For example, when the neocortex (thinking portion of the brain) is stressed by fear, anxiety, and worry, then this will be relayed to the hypothalamus, which sends signals to the pituitary gland. The latter, in turn, will send signals to the adrenal glands. Too many stress signals and responses leads to overfunctioning and eventually underfunctioning of the adrenal glands and might result in hypoadrenocorticism (a subclinical form of Addison's disease), depression, or other emotional disorders.

Some measurement of adrenal-pituitary function is helpful in the diagnosis of certain cases of endogenous depression. Let us briefly

consider the hormones of both the adrenal cortex and medulla before
describing some additional tests for endogenous depression.

1. *The Glucocorticoids of the Adrenal Cortex*
   The glucocorticoids are especially important for increased carbohydrate, protein, and fat metabolism in response to stress.
   They play a key part in reducing inflammatory conditions, maintaining water and salt balance, and proper functioning of the
   cardiovascular system and other organs, in particular the kidneys.
   Adrenocortical hyperfunction creates high levels of cortisol and
   this increases the enzyme tryptophanase. High tryptophanase
   causes reduced levels of the neurotransmitter serotonin. When
   serotonin levels drop too much then endogenous depression might
   result.
   Adrenocortical hypofunctioning lowers cortisol levels and increases glucose utilization to the point of hypoglycemia. The latter, in turn, is involved in many physical and mental/emotional
   conditions, including depression.

2. *The Catecholamines of the Adrenal Medulla*
   The inner portion of the adrenal glands (the medulla) also plays
   a major part in physical and mental/emotional health. For example, the medulla secretes such stress hormones as dopamine,
   epinephrine, and norepinephrine. See *Glossary, Catecholamines.*
   Dopamine is a percursor of epinephrine and norepinephrine and
   is believed to function in certain areas of the brain as an inhib-
   itory neurotransmitter.
   Epinephrine is released by sympathetic (nervous system) stimulation and primarily in response to *low blood sugar* (hypoglycemia) and in times of strong emotion and other stresses. The
   physiological changes induced by epinephrine include an increase in blood sugar, blood pressure, and heart rate, and stimulation of the heart muscle. Epinephrine also functions as a
   neurotransmitter in some areas of the brain. Low levels of epinephrine can be a source of endogenous depression.
   Norepinephrine is released by visceral (internal organ) stimulation and primarily in response to *low blood pressure* (hypotension) and in times of strong emotion and other stresses. The
   physiological changes induced by norepinephrine includes the
   constriction of small blood vessels and slowing of the heart rate.
   Norepinephrine is also secreted by the neurons and acts as a
   neurotransmitter. Norepinephrine, together with other amines,
   plays a role in sleep and arousal, mood, memory, learning, and

many of the functions necessary for physical homeostasis such as the regulation of blood pressure, body temperature, and food and fluid intake.

Epinephrine, norepinephrine, and dopamine are enzymatically synthesized from the amino acid tyrosine as follows: Tyrosine—dihydroxy-phenylalanine (dopa)-dopamine-norepinephrine-epinephrine. The three amino acids often recommended in the treatment of depression are tyrosine, tryptophan, and DL-phenylalanine and are described in Appendix 7 and the Glossary.

Adrenal-Pituitary Function Tests

1. *ACTH Stimulation Test*
   This is an excellent test to check on both adrenal and pituitary gland function. Since the adrenal gland is stimulated by ACTH from the pituitary, it can quickly be determined if *low* adrenal cortex output is due to lack of TSH—and pituitary failure—or lack of response—and therefore adrenal failure. A simple 24-hour (before and after) urine test differentiates between these two conditions. Normal urine contains a certain amount of so called 17-ketosteroids (*See* Glossary). If low levels of ketosteroids do not markedly increase after the intramuscular administration of 80 units of ACTH on two consecutive days, then we know that the adrenal gland is not functioning properly. If, on the other hand, there is a marked rise in ketosteroids after the administration of ACTH, then the pituitary gland fails to secrete enough ACTH.

2. *Insulin Tolerance Test*
   The insulin tolerance test is an indirect test of the function of the adrenal cortex and anterior pituitary gland. Insulin given to a normal (nondiabetic) individual quickly lowers the blood sugar level. In this test 0.1 unit of regular insulin per kg of body weight is administered intravenously.

   Blood sugar levels fall to about 50 percent of the fasting blood sugar levels (determined before the start of the test) in about 30 minutes. Normal levels are usually established in 90-120 minutes. Blood samples will be taken at 20, 30, 45, 60, 90, and 120 minutes. If there is only a slight (or delayed) *fall* in blood sugar the diagnosis is "insulin resistance." If there is a delayed *rise* in blood sugar the diagnosis is "hypoglycemic unresponsiveness."
   Insulin resistance might be due to hyperfunction of the adrenal

cortex or anterior pituitary gland, or diabetes mellitus.

Hypoglycemic unresponsiveness might be due to hyperinsulin-ism, Addison's disease, hypofunction of the anterior pituitary (Simmond's disease), pituitary myxedema, hypothyroidism, gly-cogen storage disease (Von Gierke's disease). The insulin toler-ance test is rarely used nowadays.

3. *Cortisone Suppression Test*

   This is a rather lengthy—five-day—test to determine adrenal cortical hyperfunction. A 24-hour-urine specimen is collected be-fore and after the test. The specimens are checked for 17-ketosteroids and 17-hydroxysteroids. This test involves the oral administration of cortisone derivatives (1-a-fluorohydrocor-tisone, dexamethasone, or prednisolone) every 6 hours after meals for 3 days. The administration of cortisone derivatives depresses the anterior pituitary gland. A decrease in ACTH would then also lead to a decrease in adrenal cortical output. In case of ad-enoma or carcinoma of the cortex, however, there will be no de-crease in 17-ketosteroids or ketogenic steroids. In Cushing's disease there will be a 50 percent decrease.

4. *Metyrapone Test*

   This is a good test of the pituitary's production of ACTH. The oral administration of 750 mg metyrapone every 4 hours for 48 hours inhibits an enzyme that converts 11-deoxycortisol into cor-tisol. Since this leads to decreased levels of cortisol, the pituitary gland will be stimulated to secrete more ACTH. If both the pi-tuitary and adrenal glands function normally there will be an increase of urinary ketosteroids and ketogenic steroids. In case of pituitary insufficiency there will be *no* increase of urinary steroids.

5. *Dexamethasone (DST/DEX) Test*

   This is a useful test to measure adrenal hyperfunction, and its excessive production of cortisol. Overproduction of cortisol is re-lated to depression primarily because excessive cortisol leads to an increase of the enzyme tryptophanase and eventual lowering of tryptophan and—more important—the neurotransmitter serotonin. This test is rather simple. A 1 mg tablet of dexameth-asone—a corticosteroid drug—taken between 11:00 and 12:00 P.M. usually *stops* the production of cortisone the next morning. Plasma cortisone measured between 7:00 and 8:00 A.M. should be 5 mg/dl or less. In case of Cushing's syndrome or adrenal tumors, cortisol levels will remain unchanged. It has also been reported that children who suffer from depression and continue to produce high levels of cortisone, following this test, are at increased risk for suicide.

Additional Tests for Endogenous Depression Are Rarely Needed

There is rarely a need for more than a standard blood profile and Six-Hour-Glucose-Tolerance Test (6-HrOGTT) to help make an objective distinction between exogenous and endogenous depression. This is especially so since laboratory studies are in addition to the physical examination and in-depth physical and mental history that has already been taken.

The standard blood profile helps identify infectious diseases, toxic conditions, and possible problems with the adrenal, pancreas, or thyroid gland. And the 6-HrOGTT provides additional insight into a number of depression related conditions. If these tests are negative—and other objective and subjective data supports these findings—then endogenous depression can usually be ruled out.

A few adrenal-pituitary function tests have been mentioned because occasionally one of these tests is useful to help distinguish between organic and functional adrenal disorders. If there is a serious problem with the adrenal glands there will be a number of obvious physical and mental symptoms of which depression might only be one. The chances are overwhelming that in such a case additional laboratory studies have already been requested and an appropriate diagnosis made.

It is highly unlikely that a person has depression as the primary complaint, preceding an eventual diagnosis of such major adrenal disorders as Addison's or Cushing's disease. More than likely such a diagnosis has been made already and depression identified as part of that particular disease. Most depressed people do not need adrenal-pituitary function tests.

One reason to consider these tests is that some persons do not suffer from a full-blown adrenal disorder, but simply suffer from below normal functioning of that gland. Tintera (1955) describes hypoadrenocorticism as a subclinical form of Addison's disease. Here we might find symptoms such as anxiety, nervousness, and depression as the primary outcome of adrenal cortex dysfunction, rather than adrenal cortex disease. Tintera (1955) describes significant laboratory findings as low blood sugar, low basal metabolism (-11 to -15), low blood pressure and low titer of 17-Ketosteroids (3-12 mg in men and 2-8 mg in women per 24 hours).

Prescription Drugs for Depression

One of the best and most rational teachers I know is Dr. Maxie C. Maultsby, Jr., professor of psychiatry, and director of the Rational Behavior Therapy Center at the University of Kentucky Medical School. It is he who taught me many years ago that the overwhelming majority of depressed people do not need drugs and are better off without them. My own twenty years of counseling experience has also shown that it is indeed far better for most people to work through their problems with undrugged brains.

Nevertheless some people do receive great benefit from medications for certain depressions. These are depressed people with certain organic disorders, psychotic problems, genetic abnormalities, or extraordinary—perhaps catastrophic—stresses that have virtually immobilized them. For all practical purposes, however, only those who suffer from *severe* forms of depression—depressive illness—are good candidates for drug therapy.

A brief description is provided in this Appendix of certain prescription drugs that have been used (correctly or incorrectly) in the treatment of depression. This is followed by a current list of commonly used drugs in the treatment of *severe depression*.

231

A Brief Description of Certain Prescription Drugs

Amphetamines. These are central-nervous-system stimulants that have been used in the treatment of hyperactivity in children, narcolepsy, or some forms of depression. Amphetamines—such as, Benzedrine, Dexedrine, Ritalin—can be addictive and toxic. Side effects—including rapid heart beat, restlessness, sleeplessness—have dramatically reduced the use of these drugs. High dosages of amphetamines have also caused hallucinations.

Amphetamines are chemically similar to the neurotransmitter norepinephrine, and they do raise norepinephrine levels in the brain. It has been reported that high dosages of vitamin C (more than 300 mg per day) may perhaps reduce the effectiveness of amphetamines and also of tricyclic antidepressants. Sudden withdrawal from amphetamines often results in depression. Amphetamines are popularly known as "speed."

Barbiturates. These are addictive drugs—such as, phenobarbitol—that depress brain and spinal-cord activity. Because barbiturates work on the brain stem's reticular activating system they induce sleep or lethargy. For that reason they have been used in the past to treat manic behavior.

Barbiturates are often abused and are increasingly replaced by safer drugs. It is said that the use of barbiturates increases the need for vitamin C. The sudden withdrawal of barbiturates can result in convulsions. Barbiturates are popularly known as "downers."

Hormones. These are natural or artificial complex chemicals used to treat inflammatory conditions and severe allergies. They are also used in hormone replacement therapy and play a major part in the treatment of such conditions as Addison's disease. Progesterone has been heralded in the treatment of premenstrual depression. Thyroid hormone is sometimes used in conjunction with tricyclic antidepressants in the treatment of unipolar depression. (*See* Glossary, *Addison's Disease, Premenstrual Tension, Unipolar Depression.*)

Monoamine Oxidase Inhibitors (MAO Inhibitors). Monoamine oxidase is an enzyme found in body tissues, the nervous system, and the liver. This enzyme causes the oxidation of monoamines, such as the neurotransmitters epinephrine, norepinephrine, and serotonin. The depletion of any of these monoamines are known to cause depression.

Drugs such as Furoxone, Marplan, Nardil, or Parnate, slow down the utilization of (inhibit) monoamine oxidase in the brain. This increases the availability of the neurotransmitters and is important in the prevention and treatment of certain forms of depression.

MAO inhibitors can be lethally toxic if taken with tyramine (*see*

Glossary), which is found in certain foods and other products (such as, cheeses, red wine, beer, yogurt). They also interact with other drugs and close medical supervision is required. MAOI's are often used in the treatment of unipolar depression.

Tranquilizers. These drugs calm or quiet agitated and anxious people without causing stupor. They have a calming effect by influencing the reticular formation of the brain and by reducing the levels of neurotransmitters. For example, Reserpine reduces norepinephrine levels, and Chlorpromazine reduces dopamine levels. In the treatment of anxiety—which often accompanies depression—diazepam (Valium), and chlordiazepoxide (Librium) have often been used.

A distinction is made between major and minor tranquilizers. The latter have no antipsychotic properties. A major tranquilizer used in the treatment of manic episodes in bipolar (manic) depression is lithium.

This soft silver-white metallic element is a naturally occurring salt and is found in rocks and mineral water. Lithium has been used successfully as a prophylactic medication and has enabled many bipolar depressed persons to have fairly normal lives. (*See* Glossary under *Lithium* and *Tranquilizers.*)

Tricyclic Antidepressants. These drugs are often used in the modern treatment of severe depression. They increase the levels of one or more neurotransmitters in the brain. Tricyclic antidepressants are said to cause mania in about 10 percent of depressed patients. If it is not recognized that the mania is a direct result of drug treatment, then this could result in a major diagnostic and therapeutic error. For example, a person's diagnosis might be changed from unipolar depression to bipolar (manic) depression, and the person might erroneously be placed on lithium.

Tricyclic antidepressants include Adapin, Aventyl, Elavil, Sinequan, Surmontil, and Tofranil. It has been reported that high dosages of vitamin C (more than 300 mg a day) could reduce the effectiveness of tricyclic antidepressants. These drugs are mainly used in the treatment of unipolar depression, or the *depressive phase* of bipolar depression.

Commonly Used Drugs
in the Treatment of Severe Forms of Depression

The following list includes commonly used drugs in the treatment of severe depression. They are usually *not* appropriate for the treatment of mild or moderate depression.

11. Commonly Used Drugs in the Treatment of Severe Forms of Depression

Generic Name(s)	Brand Name(s)	Prescribed for	Usual "Total" Dose per Day*	
Tetracyclic Antidepressants				
Maprotiline-Hydrochloride	Ludiomil	Depression with anxiety	Initial: Maximum: Maintenance:	75 mg 225 mg 75-150 mg
Tricyclic Antidepressants				
Amitriptyline-Hydrochloride	Amitril Elavil Emitrip Endep SK-Amitriptyline	Depression	Initial: Maximum: Maintenance:	75 mg 300 mg 50-150 mg
Desipramine-Hydrochloride	Pertofrane Norpramin	Depression	Initial: Maximum: Maintenance:	50 mg 300 mg 100-300 mg
Doxepin-Hydrochloride	Adapin Sinequan	Depression with anxiety	Initial: Maximum: Maintenance:	75 mg 300 mg 75-300 mg
Imipramine-Hydrochloride/ Imipramine-Pamoate	Janimine SK-Pramine Tipramine Tofranil	Depression with anxiety attacks	Initial: Maximum: Maintenance:	75 mg 300 mg 50-150 mg
Nortriptyline-Hydrochloride	Aventyl Pamelor	Depression with anxiety	Initial: Maximum: Maintenance:	50 mg 100 mg 50-100 mg
Protriptyline-Hydrochloride	Vivactil	Depression	Initial: Maximum: Maintenance:	15 mg 60 mg 15-60 mg
Imipramine-Maleate	Surmontil	Depression	Initial: Maximum: Maintenance:	75 mg 300 mg 50-200 mg
Quadracyclic/Tricyclic Antidepressants				
Amoxapine	Asendin	Depression with anxiety	Initial: Maximum: Maintenance:	150 mg 300 mg 50-200 mg
Monoamine Oxidase Inhibitors				
Isocarboxazid	Marplan	Depression	Initial: Maximum: Maintenance:	20 mg 40 mg 10-30 mg
Phenelzine Sulfate	Nardil	Depression with anxiety attacks	Initial: Maximum: Maintenance:	45 mg 90 mg 15-60 mg
Tranylcypromine-Sulfate	Parnate	Depression	Initial: Maximum: Maintenance:	20 mg 40 mg 10-20 mg
Lithium				
Lithium	Eskalith Lithane	Bipolar depression (manic type)	Initial: Maximum:	600-900 mg 3600 mg

	Lithium Carbonate Lithobid Lithonate Lithotabs		Maintenance:	Depends on lithium blood levels. Usual dose is from 900-1200 mg

Additional Antidepressants

Buproprion	Wellbutrin	Depression	Initial: Maximum: Maintenance:	150-600 mg 600 mg 150-400 mg
Benactyzine- Hydrochloride & Meprobamate	Deprol	Depression with anxiety	Initial: Maximum: Maintenance:	3 Tablets 6 Tablets Smallest possible dose
Amitriptyline- Hydrochloride & Perphenazine	Etrafon Triavil	Depression with anxiety	Initial: Maximum: Maintenance:	3 Tablets 6 Tablets Smallest possible dose
Amitriptyline- Hydrochloride & Chlordiazepoxide	Limbitrol	Depression with anxiety	Initial: Maximum: Maintenance:	3-8 Tablets 8 Tablets Smallest possible dose
Nomifensine- Maleate	Merital	Depression	Initial: Maximum: Maintenance:	100 mg 200 mg Smallest possible dose
Trazodone- Hydrochloride	Desyrel	Depression	Initial: Maximum: Maintenance:	100-150 mg 400 mg Smallest possible dose

*A smaller dose, perhaps ⅓ to ½, is given to adolescents and elderly persons. Only a physician can determine proper dosages. **Never self-medicate!** Some of these medications, for example, Trazodone Hydrochloride (Desyrel), are not recommended for patients below age eighteen.

Appendix **5**

Basic Facts About
Food and Calorie Control

Nutrition is a complex subject, and this is perhaps one of the reasons why it is often discussed in general terms only. For those who are interested in good physical and mental health, however, it is important to have at least a basic knowledge of such nutrients as carbohydrates, proteins, fats, water, vitamins, minerals, amino acids, and enzymes. All these nutrients are important for good health. Yet, it seems that some nutrients play a larger role than others in specific physical or mental disorders. For example, one particular carbohydrate—glucose—plays a major role in mood disorders such as depression.

Glucose provides more than energy for the cells. For example, cells recognize each other by specific carbohydrate chains, and glucoselike connections on cell surfaces are important for communication among the cells. It is said that carbohydrates determine the social behavior of living cells. Even blood groups are determined by different carbohydrate chains on the outer surfaces of red blood cells. Blood group O has a carbohydrate chain ending in five specific sugar residues. Blood group A, however, has a sixth sugar molecule—acetylgalactosamine—while blood group B has galactose as its sixth sugar. And blood group AB has both acetylgalactosamine and galactose. Even more startling there are about 150 more blood-subgroups and all of them receive their specific designations from sugar endings on the carbohydrate chains. Even bacteria are surrounded by specific carbohydrate chains and modern research is trying to determine what role sugars play on cell surfaces of tumors. That they do play a role has already been determined.

Why bring all this up? Only to emphasize that (1) there are differences between carbohydrates, that (2) food plays a major role in health and disease, and that (3) it is important to know some basic facts about food.

Some Basic Facts About Food

Carbohydrates

Carbohydrates are chemical compounds consisting of carbon, hydrogen, and oxygen. The most important carbohydrates are starches, celluloses, gums, and sugars. Glucose—a special sugar—is the body's chief source of energy. Without a satisfactory and steady amount of glucose, the brain and nervous system do not function properly. Glucose is essential for the efficient functioning of every part of the body including the repair of tissue and the transportation of nutrients. Glucose is best manufactured by the body from *complex* carbohydrates. The differences between single, double, and multiple sugars are as follows:

Monosaccharides

Monosaccharides ($C_6H_{12}O_6$) are single molecules and found in (1) *glucose* (dextrose, corn sugar, grape sugar); (2) *fructose* (fruits, honey, vegetables); (3) *galactose,* which is found in lactose (milk sugar); and (4) *raffinose* (from sugar beet).

These sugars are single molecules but they are by no means the same. Although the number of atoms (the empirical formula) are identical, the actual molecular structure (arrangement of the atoms) is different. We also find that the body responds differently to these monosaccharides. For example, fructose causes a lower rise in blood sugar levels than glucose (*see* Glossary, *Fructose*).

Thus, the best monosaccharide is fructose. The next best is galactose. Unacceptable to a Wellness Diet is glucose. Hypoglycemics and people who suffer from depression should not use glucose or products containing glucose.

Disaccharides

Disaccharides $(C_{12}H_{22}O_{11})$ are double sugar molecules found in (1) *sucrose* (beet and cane sugar); (2) *maltose* (from grain); (3) *lactose* (from milk).

The digestive process breaks these complex sugars down into hexoses. This process (called "hydrolysis"), produces the following chemical changes $(C_{12}H_{22}O_{11}+H_2)\ C_6H_{12}O_6 + C_6H_{12}O_6$. This changes *sucrose* into glucose + fructose; *maltose* into glucose + glucose; and *lactose* into glucose + galactose. None of the disaccharides are recommended for people on the Wellness Diet, or those who suffer from hypoglycemia or depression.

Polysaccharides

Polysaccharides $(C_6H_{10}O_5)_n$ are molecules that break down into two or more sugars during the digestive process and include (1) *starch* (the main storage form of carbohydrates in plants) as found in granular materials from grain and corn; (2) *dextrin* (formed during hydrolysis from starch to sugar); (3) *glycogen* (manufactured by and stored in the liver, and to a lesser extent in the muscles), which is converted by the liver as needed into glucose.

The molecules of such polysaccharides as starch, cellulose, and dextrin, are so complex that no exact formula can represent them. For example, starch has almost 1,000 hexose groups. The n at the end of the formula $(C_6H_{10}O_5)_n$ simply stands for unknown number. Commercial refined carbohydrate products containing starch or dextrin are *not* on the Wellness Diet and are *not* recommended for hypoglycemics and people who suffer from depression. In the healthy body glucose levels remain fairly constant. Excess glucose is carried by the blood stream to the liver and converted into glycogen. When the glucose stores are filled, and no additional energy is required, the rest will be converted to body fat.

Proteins

Proteins are organic nitrogenous compounds, which are found in every living cell of the body. Once energy needs have been met, protein is used for the multiple purposes that are essential for good physical and mental health. These purposes include the manufacture of *amino acids,* which are essential for the manufacture of neurotransmitters and tissue building and repair; *enzymes,* the proteins that accelerate or produce (by catalytic action) some change in certain body substances, and which are needed for the breakdown of nutrients during the digestive process; and *hormones,* the chemical substances produced by our bodies, with a specific regulatory effect on the various cells, glands, and organs, which are very important for the proper functioning of the brain and nervous system.

Lack of protein might also lead to a lack of essential amino acids, and eventually result in depression. The quality of protein is determined by the amount of essential amino acids it contains. Not all protein provides essential amino acids. This has been described elsewhere in this book. (*See* Index.) Excess protein, like excess carbohydrates, will be stored by the body as fat.

Fats

Pure fats are composed of carbon, hydrogen, and oxygen. They are found in animals and plants, and are an essential part of our diet, and the principle source of *constant* energy. Fats may be divided in saturated, monosaturated, and polyunsaturated fats. It is important to distinguish between them. Some are bad and others are good for health:

Saturated fats tend to raise blood cholesterol. These fats are *not* healthy. Saturated fats from animal sources include butter, lard, shortening, cream, and whole milk.

Monosaturated fats, such as olive and peanut oil are not recommended either.

Polyunsaturated fats, which are usually liquid and of vegetable origin, are healthy. These fats, such as, safflower oil, tend to lower blood cholesterol levels by helping our bodies to eliminate excess cholesterol.

Hydrogenated fats are also to be avoided. These are liquid fats that have been hardened to resemble saturated fat; included are some margarines and shortening. When in doubt about any of these products, refer to the Wellness Diet.

Water

Many people understand the importance of obtaining satisfactory amounts of protein, carbohydrates, fats, vitamins, and minerals, but sometimes overlook another important nutrient, namely water (H_2O).

Our body is 60 percent water. This percentage varies somewhat with age, sex, and proportion of muscle tissue. Our muscles contain about 75 percent water, and blood plasma is more than 90 percent water.

Our needs for water differ somewhat, depending on activity levels, diets (more water is needed for low carbohydrate diets), and climate. It is generally recommended that adults drink six to eight (8 ounce) glasses of water every day.

A good amount of water is derived from fruits and vegetables (they are about 80 percent water), and other food products; for instance, meat is about 50 percent water. If water does not look, smell, or taste good, then it is *not* good. However, looking, tasting, and smelling good is no absolute guarantee either.

Vitamins

Vitamins are organic chemical compounds containing essential nutrients. These are ideally supplied through a healthy well-balanced diet. Some vitamins are *water soluble* (B-Complex and C), and easily eliminated in sweat and urine. They are also quickly destroyed in varying degrees during food processing and cooking. As much as 100 percent of vitamin C may be destroyed in cooking. Water soluble vitamins are stored in very tiny amounts in the body. They need to be replaced daily. *Fat soluble* vitamins (A, D, E, K) are not soluble in water, and they are not easily excreted. As a result, it is possible to build up toxic levels. Water-soluble vitamins, however can also be toxic! It is easier to develop deficiencies of the water-soluble vitamins (for example, vitamin B), and these are also more often implicated in depression.

Vitamins assist in certain chemical responses, and act as catalysts in the processing of carbohydrates, fats, and proteins. In addition, they help with the formation of red blood cells, hormones, genetic materials, and the regulation of the nervous system. In short, they *are* essential for life.

Minerals

Minerals are chemical compounds found in most foods. They are essential for our general health, the formation of bones, teeth, and growth. They are also necessary for the regulation of body fluids, the life process of cells, and numerous important chemical reactions. Minerals are divided in *macrominerals,* which are needed in fairly large amounts, such as calcium, phosphorus, magnesium, sodium, potassium, chloride, and sulphur and *trace minerals.* These are needed in very small amounts, such as, iron, manganese, copper, iodine, zinc, cobalt, fluoride, and selenium. Be careful not to use minerals to excess, as one mineral may interfere with the proper function of another mineral, and toxic levels can build up.

Enzymes

A discussion of basic food facts is not complete without looking at *enzymatic action.* Enzymes are protein substances manufactured in cells by catalytic action. They accelerate or produce various changes in body substances and are essential for the digestive process. This begins when food enters into the mouth, followed by mastication. The taste buds then signal to the brain what kind of food the body has to deal with.

This information is important as specific foods require specific enzymes for digestion. For example, salivary amylase (ptyalin) is secreted in the saliva only whenever we eat foods that contain starch. Protein requires the hydrochloric acid found in our gastric juice and the digestive enzyme *pepsin*. Fat, on the other hand, cannot be digested without the help of the digestive enzyme *gastric lipase*. In the case of milk *rennin* is required. This enzyme is primarily found in infants.

The main feature about enzymes is that each of them is specifically designed to deal with only one type of food. They also require specific gastric pH (positive hydrogen ion) levels. A pH of 7 indicates that the solution is neutral. If it goes higher, *alkalinity* increases and when it goes lower, *acidity* increases. Ptyalin, needed for carbohydrate digestion, requires an alkaline environment. Gastric lipase, needed for fat digestion, also requires an alkaline environment. Pepsin, needed for protein digestion, requires a highly acid environment. Protein needs plenty of hydrochloric acid in the gastric juices also.

To obtain maximum benefit from foods, remember the following:

1. The digestive process in the small intestine depends on successful digestion in the stomach. The latter requires the same kind of help from the mouth, the place where digestion starts. Each sequential step depends on the preceding one.
2. When we eat foods with conflicting digestive requirements, we might obstruct enzymatic secretions.
3. Different foods require different enzymes and different lengths of time for digestion. Foods that require only a short time for digestion, such as fruit (10-60 minutes) may be held up for hours by foods that require extra time (protein up to 4 hours).
4. Combining opposite foods may lead to fermentation and putrefication.
5. During the digestive process, *carbohydrates* are broken down into sugars. But when fermentation (decomposition) takes place, they become water and poisonous substances, such as acetic acid, carbon dioxide, alcohol, and lactic acid.
6. During the digestive process *proteins* become (among many other things), amino acids. However, when protein is not properly digested, putrefication takes place, releasing poisons such as leucomaines, and ptomaines.
7. Digestive juices are quite capable of digesting *single* foods that contain a combination of carbohydrates, fats, and proteins. They

may not be able to do this effectively and efficiently for two or more foods that have different digestive enzymatic requirements.

8. Although a great variety of foods is needed for good health, it is often better to consume some of them separately, as explained below:

   (a) The following foods are considered more compatible.

   Protein with low carbohydrate vegetables

   For example, alfalfa sprouts, asparagus, broccoli, Brussels sprouts, cabbage, cauliflower, collards, corn, cucumbers, eggplants, endive, garlic, green beans, kohlrabi, lettuce, mushrooms, okra, onions, peas, radish, spinach, sweet pepper, summer squash, and turnips.

   High carbohydrate foods with low carbohydrate vegetables

   The following high carbohydrate foods are compatible with any of the low carbohydrate vegetables listed above, but *not* with protein. These high carbohydrate foods include: beets, carrots, cereals, chestnuts, dry beans, dry peas, grains, globe artichokes, Jerusalem artichokes, lima beans, pumpkin, potatoes, sprouted grains, winter squash, and yams.

   (b) The following foods are considered less compatible:

   Acids with carbohydrates
   Acids with protein
   Protein with high carbohydrates
   Protein with protein (different timing)
   Fat with protein

Computing Caloric Intake

The importance of proper weight control for physical and mental health has been well established. It is helpful to have some information on how to compute caloric intake to maintain, gain, or lose weight.

1. *To Maintain Current Weight.* Without changes in exercise or other routine habits, take your present weight and multiply this by 15. This will give the total number of calories needed to maintain your current weight. A calorie is the amount of heat needed to raise one gram of water by one degree Centigrade. If you weigh 200 pounds, and you want to maintain that weight, you need 200×15, or 3,000 calories per day. Of course, there are other factors to consider such as your occupation and sex. And, it is important to obtain professional advice in this area. This will, however, give you at least an idea.

2. *To Lose Weight.* You can continue to consume the same number
of calories as computed for weight maintenance, but now you
add the additional expenditure of calories through vigorous exercise. Alternately, you can reduce your caloric intake below the
minimum required for weight maintenance. To lose one pound
per week you need to consume 600 calories less per day than
needed for weight maintenance as described in paragraph one.

3. *To Gain Weight.* Increase the number of calories that are required to maintain your present weight as explained in paragraph one. You can, in addition, reduce caloric expenditure by a
reduction in exercise. The latter, however, is usually not recommended, as exercise is vitally important for good health and for
any weight control program.

4. *Caloric Content of Some Foods.* To insure that you get approximately 60 percent of your daily caloric intake in complex carbohydrates, 20 percent in protein, and 20 percent in fats, use the
following abbreviated list of the caloric content of the foods that
may be part of the Wellness Diet:

12. Calorie Content Chart

Food	Calories per Ounce
Apples—fresh	13
Apricots—fresh	12
Artichokes—green	5
Asparagus—fresh	5
Avocado	24
Bananas	22
Beans	26
Beets—boiled	13
Blackberries—fresh	8
Bluefish	40
Bran—cereal	88
Bread—whole wheat	68
Broccoli	4
Brussels sprouts—boiled	5
Butter—fresh (use sparingly)	207
Cabbage—boiled	5
Carrots	6
Cauliflower	3
Cherries—red	14
Chicken—broiled	28
Coffee—decaffeinated	0
Codfish	25
Corn	24
Cucumbers	3
Eggs—fresh, boiled	42
fresh, poached	45
white	11
yolk	99

Figs—fresh	12
Flounder	22
Grapefruit—fresh	6
Grapes	15
Haddock	28
Halibut	37
Hazelnuts	181
Lemon	2
Lettuce—raw	3
Milk—skim, fluid	10
skim, dry	100
Mustard greens	3
Oatmeal—cooked	13
Okra	9
Oranges—fresh	10
Peaches—fresh	11
Pears—fresh	12
Peas—fresh, cooked	14
Pecans	195
Peppers	5
Pineapple—fresh	13
Plums—fresh	9
Potatoes—boiled	21
Raspberries—fresh	7
Rhubarb	2
Rice—brown, cooked	35
Spinach—cooked	7
Soybean flour	123
Squash—cooked	12
Strawberries—fresh	8
Sunflower oil	270
Tomatoes—fresh	4
Tuna fish—fresh	60
Turnips—cooked	3
Vinegar	1
Walnuts	156
Watercress—fresh	4
Wheat	103
Yogurt—low fat, natural	15

Recommended Food Sources of Vitamins, Minerals, and Amino Acids in the Treatment of Depression

All people, but especially those who suffer from physical and mental/emotional problems, should have a diet that is *wellness* rather than *illness* oriented. The Wellness Diet described in this book provides a general listing of recommended and not recommended foods. This Appendix provides more than 75 specific foods that contain the 15 vitamins, 5 minerals, and 3 amino acids that are believed to be helpful in the prevention and treatment of some forms of depression.

This Appendix is helpful in several ways. It gives an idea of the many different foods that are available, and reminds us that the vitamins, minerals, and amino acids in our foods are needed for very *specific* biological functions.

Several commonly used unhealthy foods have been excluded from the list. Nevertheless, this list contains many more foods than used by most people. Although this Appendix highlights the vitamins, minerals, and amino acids believed to be helpful for those who have stress-related problems—and depression in particular—it should be noted that when a variety of these foods are eaten, we obtain all the necessary vitamins, minerals, and amino acids for good health.

Below is a brief listing of *all* the necessary vitamins and minerals and some important dietary sources. A good diet is our most potent weapon to maintain good health and is our first line of defense against disease!

13. Recommended Food Sources of Vitamins, Minerals, and Amino Acids in the Treatment of Depression

Vitamin	Biological Functions Include	Specific Actions for Depression Treatment Include	Important Dietary Sources Include
A₁ Retinol A₂ Dehydroretinol	Anti-infective protector vitamin necessary for normal growth, eyesight, healthy skin.	Assists immune system. Increases resistance to infections. Stress reductive.	Apples, apricots, asparagus, broccoli, butter, carrots, papaya, peppers, milk, liver, salmon, egg yolk.
B₁ Thiamine	Antineuritic and appetite stimulating vitamin. Necessary for proper functioning of heart, brain, and nervous system, and carbohydrate metabolism.	Assists immune system. Increases resistance to infections. Increases energy. Tranquilizes; relieves depression caused by B₁ deficiency. Stress reductive.	Almonds, artichoke, asparagus, beans, beef liver, egg yolk, garlic, grapefruit, fish, meat, milk, whole grain.
B₂ Riboflavin	Antidermatitis vitamin. Necessary for the maintenance of healthy hair, skin, and tissues. Necessary for carbohydrate, protein, and fat metabolism.	Aids healthy functioning of gastrointestinal system, prevents derangement of Central Nervous System, brings harmony to emotions, reduces extremes of depression. Stress reductive.	Apricots, apples, almonds, beef, beets, brussels sprouts, carrots, cheese, eggs, grapefruit, kelp, liver, milk, mustard greens, spinach, wheat germ.
(B₃) Niacin Nicotinic Acid	Anti-insomnia, dermatitis, and pellagra vitamin. Necessary for healthy brain and nervous system. Necessary for carbohydrate, protein, and fat metabolism. Note: This vitamin is "perhaps" promising in the treatment of schizophrenia. Niacin therapy has been given credit in helping some people suffering from schizophrenia.	Aids the synthesis of sex hormones, and cortisone, thyroxine, and insulin. Aids metabolism, increases energy. Is part of enzyme system. Promotes oxidative processes. Relieves depressions that are caused by B₃ deficiencies. Stress reductive.	Almonds, barley, bran, beef liver, dates, eggs, figs, fish, kidney, prunes, wheat germ.
B₅ Pantothenic Acid	Anti-infection and anti-stress vitamin. Important for the release of energy from carbohydrates, fats, and proteins. Important for	Aids in the release of tension. Has calming effect on the stomach. Important for proper functioning of adrenal glands. Relieves hypo-	Bran, chicken, broccoli, brown rice, egg yolk, green vegetables, honey, meat, wheat germ, whole grains.

	healthy hair, skin, and tissue growth. Note: Unexplainable fatigue may be caused by B5 deficiency.	glycemia (and depression) caused by B5 deficiency. Stress reductive.	
B6 **Pyridoxine** **Pyridoxal** **Pyridoxamine**	Antianemia vitamin. Necessary for the assimilation of carbohydrate, protein, and fat. Important for teeth, gums, and blood vessels, nervous system, and red blood cells.	Aids in the conversion of tryptophan to niacin. Important for the proper function of adrenal cortex. Relieves depressions that are caused by B6 deficiencies. Stress reductive.	Avocados, beef, brown rice, cabbage, egg yolk, honey, green leafy vegetables, whole-grain cereals.
B12 **Cyanocobalamin** **Cobalamin**	Antipernicious anemia, antineuritic vitamin. Necessary for carbohydrate, protein, and fat metabolism. Note: Strict vegetarians may have a special need for B12 supplementation.	Aids healthy functioning of nervous system. Relieves depressions that are caused by B12 deficiencies (which may be due to nutrient malabsorption, and then best treated with injectable B12). Stress reductive.	Cheese, eggs, meat, milk, raw bran, saltwater fish.
C **Ascorbic Acid**	Antiscorbutic (scurvy), anti-infective protector vitamin. One of the most versatile vitamins. Necessary for wound healing, cells, and blood vessels, teeth, gums, shock, and so forth. Helps body to absorb iron. Note: Only small amounts are stored in the liver, intestinal walls, and adrenal cortex, and requires "daily" replenishment.	Aids in the overall health of the "total" body. Increases resistance to infections. Aids in decreasing blood cholesterol, and various viral and bacterial infections. Reduces incidence of blood clots in the veins. Promotes life extension by helping protein cells to stick together. Stress reductive. Note: Shortage of vitamin C produces numerous physical disorders, including "impaired adrenal function"!	Alfalfa, almonds, apples, asparagus, bananas, blueberries, brussels sprouts, cabbage, cantaloupe, carrots, collards, cranberries, currents (black), endive, grapefruit, lemons, milk (human), oranges, papaya, pineapple, radish, rhubarb, spinach, tomatoes, watercress, watermelons.
D **Calciferol** **Ergosterol** **Viosterol**	Antirachitic (rickets) antiosteomalacia, senile osteoporosis, and tooth decay vitamin. Necessary for healthy thyroid and parathyroid glands. Note: Vitamin D can be made in the oils of the skin only before suntanning. It is important to obtain it through dietary sources.	Aids in assimilating Vitamin A, the utilization of calcium and phosphorus.	Butter, fish liver oils (especially cod liver), egg yolk, salmon, sardines, tuna, milk.
E **Tocopherol**	Antioxidant, antisterility, anticoagulant vitamin.	Aids brain cells in getting needed oxygen, as anticoagulant functions and vasodilator. Counteracts sterility in both	Almonds, avocados, butter, cod liver oil, egg yolk, sunflower seeds, pecans, vegetable oils (wheat germ, sunflower,

		sexes. Helps to regulate the pituitary gland (synthesis of TSH), as well as the thyroid gland. May help with variety of nervous symptoms, heart disease, and circulatory disorders. Stress reductive.	safflower, soybean), walnuts.
F **Unsaturated Fatty Acids Linoleic Linolelic**	Antiacne and eczema vitamin. Important source of necessary oil in the diet. Necessary for proper metabolism. Polyunsaturated fatty acids are needed to prevent tissue breakdown when saturated fatty acids are used in the metabolic process instead of polyunsaturated ones.	Aids in maintaining proper resilience and lubrication of the cells. Helps prevent allergic conditions, and cholesterol deposits in arteries; burns saturated fats; helps make calcium available to the cells. Stress reductive.	Almonds, avocados, butter, cod-liver oil, egg yolk, sunflower seeds, pecans, vegetable oils (wheat germ, sunflower, safflower, soybean), walnuts.
H **Biotin**	Antidermatitis and eczema vitamin. Necessary for synthesis of vitamin C. Necessary for carbohydrate, fat and protein metabolism.	Aids in the utilization of other B vitamins. Relieves depression caused by a deficiency of this vitamin.	Beef liver, brown rice, egg yolk, lentils, milk, nuts, whole grains.
M **Folic Acid** **(Folate)**	Antianemia vitamin. Necessary for growth and division of blood cells. Important in red blood cell formation. Note: Folic acid deficiency may lead to depression.	Aids metabolism of proteins. Significant for the production of nucleic acids (RNA/DNA). Important for amino acid and sugar utilization. Needed for a healthy nervous system. Stress reductive.	Apricots, avocados, beans, cantaloupe, carrots, dates, dark rye flour, deep-green leafy vegetables, egg yolk, pumpkins, salmon, spinach, tuna, whole grains.
Choline **Member of B-complex family and a fat emulsifier** *NOTE:* **Works with Inositol**	Anticirrhosis and fatty liver vitamin. Important for nerve transmission, and the regulation of liver and gallbladder. There is increased speculation that a deficiency of choline may be related to Alzheimer's disease. Low levels of ACh are found in Alzheimer's patients. Necessary for the manufacture of the neurotransmitter acetylcholine.	Aids metabolism and transport of fat. Deficiency may be related to high blood pressure, hardening of the arteries, and hemorrhaging kidneys. Aids healthy functioning of brain cells. Stress reductive.	Egg yolks, fish, green leafy vegetables, lecithin, legumes, liver, meats, soy beans, whole grains.
Inositol **Member of B-complex family, and fat emulsifier** *NOTE:* **Works with choline**	Antieczema and hair loss vitamin. Important for metabolism of fats. Necessary for formation of lecithin and for hair growth.	Aids metabolism of fats, including cholesterol, and redistribution of body fat. Aids healthy functioning of brain cells. Acts as a natural tranquilizer. Stress reductive.	Cabbage, cantaloupe, dried lima beans, grapefruit, lecithin, liver, raisins, wheat germ.

Mineral	Biological Functions Include	Specific Actions for Depression Treatment Include	Important Dietary Sources Include
Calcium (Ca) Note: Requires Vitamin D and phosphorus for metabolism.	Antistress, acid-binding mineral. Important for the development and maintenance of strong bones and teeth. Important for blood clotting, muscle, nerve, and heart function.	Aids in general mineral metabolism. Necessary for normal nerve and muscle responses. Helps to reduce fatigue. Increases mental alertness. Has tranquilizing effect. Stress reductive.	Almonds, beans, carrots, cheese, cauliflower, broccoli, brown rice, cashews, cabbages, eggs, garlic, grapefruit, lettuce, milk, pecans, raisins.
Chromium (Cr)	Antiatherosclerotic, anti-glucose intolerance mineral. Necessary for insulin effectiveness. Important for fatty acids, cholesterol, and protein synthesis. Necessary for manufacture of the glucose tolerance factor (GTF) and thus regulation of blood sugar.	Aids enzymes in metabolism of energy. Aids in the utilization of carbohydrates, and the control of both hyper and hypoglycemia. Stress reductive.	Black pepper, beef, beets, whole wheat bread.
Magnesium (Mg)	Antistress, acid binding mineral. Important as a catalyst in the utilization of carbohydrates, fats, and proteins. Necessary for nerve functioning. Helps maintain body balance with sodium chloride, and with calcium and phosphorus. Important for healthy bones, teeth, nerves and muscles.	Aids nervous system as a natural tranquilizer. Reduces anxiety, depression, and hyper-activity. Stress reductive.	Almonds, cashews, nuts, brown rice, oatmeal, pecans, pineapple, green vegetables, tuna, kelp.
Manganese (Mn)	Antineuritic and nerve nourishing, acid-binding mineral. Important for manufacture of carbohydrate and fat. Combines with choline to help digest fat. Important in prevention of digestive problems, male and female sterility, impotence, poor equilibrium, and so forth.	Aids in normalizing blood sugar levels. A manganese deficiency may be found in patients suffering from diabetes or pancreas disturbances. Stress reductive.	Almonds, bananas, beets, eggs, herring and egg yolks, whole grains, leafy vegetables, walnuts.
Zinc (Zn)	Antigrowth retardant and wound healing mineral. Important component of insulin and male fluid. Necessary for proper growth, sexual development and healing of wounds.	Aids in digestion and metabolism of phosphorous, and the healing of wounds. Helps to maintain normal blood sugar levels. Stress reductive.	Beef, brown rice, barley, beets, eggs, herring and ocean fish, liver, soybeans, sunflower seeds, whole wheat.

Amino Acids	Biological Functions Include	Specific Actions for Depression Treatment Include	Important Dietary Sources Include
Tryptophan	Anti-insomnia and pain amino acid.	Aids in the overall health of the body by	Found in most foods, however, excellent

This essential amino acid is necessary to synthesize the neurotransmitter serotonin.

helping to provide natural sleep. May relieve depression caused by serotonin deficiency.

The body converts tryptophan into Niacin (B_3), and serotonin. Stress reductive.

sources are lean meats, poultry, fish, and wheat germ.

Tyrosine

Antistress amino acid. This nonessential amino acid is necessary for the manufacture of the excitatory neurotransmitter norepinephrine.

Aids in the regulation of blood pressure and mood. Especially important and effective for people who are under chronic stress. May relieve depression caused by norepinephrine deficiency. Stress reductive.

Found in most foods, however, excellent—and needed—sources include lean meats, poultry, fish, pecans, pumpkin and sesame seeds, soy flour, lentils.

Phenylalanine

Antidepression amino acid.
This essential amino acid is necessary to manufacture phenylethylamine (PEA) a natural brain stimulant, and neurotransmittertype substance.

Note: Phenylalanine turns into the excitatory neurotransmitters norepinephrine and dopamine.

Aids in the regulation and control of pain thresholds and mood. Inhibits enzymes that break down the natural opiate, endorphin. Aids memory, alertness.

Found in most foods, however, best sources include lean meats, poultry, fish, soy flour, almonds, brazil nuts, pumpkin, sesame, sunflower seeds, raw lima beans, chick peas, lentils.

14. Vitamins and Recommended Food Sources

A_1	Retinol	Apples, apricots, butter, egg yolk, cheese, green
A_2	Dehydroretinol	leafy vegetables, liver, milk and others.
	Carotene: precursor of vitamin A	The body can use certain foods such as squash, pumpkins, carrots, and convert carotene to vitamin A as needed.
B_1	Thiamine	Almonds, beans, beef liver, egg yolk, fish, peas, whole grains.
B_2	Riboflavin	Apricots, apples, almonds, beef, milk, wheat germ.
B_3	Niacin (Nicotinic acid)	Almonds, barley, bran, beef liver, eggs, milk, wheat germ.
B_5	Pantothenic acid	Bran, chicken, broccoli, honey, meat, wheat germ, whole grains.
B_6	Pyridoxine Pyridoxal Pyridoxamine	Avocados, beef, brown rice, cabbage, green leafy vegetables, eggs, liver, whole grain cereals.
B_{12}	Cyanocobalamin Cobalamin	Eggs, fish, milk, liver.

C	Ascorbic acid	Fruits and vegetables, especially citrus fruits. (Up to 100 percent of vitamin can be destroyed in cooking!)
D	Calciferol Ergosterol Viosterol	Butter, fish liver oils—especially cod liver—egg yolk, milk.
E	Tocopherol	Butter, cod-liver oil, egg yolk, sunflower seeds, pecans, sunflower, safflower and wheat-germ oil.
F	Unsaturated fatty acids. Linoleic Linolelic	Almonds, avocados, cod-liver oil, safflower, soybean, sunflower oils.
G	Riboflavin (B_2)	See vitamin B_2
H	Biotin	Beef liver, brown rice, soybeans. Also produced in the intestines if healthy intestinal flora exists.
K	Menadione	Alfalfa, egg yolks, green vegetables, liver, milk.
M	Folic Acid (B_9) Folate Pteroylglutamic Acid	Asparagus, avocados, broccoli, green leafy vegetables, nuts, potatoes, wheat germ.
PABA	Para-amino-benzoic acid (B_x)	Eggs, milk, liver, molasses, wheat germ, yogurt. Also synthesized in intestines, if healthy intestinal flora is present.
Choline	B-complex vitamin	Egg yolks, fish, green leafy vegetables, lecithin, legumes, liver, soybeans, wheat germ.
Inositol	B-complex vitamin	Citrus fruits, lecithin, liver, milk, whole grains, nuts, wheat germ.

15. Minerals and Recommended Food Sources

Calcium (Ca)	Almonds, beans, broccoli, cabbage, green leafy vegetables, lettuce, milk, sunflower seeds, walnuts.
Cobalt (Co)	Green leafy vegetables, liver.
Chromium (Cr)	Beef, brown rice, buckwheat, legumes, millet.

Copper (Cu)	Almonds, beans, green leafy vegetables, peas, prunes, whole grains.
Chlorine (Cl)	Avocado, cabbage, endive, cucumber, pineapple, oats, watercress.
Fluorine (F)	Almonds, carrots, cheese, garlic, green vegetables.
Iodine (I)	Artichokes, egg yolk, garlic, citrus fruits, fish, watercress.
Iron (Fe)	Alfalfa, apricots, bananas, beets, egg yolk, spinach, sunflower seeds, walnuts, whole grains.
Magnesium (Mg)	Alfalfa, apples, almonds, beet tops, brown rice, endive, green leafy vegetables, sunflower seeds, whole grains.
Manganese (Mn)	Beets, Brussels sprouts, grapefruit, green leafy vegetables, wheat germ.
Molybdenum (Mo)	Brown rice, buckwheat, millet, legumes, whole grains.
Lithium (Li)	Kelp, lithium-rich mineral water.
Phosphorus (P)	Butter, egg yolks, fish, corn, legumes, nuts, seeds, whole grains.
Potassium (K)	Bananas, milk, nuts, potatoes, sunflower seeds, green leafy vegetables, oranges, whole grains.
Sodium (Na)	Asparagus, kelp, lettuce, sea salt, watermelon.
Silicon (Si)	Alfalfa, almonds, apples, beets, kelp, strawberries, onions, sunflower seeds.
Selenium (Se)	Eggs, fish, garlic, whole grains, vegetables (most).
Sulfur (S)	Fish, beef, onions, radishes, soybeans, string beans, watercress.
Zinc (Zn)	Eggs, green leafy vegetables, milk, pumpkin seeds, sunflower seeds, onions, nuts, wheat germ.

In summary, a varied diet rich in *fresh fruits, vegetables, nuts, seeds, whole grains,* and supplemented with some *fish, poultry, lean meat, low-fat milk,* and *eggs* provides the vitamins, minerals, and amino acids needed by the body.

Appendix 7

Food Supplements
for Depression

This Appendix lists the vitamins, minerals, and amino acids that are often recommended as a *routine dietary measure* in the overall treatment of depression. Merely taking these food supplements, however, is not a magical solution to depression. The food supplements described in this Appendix are not so much intended for the biological treatment of a specific depression, as they are part of the Wellness Diet described earlier in this book.

This does not detract from orthomolecular psychiatrists, and other health specialists, who often prescribe large doses of specific food supplements for the treatment of specific types of depression. Those interested in learning more about megavitamin treatment may wish to contact some of the organizations listed in Appendix 8.

The main purpose of this discussion is to present a safe and sane approach to the use of food supplements as a small—but important—part of the Wellness Diet. In most instances it is best to take food supplements in balanced and natural multivitamin and multimineral preparations. In excessive dosages (and what is insufficient for one person may be excessive for another), most food supplements, and especially minerals, are toxic. In the right amounts—for persons who do not have physical conditions to preclude their use—food supplements can be a great blessing. Wrongly used they can be a curse.

For example, when taken in the right amount *choline* and *calcium* can have a *tranquilizing* effect, but in excessive amounts they can have a *depressive* effect. The bottom line is that *we need moderation in all things,* including food supplements. Obviously we need to know average safe dosages (what is safe for most people, most of the time), what physical conditions might preclude the use of certain food supplements, and what the warning signs are in case of excess usage. Much has been said for or against the use of food supplements and myths are propagated by opponents and adherents alike. The consumers are therefore left with the task of educating themselves on the possible merits of food supplements.

Some Important Considerations
Before Using Food Supplements

Supplemental Needs Differ From Person to Person. As dietary needs differ from person to person, so do supplemental needs. There is an obvious relationship to health status, age, and sex. For example, children have different requirements than adults. The dosages listed in this Appendix are *for adults only.* Pregnant women too have special requirements.

Certain Vitamins Work Together. Vitamins act as enzymes and are important for proper metabolic functioning. They often work together, which makes it important to take several vitamins at one time. Yacenda (1984) has described how vitamin combinations affect body systems:

1. *Immune System*: Vitamin C, bioflavonoid, B_6, A, pantothenic acid, and D.
2. *Nervous System*: D, E, $B_{1,2,3}$, B_{12}, choline, inositol and folacin.
3. *Antioxidant Activity*: A, C, and E.
4. *Energy Metabolism*: E, K, and B-Complex.

It Is Possible to Take Too Many Food Supplements. Although millions of people take daily dosages of food supplements without any known side effects, there are faddists who attempt to scare people out of taking them. Some extremists think that food supplements should not be sold on the open market. Yet it is well known that aspirins (and many other over-the-counter drugs) are far more dangerous. Obviously most anything can be abused or misused, and this also holds true for food supplements. Some known side effects to certain food supplements are described in the listing at the end of this Appendix. Be especially careful not to exceed the maximum dosage of vitamins A, D, and E. It is important to take food supplements under the supervision of a nutritionally oriented physician.

World Renowned Medical Experts Support the Use of Food Supplements. It has been shown repeatedly that the therapeutic use of food supplements is helpful in the reduction of stress and in the treatment of a number of physical and psychological disorders, such as depression (Airola, 1977; Brennan 1971; Langer 1984; Lesser 1981; Mandell and Scanlon 1980; Mindell 1979; Newbold 1975; Sheinkin and Schachter 1980; Wright 1979, 1984). Vitamins, minerals, and amino acids are important for both the prevention, and the treatment of many physical and mental/emotional problems.

Those who believe that megadoses of vitamins and minerals are not useful are disagreeing with such *world renowned experts* as Nobel Prize winner Dr. Linus Pauling; Nobel Prize winner Julius Axelrod, Ph.D., Chief of Pharmacology of the National Institute of Mental Health; Nobel Prize winner Andrew V. Schally, Ph.D., professor of Medicine, Tulane University; Christiaan Barnard, M.D., internationally recognized heart transplant surgeon, University of Capetown; Michael DeBakey, M.D., Chancellor of Baylor College of Medicine, and pioneer in cardiovascular surgery; Robert A. Good, M.D., famous immunologist, and a lengthy list of other experts who have endorsed the use of megadoses of vitamins and minerals for optimum health!

Today it is a matter of great importance to use food supplements. Personally, I recommend that people commit themselves to the Wellness Diet described earlier, prior to carefully selecting a program of food supplements. The treatment of depression should routinely include proper diet *and* food supplements. Bricklin (1983) sums it up this way:

> . . . depression can be a kind of nonspecific result of generally bad nutrition and may respond to a more sensible diet that cuts out junk food, drastically cuts down on sugar and maximizes foods with honest nourishments. Multivitamin and multimineral supplementation (including magnesium) should be used as a routine dietary measure.

Minerals Are Important. In addition to vitamins, certain minerals also are helpful in the treatment of depression—especially if the depression has an endogenous basis—due to hypoglycemia, for example, which in turn could be influenced by low levels of chromium, or disturbed calcium-magnesium, calcium-phosphorous, sodium-potassium, or zinc-copper ratios. Mineral needs are best determined by a professional nutritional evaluation, including blood chemistry and sometimes a hair analysis. A computer hair analysis by itself, however, is not sufficient evidence.

Amino Acids Are Important. An important breakthrough in food supplements for depression (and other disorders) is found in the manufacture of amino acids, the smallest molecules that comprise a protein. They are often referred to as the building blocks of protein and take up three quarters of a person's solid weight. About 50 percent of the dry weight of body cells is composed of amino acids. Proteins differ from carbohydrates and fats because they have a nitrogen (amino) group. Threonine, tryptophan, valine, lysine, leucine, isoleucine, methionine, and phenylalanine are called "essential" because the body cannot manufacture them. The other fourteen amino acids necessary for adults can be manufactured by the body. Sometimes there is confusion about the total number of amino acids. There are actually twenty-four amino acids, but two of these are not considered important for adults.

People who get about 20 percent of their daily caloric intake in the form of animal protein get all of the essential amino acids. Those who strictly depend on vegetable protein need to carefully balance their foods. They do this by combining, for example, rice and sesame seeds or rice and beans. The basic rule of obtaining all of the essential amino acids is to take seed foods *and* cereal foods at the same time, or seed foods *and* legumes at the same time (*see* the Wellness Diet).

Without amino acids people cannot live. They are essential for the manufacture and maintenance of cell tissue, hormones, blood cells, antibodies, muscle, and bone—in short, every part of the body. Many health-conscious people take a balanced amino-acid formula (a complete amino-acid complex) approximately thirty to sixty minutes *before* one or more balanced meals. Vitamins and minerals obtained from the meal enable the amino acids to do their job!

Deficiencies of certain amino acids can lead to serious disorders. Taurine, for example, a nonessential amino acid (derived from methionine), may be lacking in some vegetarian diets. Also a rare intestinal disorder may cause taurine deficiency and cause severe depression. Taurine is often considered an anti-seizure nutrient. Mother's milk is high in taurine. Commercial formulas deficient in this amino acid have resulted in convulsions in babies. It has also been reported that irregular heartbeats have been normalized with the use of taurine.

Depression is sometimes related to a shortage of certain neurotransmitters in the brain. Again and again we are reminded that various nutrients—including amino acids—are needed to manufacture these neurotransmitters. The brain needs certain nutrients (including amino acids) from the bloodstream to manufacture certain neurotransmitters.

Obviously, diet is of the utmost importance in the treatment or prevention of depression. Brain cells live in very delicately balanced chemical environments. Even slight imbalances of vitamins, minerals, and/or amino acids are sufficient to effect our thinking and emotive feelings negatively.

Many vitamins, minerals, and amino acids depend on each other for proper functioning. We know, for example, that a lack of the neurotransmitter serotonin may lead to depression. Serotonin, in turn, requires the amino acid tryptophan. On the other hand, tryptophan requires B_2 for its metabolism, and B_6 is also necessary for the conversion to serotonin. Another source of depression has been found in low levels of norepinephrine. That neurotransmitter, however, depends on the amino acid tyrosine.

It is *not* recommended to use megadoses of single amino acids without the help of a health professional. It is also possible to obtain a so-called *amino-acid chromatogram* of the urine and blood serum. The chromatogram is a record that shows the different levels of amino acids in the body. A physician might order this test both *before* and *after* (four weeks of) amino-acid treatment. Severe kidney and/or liver dysfunctions and some other conditions preclude the use of amino-acid treatment.

Food Supplements Are Sometimes Safer than Foods. Some foods are consistently high in certain vitamins, minerals, and/or amino acids. However this does not mean that they are safe to consume in large quantities—if at all. For example, calcium from supplements is healthier than from high-fat calcium-rich foods such as whole milk. However, even low-fat milk may not be the answer.

A great number of people cannot digest milk properly and some are allergic to it. Others are endangered by the xanthine oxidase (XO) enzyme that is found in cow's milk. This enzyme, found in fat globules, normally poses no danger. The fat globules are too large to pass through the intestinal wall and into our bloodstream. Homogenized milk, however, breaks the globules down into smaller parts that do enter our bloodstream and may contribute to atherosclerosis (Newbold 1975). Food supplements are often ideal for those who are allergic to such common products as wheat, corn, soy, and yeast. It is now possible to purchase some very excellent vitamin supplements that are sugar, corn, wheat, soy and yeast free!

Food Supplement Withdrawal. It is unwise to suddenly stop taking megadoses of vitamins, minerals, or amino acids. It is important to slowly taper off and give the body a chance to adjust. Reports reveal varied symptoms that might come about as the result of too quickly stopping the use of megadoses of food supplements.

Be Careful of Propaganda for or Against Food Supplements. Recommended dosages of food supplements for depression are therapeutic dosages, and they far exceed the U.S. Recommended Daily Allowances (RDA), which are nontherapeutic and are based on ideal conditions.

Recently the FDA stated that ". . . average or normal eaters probably never need supplemental vitamins, although many think they do" (HHS Publication, FDA, No: 70-2117, 1982).

In my estimation this advice is irresponsible. What is an average or normal eater? If only the FDA could define a normal eater and what they mean by "probably never." Many people in this country do *not* get a balanced diet. They eat much junk food, are often addicted to such harmful substances as caffeine, nicotine, and sugar, and use too many over-the-counter, FDA-approved (but nontheless unhealthy) drugs.

The actual average eater probably purchases groceries in the average supermarket. Yet the health-conscious shopper can use only a small section of a large supermarket, since most foods there are processed and lack essential nutrients.

Although there is no reason to doubt the sincerity of the FDA, there is good reason to think twice about the true value of pamphlets that attack vitamin supplementation, and basing the whole thesis (of no need for supplementation) on a pathetically unscientific reference to average or normal eaters. Here is the final statement in the aforementioned pamphlet.

> Even though the widely seen and identified vitamin deficiencies of 30 years ago have all but disappeared, the American consumer is approached from all sides with misinformation about the almost universal "need" for supplements of vitamins.

Although it is debatable whether vitamin deficiencies have completely disappeared, we could ask the question: Has nutrition improved in our society? Is it because more American households use vitamins? Is it because people are starting to eat less of the so-called normal and average foods that have been so widely recommended and hailed as safe, healthy, and good for us?

Is it because millions of people have nothing whatsoever to do with the so-called normal diet and have learned to become "abnormal" by staying away from processed foods, refined carbohydrates, and FDA approved over-the-counter drugs? Is it because nearly half of all Americans use vitamin supplements?

On the other side of the coin we have people who are far too intent on selling a lot of food supplements. We also have consumers who have a mistaken faith in food supplements. Obviously massive commercial interests are at stake. The food supplement market is worth about three billion dollars a year. That is less, however, than 1 percent of the 400-billion-dollars-a-year medical industry.

Also, unqualified people have gone into nutritional counseling. Faddists, too, have always been here, and they will stay around. The information presented in this book, however, is based on the work of scientists and medical experts, and on my own day-to-day professional experiences.

It is also difficult to refute world-renowned medical experts, researchers, and Nobel Prize winners who evaluated the food supplement formulas of United Sciences of America. Their endorsement of megadoses of vitamins and minerals was based, among other things, on state-of-the-art use of the world's largest computerized data base in clinical nutrition. This project is said to have involved more than 5 million references in 14,200 medical and scientific journals from 148 countries.

Highly qualified, independent researchers have come up with startlingly different findings than those of powerful special interest groups. Many are the testimonies of researchers and health practitioners about the relationship of the nation's diet and ill health. In the next paragraphs a dozen of those people are mentioned by name.

Cheraskin and Ringsdorf (1975) believe that there is a direct relationship between improper diet and the increase of mental illness, learning disabilities, and substance abuse. Robinson (1976), writing in the *Journal of the American Dietetic Association* (JADA), maintains that "the very affluence [in America] is creating imbalances that contribute to many chronic diseases." Ballentine (1979) in a review of the American diet, stated that only 50 percent of the people in this country had an "adequate" diet. Bylinski (1978) concluded that it takes only slight nutritional factors to affect our thinking and emotions.

The same has been found by many others, including Brennan (1977), Kunin (1980), Langer (1984), Newbold (1975), Ross (1975), Sheinkin and Schachter (1980), Tintera (1955; 1967), and others.

American dieticians, as revealed by an earlier mentioned study (Worthington-Roberts and Breskin 1984), do take food supplements, and we can assume that their knowledge of the average diet must have convinced them of the need.

What we need is not a so-called normal or average diet, but a well-balanced nutritious diet, geared to our own special needs. In summary, don't be persuaded by propaganda for or against food supplements. Remember that the entire subject of proper diet and nutrition has been hotly debated in congress, in professional meetings, and among scientists and lay persons.

Unfortunately, the professionals of different persuasions have found it difficult to cooperate. To enable us to take greater responsibility for our own health, I highly recommend use of the References section of this book as a recommended reading list, and to make appropriate use of the *Directory of Organizations,* listed in Appendix 8.

On the following pages is a description of often-recommended therapeutic dosages of food supplements for depression.

16. Supplementary Vitamin, Mineral, Amino-acid Regimen for Depression

Vitamins	Often Recommended Daily Dosage	Warning Signs/Excess Oral Usage Include
A **(A₁)** **(A₂)**	5,000-15,000 I.U.	Severe headache, anemia, loss of appetite, loss of hair, enlargement of the liver, pressure inside the skull, nose bleeds, mental disturbances, nausea, vomiting, fatigue, dizziness, peeling of the skin. Pregnant women must not exceed 5,000 I.U.
B₁ **(Thiamine)**	10-100 mg	Headache, trembling, rapid pulse, insomnia, low blood pressure, restlessness, sweating. Extra care needed if suffering from diabetes.
B₂ **(Riboflavin)**	10-100 mg	Itching, tingling in extremities. These may also be symptoms of B₅ shortage.
B₃ **(Niacin/ Niacinamide)**	20-100 mg	Nausea, vomiting, tingling, itching, diarrhea, ulcers. High levels of uric acid and sugar in blood. Flushing is a common side effect of niacin. Extra care needed if suffering from diabetes, gout, glaucoma, ulcers, liver disorders.
B₅ **(Pantothenic acid)**	50-100 mg	Gastrointestinal problems, headaches.
B₆ **(Pyridoxine)**	20-100 mg	Numbness, burning, and tingling pains in hands and feet. Loss of muscle coordination, clumsiness, night restlessness, unsteadiness, fatigue and nerve damage. Reduces effectiveness of certain drugs, such as, phenobarbitol, Dilantin, and Levodopa.
B₁₂ **(cobalamin)**	25-100 mcg (Ug)	Unknown oral toxicity. Rare allergic reactions, such as eczema.
C **(ascorbic acid)**	300-1,000 mg	Diarrhea, peptic flare-up, increased risk for gout, kidney stones, abdominal cramps, fatigue, headache, nausea, sleepiness, insomnia, reduced copper levels in blood (anemia) erosion of

		tooth enamel with chewable tablets. Extra care required if suffering from diabetes, kidney problems, or when taking tricyclic antidepressants.
D (calciferol, ergosterol, viosterol)	400-600 I.U.s	Frequent urination, joint pains, loss of appetite, nausea, headache, vomiting, high blood pressure, itching, dizziness, dry mouth. The lower therapeutic dose will most likely be prescribed if suffering from heart disease. With extremely high dosages, calcium might deposit in the kidneys.
E (D-alpha tocopherol)	400-800 I.U.s	Blurred vision, elevated blood pressure, muscle weakness, hypothyroid functioning, chapped lips, fatigue, weakness. Might be contraindicated if suffering from rheumatic heart disease. Warning signs more likely to occur above 1,200 I.U.s.
F (unsaturated fatty acids)	10% of total calories	(Most nutritionists do not consider this a vitamin.)
BIOTIN	150-300 mcg (Ug)	May decrease production of acid in the stomach. Biotin is made in the intestines—usually this is satisfactory.
Folic Acid	400 mcg (Ug)	Allergic reactions such as rash or hives, nervousness, digestive disturbances. Folic acid could mask symptoms of B_{12} deficiency. Therefore, this vitamin must be taken with B_{12} to prevent irreversible nerve damage. People on Dilantin most likely will be told by their physicians not to exceed the RDA of 400 mcg per day.
Choline	250-500 mg	At very high dosages (of 3000 mg. or more) might lead to depressive reactions. Choline is not considered a vitamin by most nutritionists.
Inositol	250-500 mg	Unknown. Inositol is not considered a vitamin by most nutritionists. Both choline and inositol are part of the so-called B-complex, together with biotin, pantothenic acid, thiamine, and riboflavin. (Lecithin supplies both choline and inositol.)

Note: The above fifteen vitamins are an important routine dietary adjunct in the overall treatment of depression. *Occasionally* it is determined that there is a specific deficiency of a given vitamin and in that case a single food supplement is prescribed by the physician. As a rule, however, all of the above vitamins are taken together in a multivitamin preparation. Actually it is important to do so as they work synergistically and all of them are stress reductive. On the other hand, certain vitamins (minerals and amino acids) might be contra-indicated for people who suffer from certain disorders such as diabetes, glaucoma, heart disease, high blood pressure, kidney disorders, liver disorders, and ulcers. This could mean that they can take only small (if any) dosages under strict medical supervision. On the other hand, these people might greatly benefit from specific food supplements that are designed to help their particular ailment. Regardless of a person's physical condition it is important to obtain the advice of a nutrition-oriented physician when considering food supplements.

It is always best to take the lowest possible therapeutic dosage, which is sufficient for most people in any case. If very large dosages of food supplements are needed they are usually prescribed by an orthomolecular specialist (see Appendix 8, Directory of Organizations).

The possible adverse effects of vitamins, minerals, and amino acids are real, yet they are few and mild when compared to those of anti-depressant drugs. Also, the good news is that when food supplements are taken in the dosages described in these pages, that few (if any) adverse reactions have been reported.

Adverse reactions usually are found in far higher dosages than those mentioned here. Other good news is that adverse reactions or side effects usually disappear upon discontinuation of the food supplements. Nevertheless, while the therapeutic dosages listed are below those that normally might elicit warning signs, it is important not to overlook individual differences and to be alert for untoward signs or symptoms. Remember that one person's blessing can be another person's curse.

Minerals	Often Recommended Daily Therapeutic Dosage	Warning Signs/Excess Oral Usage Include
Calcium	1000-1500 mg	Hypercalcemia unlikely under 2000 mg. Kidney stones, constipation, vomiting, loss of appetite, fatigue, depression. High calcium intake is contraindicated in many conditions. This includes Addison's disease, Cushing's syndrome, hyperparathyroidism, hyperthyroidism, and hypothyroidism.
Chromium	50-200 mcg (Ug)	Allergic reactions.

Magnesium	500-750 mg	The low dosage will probably be prescribed with kidney malfunctions.
Manganese	2.5-5 mg	High dosages may be toxic.
Zinc	15-40 mg	The use of 50 mg or more daily might inhibit copper absorption, and result in anemia. High dosages might be toxic and interfere with immune cell activity.

Note: The above minerals are often considered an important routine dietary adjunct in the overall treatment of depression. *Occasionally* it is determined that there is a specific deficiency of a given mineral, and in that case a single food supplement might be prescribed by the physician. As a rule, however, all of the above minerals—plus others— are taken in a multimineral preparation. This is important because minerals work synergistically and are best taken in balanced amounts.

Amino acids	Often Recommended Daily Therapeutic Dosage	Warning Signs/Excess Oral Usage Include
Tyrosine	500 mg (midmorning)	Toxic at very high dosages.
Phenylalanine	500 mg (midafternoon)	Toxic at very high dosages. Phenylalanine is not to be taken by those who have PKU, or high blood pressure as it has a vaso-constrictive effect.
Tryptophan	500 mg (midevening) (1000 mg [under medical super-vision] is usually prescribed for sleep)	Possible liver damage with doses as low as 1000 mg?

Note: The above three amino acids have been identified as helpful in the overall treatment of depression. They are *not* a routine dietary adjunct in the overall treatment of depression. Rather they are to be taken as required only.

Amino-acid imbalances are more readily found in individuals who have vitamin and mineral deficiencies. The Wellness Diet (supplemented by vitamins and minerals) is therefore the first step to take. A health practitioner might recommend only one of the above three amino acids. In most cases this will be tyrosine. This particular amino acid is converted in another amino acid called L-Dopa, which is responsible for improved brain function and a reduction or elimination of depression and nervousness. Some of the L-Dopa will also be converted into the Catecholamines (dopamine, norepinephrine, and epinephrine) discussed in Appendix 3. Tyrosine is known as the anti-stress amino acid. It reduces anxiety, improves mental agility, and raises moods without the side effects that are so common with drugs such as amphetamines and tranquilizers.

Phenylalanine is usually taken as DL-Phenylalanine (a ratio of 50/50 of both the D and L form) and is believed as effective as the tricyclic antidepressant Imipramine (*see* Appendix 4) in three equal dosages of 150-200 mg per day (*Nutrition News* 1983). Phenylalanine is contraindicated for those with phenylketonuria. (*See* Glossary for further information on phenylalanine, phenylketonuria, and Imipramine.)

Tryptophan has many wonderful uses, one of which is its direct conversion into the important neurotransmitter serotonin. Tryptophan is often lacking in the diet of many people because it is the least common essential amino acid in our food. Also if people have a niacin (Vitamin B_3) deficiency, much of the tryptophan will be used to convert it into niacin. For the conversion of tryptophan into serotonin vitamin B_6 is required.

For maximum effectiveness it is best to take amino acids on an empty stomach or one hour before a meal. Another way is to take them midmorning, midafternoon, and midevening. All of the amino acids require vitamin B_6 for their synthesis. To prevent toxic levels of individual amino acids it is often recommended to also take a balanced formula of all 24 amino acids.

Some Practical Advice

Now I would like to give you some practical advice. Once you get the okay from your physician that you can safely take the higher dosages of food supplements, find a reputable health-food store and purchase natural formulas that have already been balanced.

Usually it is not necessary to obtain vitamins and minerals separately. Not only is this an expensive and cumbersome method, but it also more readily results in an imbalanced intake of food supplements. There are, however, exceptions: for example, if a specific deficiency has been determined or when certain physical conditions prevent the proper absorption of oral food supplements. *As a rule, the safest way to use food supplements is through multivitamin and multimineral supplementation.* Remember that food supplements are only *supplements.* Appropriately used they will provide many benefits.

Appendix **8**

Directory of Organizations

United States

Allopathic Medicine

American Medical Association
535 N. Dearborn St.
Chicago, IL 60160

Objective: The promotion and dissemination of Western conventional (allopathic) medicine.

Publication: The Journal of the American Medical Association (JAMA) and others.

Audience: Professionals (MDs and DOs).

Alternative Medicine

American Foundation for Alternative Health Care
25 Landfield Ave.
Monticello, NY 12701

Objective: To serve as an alternative health-care information resource center.
Audience: Professionals and laypersons.

Gerson Institute
P.O. Box 430
Bonita, CA 92002

Objective: The dissemination of information on general nutritional health and Gerson therapy in particular. Gerson therapy is aimed at the prevention of disease and the restoration of health through natural healing mechanisms. This therapy is especially aimed at cancer and other degenerative diseases.
Publication: Newsletter.
Audience: Professionals and laypersons.
Training: Available for physicians.

Christian Counseling

American Association of Pastoral Counselors (AAPC)
9508A Lee Hwy.
Fairfax, VA 22031

National Association of Christian Marriage Counselors
P.O. Box 782
Terrell, TX 75160

North American Association of Christians in Social Work
Box 90
St. Davids, PA 19087

United Association of Christian Counselors International (UACCI)
3837 Walnut St.
Harrisburg, PA 17109

The above listed Christian organizations provide a wide variety of professional services to both the professional membership and the public at large, including professional certification, the development of professional standards, ongoing training and education programs, and the enforcement of ethical standards. The members are committed to further God's answers to our personal and interpersonal problems. In most cases these organizations also provide referrals.

Depression Self-Help

International Association for Clear Thinking (I'ACT)
3939 West Spencer Street
P.O. Box 1011
Appleton, WI 54911

Objective: The promotion and dissemination of information on various self-help techniques and in particular rational self-counseling. Chapters are located in the United States, Canada, Great Britain, and the Netherlands (Associatie van Rationele Denkers, Grootmede 92, 4337 AE Middelburg, Netherlands).
Publications: Newsletter and various pamphlets. Also books (including this one) may be purchased from I'ACT.
Audience: Laypersons.
Training: Residence training programs, workshops, and seminars.
Referrals: A listing is available of both professional and nonprofessional helpers.

Rational Behavior Therapy Center (RBT Center)
University of Kentucky Medical Center
820 South Limestone
Lexington, KY 40536

Objective: The promotion and dissemination of information on rational behavior therapy (RBT). This is a drugless therapy for depression and certain other mental/emotional problems. Training and certification of professionals in RBT is also available.
Publications: Newsletter and many books and pamphlets. Most of these are written by Dr. Maxie C. Maultsby, Jr., Professor of Psychiatry and founder of RBT.
Audience: Mainly professionals and paraprofessionals in the field of mental health.
Training: Ongoing training programs for professionals and paraprofessionals are held in Lexington, Kentucky, and elsewhere.
Referrals: A listing is available of trained RBT professionals in the United States and abroad.

Hypoglycemia (low blood sugar)

Adrenal Metabolic Research Society of Hypoglycemia
Foundation, Inc.
153 Pawling Ave.
Troy, New York 12180

Objective: The dissemination of information on hypoglycemia and hyperinsulinism.
Publication: Newsletter, "Homeostasis," books, and pamphlets.
Audience: Professionals, paraprofessionals, and laypersons.
Referrals: To physicians in the U.S.

Medical Consumer Information

People's Medical Society
14 East Minor Street
Emmaus, PA 18409

Objective: To improve the quality and availability of medical care for all persons.
Publication: People's Medical Society Newsletter.
Audience: Laypersons.

Center for Medical Consumers and Health Care Information, Inc.
237 Thompson Street
New York, NY 10012

Objective: The evaluation of medical treatment.
Publication: Newsletter, "Health Facts."
Audience: Laypersons.

Medical Ecology

American Academy of Environmental Medicine
P.O. Box 16106
Denver, CO 80216

Objective: The dissemination of information on ecologic illness.
Publications: Clinical Ecology, quarterly; Newsletter, quarterly; AAEM Directory, annual.
Audience: Physicians, engineers, nurses, and others interested in environmental medicine.
Training: Annual scientific meetings for physicians, nurses, and technicians in basic aspects of clinical ecology.

Human Ecology League
7330 N. Rogers Ave.
Chicago, IL 60626

Objective: To serve as grassroots environmental health movement and to collect and disseminate information on ecological illness.
Publication: Human Ecologist, magazine.
Audience: Professionals and laypersons.
Referrals: Publishes a directory of physicians who practice clinical ecology.

International Academy of Preventive Medicine
P.O. Box 70937
1408 Edgecliff Ln.
Pasadena, CA 91107

Objective: To stimulate discussion of preventive medicine among health professionals and health-related professionals with doctorate degrees, and to disseminate information on new developments in preventive medicine to the membership.
Publication: Professional newsletter.
Referrals: An annual directory is available to the membership.

Wellness and Health Activation Networks
P.O. Box 923
Vienna, VA 22180

Objective: To help individuals achieve and maintain wellness and to prevent illness.

National Wellness Association
South Hall
University of Wisconsin
Stevens Point, WI 54481

Objective: Act as a clearing house for information on fitness, health, and wellness for health and wellness professionals.
Publication: Newsletter, "Wellness Management."
Audience: Professionals.
Referrals: An annual directory is published.

Nutrition Information Resources

American Association of Nutritional Consultants
2375 E. Tropicana, Suite 270
Las Vegas, NV 90109

Objective: Provide certification and exchange of information for its membership.

Publications: The Nutrition and Dietary Consultant, monthly; Directory, annual.

Audience: Professional nutritional consultants.

American Dietetic Association
430 N. Michigan Ave.
Chicago, IL 60611

Objective: To provide direction and leadership in the field of dietetics.

Publication: Journal, monthly.

Audience: Mainly dieticians in hospitals, colleges, school food services, and similar settings.

Cooking for Survival Consciousness
Box 26762
Elkins Park, PA 19117

Objective: Provide information about food and cooking for the maintenance of health and the prevention of illness.

Publications: CSC Philadelphia Holistic Health Resource Guide and Directory, quarterly; CSC Reports, quarterly, and *I Choose to Be Well Diet Cookbook*.

Audience: Professionals and laypersons.

Training: Conducts seminars, classes, and holds annual symposium.

Feingold Association of the United States
P.O. Box 6550
Alexandria, VA 22306

Objective: To disseminate information on the Feingold Diet for children and adults who suffer from anxiety, aggression, overactivity, sleep disturbances, learning disabilities, and retardation.

Publication: Pure Facts, newsletter.

Audience: Mainly laypersons.

Training: Annual convention. Also offers specialized children's services, and provides assistance in the formation of local groups.

Natural Food Associates (NFA)
P.O. Box 210
Atlanta, TX 75551

Objective: To disseminate information on the values of natural, chemical-free food and preventive measures to metabolic disease.

Publications: Natural Food and Farming, magazine; Natural Food News, newspaper.
Audience: Professionals and laypersons.

Nutrition Education Association (NEA)
3647 Glen Haven
Houston, TX 77225

Objective: To disseminate information on the importance of good nutrition for good health.
Publications: Crackdown on Cancer with Good Nutrition; Switchover; The Anti-Cancer Cooking Plan for Today's Parents and Their Children, as well as various brochures.
Audience: Professionals and laypersons.
Training: Home study course in nutrition and Annual Nutrition Education Conference.

International College of Applied Nutrition (ICAN)
P.O. Box 1000
San Gabriel, CA 91776

Objective: Provide post-graduate education in nutrition for professionals.
Publication: Journal of Applied Nutrition.
Audience: Professionals with doctorate degrees.

Southern Academy of Clinical Nutrition
P.O. Box 266
Keystone Heights, FL 32656

Objective: Health education.
Audience: Laypersons.
Referrals: To nutritionally oriented physicians.

American Society for Clinical Nutrition
9650 Rockville Pike
Bethesda, MD 20814

Objective: To promote the teaching, research, and reporting of progress in clinical nutrition.
Publication: American Journal of Clinical Nutrition.
Audience: Physicians and scientists interested in clinical nutrition research.

Orthomolecular Medicine

Academy of Orthomolecular Medicine
1691 Northern Blvd.
Manhasset, NY 11030

Objective: The dissemination of information on orthomolecular
    psychiatry.
Publication: Journal of Orthomolecular Psychiatry and Medicine.
Audience: Professionals.
Referrals: To members of the academy.

The Huxley Institute for Biosocial Research
900 N. Federal Hwy. #330
Boca Raton, FL 33432

Objective: The dissemination of information on various disorders
    amenable to diet and nutrition, including allergies, depression,
    hypoglycemia, and schizophrenia.
Publication: "Newsletter of the Huxley Institute."
Audience: Professionals and laypersons.
Training: Available for physicians and allied health professionals.
Referrals: To orthomolecular and nutritionally oriented psychiatrists.

Orthomolecular Medical Society
P.O. Box 7
Agoura, CA 91301

Objective: Research in orthomolecular medicine.
Referrals: The names of physicians and other health specialists in
    orthomolecular medicine are available to the members of the
    society.

Wholistic Approach in Medicine

American Holistic Health Sciences Association
1766 Cumberland Green, Suite 208
St. Charles, IL 60174

Objective: To disseminate holistic health information.
Publication: Bulletin of Society for Nutrition and Preventive Medi-
    cine, quarterly; Herald of Holistic Health, quarterly.
Audience: Professionals.
Training: Annual convention.

American Holistic Nurses Association (AHNA)
Box 116
Telluride, CO 81435

Objective: To disseminate information on holistic health care.
Publication: Beginnings, monthly newsletter; Journal of Holistic Nursing, annual.
Audience: Registered, licensed, practical, vocational, and student nurses.
Training: Quarterly meetings.
Referrals: Maintains listing of holistic nursing schools.

Directory of Organizations

Great Britain

British Holistic Medical Association (BHMA)
179 Gloucester Place
London, NW1 60X

Objective: Research effectiveness of wholistic medicine. Teach patients how to reduce stress. The latter is seen as the main culprit behind many disorders.
Audience: Professionals and laypersons.
Training: Has been conducted for selected patients in London.
Referrals: Provides referral listing (SSAE) of wholistic-minded physicians (GP's).

Allergy

Action Against Allergy (AAA)
43 The Downs
London, SW 20 8HG

National Society for Research into Allergy
P.O. Box 45
Hinckley
Leicester, LE10 1JY

Children

Hyper-Active Children's Support Group
59 Meadowside
Angmering
Littlehampton
West Sussex, BN16 4BW

Complementary Medicine

Institute for Complementary Medicine
21 Portland Place
London, W1N 3AF

Counseling and Psychotherapy

British Association for Counseling
37a Sheep Street
Rugby
Warwickshire, CV21 3BX

British Association of Psychotherapists
121 Hendon Lane
London, N3 3PR

National Council of Psychotherapists
1 Clovelly Road
Ealing, London W5

Cancer

Bristol Cancer Help Centre
Grove House
Cornwallis Grove, Clifton
Bristol, BS8 4PG

The Association for New Approaches to Cancer
231 Kensal Road
London, W10 5DB

Wessex Cancer Help Centre
42 North Street
Havant
Hants, P09 1PT

Green Gates Holistic Health Centre
136 Muswell Hill Road
London, N10 3JD

Gerson Nutritional Therapy for Cancer
97 Bedford Court Mansions
Bedford Avenue
London, WC1B 3AE

Chiropractic

British Chiropractic Association
5 First Ave.
Chelmsford
Essex, CM1 1RX

Depression Self-Help

Depressives Associated (DA)
19 Merley Ways
Wimborne Minster
Dorset, BH21 1QN
Great Britain

Objective: The promotion of (sharing-caring) self-help services for
depressives, run by ex-depressives. This is one of the most suc-

cessful organizations of its kind in the world. The founder and executive director, Janet Stevenson, S.R.N., has set an extraordinary example of dedicated leadership and self-less service to others.

Publication: Newsletter and various pamphlets.

Audience: People suffering from depression, and their relatives.

Training: Self-help methods are disseminated mainly in group meetings.

Referrals: Referrals are made to DA group meetings throughout Great Britain.

Homeopathy

British Homeopathic Association
27a Devonshire Street
London, W1N 1RH

Naturopathy

British Naturopathic and Ostheopathic Association
6 Netherhall Gardens
London, NW3 5RR

Nutrition

Community Health Foundation
188-194 Old Street
London, EC1V 8BP

The Nutrition Association
24 Harcourt House
19 Cavendish Square
London, W1M 9AB

International Academy of Nutrition
(Orthomolecular)
P.O. Box 8
Liphook
Hampshire, GU30 7JD

Osteopathy

British School of Osteopathy
1-4 Suffolk Street
London, SW1Y 4HG

European School of Osteopathy
104 Tonbridge Road
Maidstone
Kent, ME16 8SL

General Council and Register of Osteopaths
16 Buckingham Gate
London, SW1E 6LB

Glossary*

abate To reduce in intensity.

absorption The uptake of nutrients by the intestines and their release in the bloodstream.

acetic acid A colorless liquid; the basic component of vinegar.

acetylcholine A chemical compound which functions as a neurotransmitter. See *neurotransmitters*.

acid Water-soluble sour substance.

acquired immune deficiency syndrome (AIDS) A very serious disease of the immune system with an extremely high fatality rate. It is believed that a virus (HIV) is the cause of the disease that attacks and destroys the immune system, leaving the sufferer unable to fight off infections. Early symptoms include severe tiredness, chills, fever, swollen glands, swollen spleen, night sweats, loss of appetite with corresponding weight loss, and diarrhea, and often depression. See *AIDS dementia complex*.

acromegaly Abnormal enlargement of the physical extremities.

ACTH See *adrenocorticotropic hormone*.

acute Coming on suddenly and severely.

acute organic brain syndrome Sudden mental confusion and disorientation.

*Some entries, although not in the text, are included because they are part of the professional vocabulary on depression, or helpful as crossreferences. The Glossary is useful to laypersons and counselors alike.

Adapin   Trade name for the antidepressant drug doxepin hydrochloride.

ADC   See *AIDS dementia complex.*

addict   Anyone who cannot be deprived of a particular substance without withdrawal symptoms.

addiction   Dependence on a particular substance in which deprival leads to withdrawal symptoms. See *iatrogenic drug abuse.*

Addison's disease   A disease caused by failure or underfunctioning of the cortex of the adrenal glands. See *adrenal glands,* and *hypoadrenalism.*

adenohypophysis   The anterior lobe of the pituitary gland. See *anterior pituitary gland,* and *pituitary gland.*

adenoma   Benign tumor in which the cells are derived from glandular tissue, or from glandular structures.

adjustment reaction   An acute mental-emotional, or behavioral response to severe stress. The reaction may be mild, moderate, or severe, and may include anxiety and/or depression, as well as various physical ailments. Adjustment reactions are more common among adolescents than older age groups. Also see *neurotic disorder.*

adolescence   The period between sexual maturity and adulthood.

adrenal glands   Triangular shaped endocrine glands located atop the kidneys; there are two major parts: an outer cortex and inner medulla.

adrenaline   Official British pharmaceutical name for epinephrine. See *epinephrine.*

adrenergic   Nerve fibers that release norepinephrine as a neurotransmitter. See *neurotransmitters,* and *norepinephrine.*

adrenocorticotropic hormone (ACTH)   A hormone secreted by the anterior pituitary gland and essential for proper functioning of the adrenal cortex and its secretions of corticosteroids. See *anterior pituitary gland,* and *corticosteroid.*

affect   Emotional reactions to perceptions and thoughts; the emotional tone behind an expressed emotion or behavior.

affective disorders   Mood disorders. The most common ones are anxiety, depression and elation. Depressive illnesses such as bipolar and unipolar depression are affective disorders. See *depressive illness.*

afferent   Carrying toward the center, especially a nerve carrying a sensory message to the brain.

afferent neuron   A nerve, also known as sensory neuron, which carries messages toward the central nervous system from receptor cells.

afterbrain   The back and lower parts of the brain; includes pons and cerebellum.

aggression   Offensive, hostile actions toward self or others.

aggressive reaction   A response to frustration directed to its source or some substitute.

agitation   Restlessness and increased physical and mental activity, intermingled with anxiety and fear.

AIDS   See *acquired immune deficiency syndrome.*

AIDS dementia complex (ADC)   A form of dementia (progressive mental decline) that strikes AIDS victims. It may come as an early warning sign or manifest itself at any given time during the course of the disease. It is alleged that ADC could be the first and even the only indication of AIDS. In ADC it appears that the AIDS virus attacks the brain cells directly, attaches itself to receptor molecules on the neurons, or in some other way interferes with the proper functioning of the neurotransmitters. Treatment at present is with AZT and perhaps with Peptide T. Symptoms of ADC include: Apathy, clumsiness (dropping things), confusion about normally routine events, delusions, difficulty with concentration or doing complex sequential mental tasks, forgetfulness (for example, recent events or familiar names), hyperactivity, impulsiveness, irritability, leg weakness (difficulty walking), loss of spontaneity, manic symptoms as found in the manic phase of bipolar depression (including grandiose thinking and delusions), lack of insight, and slowness in picking up auditory signals from the ear to the brain. See *AIDS, Alzheimer's disease, bipolar depression, depressive illness, dementia, neurotransmitters, Pick's disease,* and *senile dementia.*

alarm reaction   The first stage of the so-called general adaptation syndrome. During this state adrenaline is released and the body prepared for fight or flight. See *general adaptation syndrome.*

albumin   A water-soluble protein found in body tissues and fluids. Albumin is composed of nitrogen, carbon, hydrogen, oxygen, and sulphur. Normal blood serum level is 4.0 to 5.5 g/dl (40-55 g/L).

aldosterone   One of the mineralocorticoid hormones released by the adrenal cortex for the regulation of sodium and potassium, and optimum water balance in the body. The normal urine level of aldosterone is 2-26 mcg/24 hr (6-72 nmol/24 hr).

aldosteronism   Also known as hyperaldosteronism, the condition results from adrenal cortex disease, or other disorders, and leads to increased blood pressure, sodium retention, and other problems, such as alkalosis.

alkali   A substance that will neutralize acids to form salts. It is a general term for a compound that has the properties of a base, for example calcium-hydroxide.

alkalosis   An abnormal condition due to the accumulation of base in the body or a loss of acid from the body.

allergen   Any substance that induces an allergy.

allergy   Hypersensitivity reaction of body tissues to specific substances, including pollen, chemicals, drugs, additives, foods, fruit, yeast, and so forth.

allness thinking   Self-defeating thoughts based on the erroneous perception that human beings can be all-knowing, and reflected in such words as *always, everybody, never,* and so forth.

allopathic   See *allopathy.*

allopathy   The conventional Western system of medical practice in use by most physicians in the U.S.A. The primary form of treatment is with chemical substances such as antibiotics which are incompatible with or actively oppose the symptoms of a given disease. Allopathy has proved more beneficial for the treatment of infectious diseases than for degenerative or other stress-related disorders.

alternative medicine   Any of the various methods used for the prevention and treatment of disease which are different from allopathy. Alternative medicine is becoming increasingly popular, especially in Europe, and includes such practices as acupuncture, chiropractic, herbalism, homeopathy, and naturopathy. Most popular is the wholistic or "total" approach. See also *allopathy* and *wholistic.*

Alzheimer's disease   A progressive disorder with loss of mental ability, especially memory and concentration. There are progressive stages, namely the early confusional, delayed confusional, early dementia, middle, and late dementia phase. Alzheimer's disease may be seen as "presenile dementia," as decline in intellectual functioning may start in forties or fifties versus approximately seventy-five in senile dementia.

amenorrhea   Absence of menstrual flow or an abnormal stoppage of menstrual flow. It is often due to physical and/or emotional problems, for example, anorexia nervosa.

amine   Any of a group of compounds prepared from ammonia; organic compounds containing nitrogen. See *monoamines.*

amino acid   Organic compounds that form the basic building blocks of protein, consisting of an amino group (NH_2) and a carboxyl group (COOH).

amino-acid supplement   A food supplement that contains the complete amino-acid complex.

Amitril   Trade name for the antidepressant amitriptyline-hydrochloride.

amitriptyline   Antidepressant drug known under the trade name of Elavil, Amitril, Emitrip, Endep, SK-Amitriptyline.

amphetamine   Central nervous stimulant sometimes used in the treatment of depression and other disorders.

amygdala   Part of the brain's limbic system (also known as the feeling system), consisting of an almond shape mass of gray matter on the bottom sides of the cerebellum. See *cerebellum.*

anabolism   The phase of metabolism that involves the conversion of simple organic substances into complex organic substances; the process of building up energy. See *catabolism* and *metabolism.*

anaclitic   Leaning against or depending on someone or something; the development of a child's love for a parent, especially the mother.

androgen   Male hormone responsible for sexual development and produced by testes and adrenal cortex, includes androsterone and testosterone.

anorexia   Lack or loss of appetite, or desire.

anorexia nervosa   Lack or loss of appetite due to emotional problems; found mostly in adolescent girls who have an abnormal body image with an obsession for leanness and fear of obesity. Symptoms include emaciation, amenorrhea, and so forth.

anterior pituitary gland   The front lobe of the pituitary gland which is located at the base of the brain and controlled by the hypothalamus. The hormones released by the anterior pituitary gland include FSH, TSH, ACTH, LH, and LTH.

antibody   A complex molecule known as immunoglobulin which is produced by lymph tissue and reacts against bacteria or other infectious organisms in the body.

antidepressants Drugs used in the prevention and treatment of depression. Included are the tetracyclic, quadracyclic, and tricyclic antidepressants, such as, Amitril, Elavil, Norpramin, Adapin, Sinequan, Tofranil, Aventyl, and so forth. Any one of these drugs may produce adverse or side effects, for instance, tricyclic antidepressants cause mania in about 10 percent of the depressed patients. If it is not recognized that the mania is a direct result of the drug, then this could lead to major diagnostic and therapeutic errors.

antioxidant A substance that protects other substances from oxidation.

anxiety Generalized state of mild-to-severe worry and apprehension. A symptom of many neuroses, the cause is often difficult to identify. A distinction is to be made of endogenous and exogenous anxiety. Physical symptoms include dizzy spells, lightheadedness, faintness, loss of balance, palpitations, chest pains and headaches; emotional symptoms include obsessions, compulsions, derealization, depersonalization, panic reactions, phobias, fears, and depression. About 13 million people in the USA suffer from anxiety disorders. See *panic disorder.*

anxiety neurosis Irrational behavior with anxiety as the principal complaint.

apathy Indifference and lack of interest; especially the absence of excitement. The suppression of emotion, concern and passion normally found under similar circumstances.

arteriosclerosis A disorder of the arteries resulting in decreased blood flow and other physical and mental symptoms. Includes calcification, loss of elasticity, and hardening of the arterial walls.

ascorbic acid Vitamin C; A water-soluble vitamin which is essential for normal connective tissue, bone and skin development. Necessary for wound healing, cell and blood vessels and numerous other functions. Vitamin C is stress-reductive. A shortage of vitamin C produces many physical problems, including impairment of adrenal function. Normal value in blood plasma is 0.5 to 2.0 mg/dl. Ascorbic acid is important for the formation of the neurotransmitters norepinephrine and serotonin. Dosages above 300 mg. per day, however, might reduce the effectiveness of tricyclic antidepressants. See *antidepressants.*

Asendin Trade name for the antidepressant drug Amoxapine.

atherosclerosis A disorder of the arteries resulting in decreased blood flow and other physical and mental symptoms. Includes plaque formation on the walls of the arteries, consisting of cholesterol and any of a group of greasy organic compounds.

atypical depression A chronic subclinical form of unipolar depression. Usually external circumstances lead to the start of the depression. There may be a relationship with personality disorders especially *borderline personality disorder.* Characteristics of the dependent, narcissistic, and hysterical personality may also be found. The individuals are extremely sensitive to rejection, mood is worse in the evening, appetite is good, and there are periods of deep and long sleep. They can often function in the world of work. Anxiety, panic attacks, and phobias (agoraphobia) are often present. More women than men have atypical depression. Many of the characteristics of neurotic depression might be found including: chronic low self-esteem, dysphoric mood, manipulative suicidal gestures, extreme sensitivity to separation from loved objects, low threshold for alcohol, and for sedative-hypnotics (barbiturates, minor tranquilizers, chloral hydrate). Tricyclic antidepressants are commonly prescribed for atypical depression, as well as MAOi's (Phenelzine). Psychotherapy, however, is important for resolving underlying character pathology. See *dysthymia* and *neurotic depression*. Compare with *depressive illness*.

autonomic nervous system That part of the nervous system that controls involuntary functions such as breathing and digestion. Also known as involuntary or vegetative nervous system, it is divided into the sympathetic nervous system (which is responsible for such functions as the constriction of the peripheral blood vessels, increase of blood pressure and heart rate, and dilation of pupils) and the parasympathetic system (which is responsible for slowing the heart rate, inducing the secretion of insulin, digestive juices, and bile, and other functions such as the dilation of the peripheral blood vessels). See *nervous system*.

Aventyl Trade name for the antidepressant drug nortriptyline-hydrochloride.

avitaminosis Vitamin deficiency due to lack of a vitamin in the diet, or malabsorption or poor utilization.

axon That process of a nerve cell along which a nerve impulse passes away from the cell body to the site of action or response; a nerve fiber extending from the cell body of a neuron. Also see *neuron, neurotransmitters,* and *synapse*.

B cell A white blood cell developed in the bone marrow which is important to the body's immune system, fighting off bacteria and other foreign substances. Also see *blood cell*.

bacteria Small, one-celled microorganisms found in air, soil, and water. They may be harmless, harmful, or beneficial to the body; they are rod-shaped (bacillus), spherical (coccus), spiral (spirochete), or comma-shaped (vibrio).

barbiturates Drugs that decrease brain and spinal cord activities, used for sedation and potentially habit forming.

basal body temperature Lowest body temperature which is found in the morning before rising or performing any activity. Armpit temperature (taken for ten minutes) should be in the range of 97.8 to 98.2 degrees Fahrenheit.

basophil A type of white blood cell. Normal value is 0 to 0.5% of total white blood cell count.

behavior modification A method for changing unwanted behavior into wanted behavior. Appropriate behavior is rewarded and thus reinforced, while inappropriate behavior is ignored or punished and thus extinguished.

biochemical Pertaining to any aspect of a chemical process in a living organism.

bioflavonoid Chemical substances found especially in fruits and which are essential for the metabolism of vitamin C, and for the walls of the tiny blood vessels known as capillaries.

biotin B-complex vitamin which is important for body growth and synthesis of vitamin C, and necessary for carbohydrate, fat, and protein metabolism. Relieves depression caused by a deficiency of this vitamin.

bipolar depression A mental/emotional disorder which is characterized by up and down mood swings. An endogenous disorder it is sometimes classified as manic depression, manic, depressed, or mixed type. An up or down mood swing may be dominant at a given time, or they may alternate, or both may be present. Medication especially in conjunction with psychotherapy and a proper diet have been found helpful. See *endogenous depression.*

blood-brain barrier A natural barrier between brain tissue and circulating blood; the prevention of large molecules in the blood to enter the brain or the fluid that surrounds the brain.

blood cell Any of the cells that are found in blood. There are two types, namely erythrocytes (red cells) and leukocytes (white cells). The latter are made up of granulocytes, lymphocytes, and monocytes. Also found in the blood are so called platelets which are disc-shaped structures that are essential for blood coagulation. See *blood count.*

blood count A measure of the numbers of different cells found in the blood. They are measured per one cubic centimeter of blood (mm), or as the number of cells per liter (L). Counting the number of different blood cells is helpful in the diagnosis of illness. The following are normal values: Red cells in a male from 4.6 to 6.2 mil/mm³ (4.6 to 6.2×10^{12}L). Red cells in a female from 4.2 to 5.4 mil/mm³ (4.2 to 5.4×10^{12}L). White cells, male or female 5000 to 10.000/mm³ (5 to 10×10^9L). Specific types of white blood cells (differential leucocyte count).

Neutrophils from 60 to 70% of total number of white cells.
Lymphocytes from 20 to 30% of total number of white cells.
Monocytes from 2 to 6% of total number of white cells.
Eosinophils from 1 to 4% of total number of white cells.
Basophils from 0 to 0.5% of total number of white cells.
Platelet count is from 150,000 to 350,000 (150 to 350×10^6L).
See *erythrocytes, hemoglobin, hematocrit, leucocytes, leucopenia, lymphocytes.*

blood plasma The lymph or fluid portion of the blood.

blood urea nitrogen (BUN) Primarily a kidney function test, it indicates the amount of urea nitrogen in the blood. Great increases may be found in acute kidney inflammation (nephritis) and other kidney disorders. Very low levels may be a sign of inadequate protein intake or liver disease. During pregnancy the values are below normal. Normal values, usually determined from blood serum, range from 10 to 18 mg/dl urea nitrogen.

body temperature Heat intensity of the body as controlled by the hypothalamus in the brain. Body temperature varies with many internal and external influences, such as time of day (lowest on awakening), surrounding air temperature, level of activity, metabolism, and illness. Normal value in adults is 98.6°F (37°C) with a range of 96.5°F to 99°F measured orally. See *basal body temperature.*

brain The total mass of highly developed nervous tissue found at the upper end of the central nervous system and located within the skull with a weight of about 1400 grams for an adult. The brain consists of two hemispheres and can be divided into the hindbrain (cerebellum, pons varolii, and medulla oblongata), midbrain, and forebrain (diencephalon and cerebellum, pons, and medulla oblongata. Each hemisphere has special functions. The left hemisphere is more rational and analytical and the right hemisphere is more artistic, intuitive, and visual. One of the two hemispheres is usually more dominant in a given person. Left or right hemisphere dominance may perhaps have some influence on moods. So-called right-brain thinkers—the more creative types—may well be more optimistic, extroverted, and happy. See *central nervous system, cerebellum, cerebral cortex,* and *cerebrum.*

bulimia Insatiable overeating, which may be of an endogenous nature (lesion of the hypothalamus), or an exogenous nature as found in people with emotional difficulties. Periods of overeating may also alternate with periods of not eating as in the case of anorexia nervosa. Depression is often found in those suffering from bulimia. See *anorexia nervosa.*

buproprion An antidepressant marketed under the trade name of Wellbutrin.

C: vitamin See *ascorbic acid.*

caffeine A central nervous system alkaloid stimulant found in coffee, tea, many carbonated beverages, and numerous other products, including various drugs. It is addictive and harmful to health.

calcium Important mineral for the transmission of nerve impulses and many other functions. It aids general metabolism, helps reduce fatigue, and has a tranquilizing effect. It is stress-reductive and important in dietary treatment of depression. Normal values in blood serum range from 8.5 to 10.5 mg/dl.

calciferol One of the D vitamins (D_2) also known as ergocalciferol and found in milk and fish liver oils. See *D: vitamin.*

calorie A measure of a unit of energy; the amount of heat required to raise one gram of water by one degree on the centigrade scale.

candidiasis A fungus infection caused by the fungus candida albicans, and resulting in numerous physical and mental problems including endometriosis, gastrointestinal complaints, poor memory, feelings of unreality, mood swings, and depression.

carbohydrate Chemical compound consisting of carbon, hydrogen, and oxygen; the body's chief source of energy. Carbohydrates include starches, celluloses, gums, and sugars. The latter can be classified into monosaccharides, disaccharides, polysaccharides, and heretosaccharides. Disturbances of carbohydrate metabolism are found in certain depressions. Some people can become fatigued by the excessive use of carbohydrates, especially refined carbohydrates, with insulin overreacting to high blood-sugar levels. Fatigue and depression may also result from low levels of serotonin. This condition can be altered by an increase in tryphophan. This amino acid, however, needs carbohydrate to help it reach the brain. See *carbohydrate connection, tryptophan,* and *serotonin.*

carbohydrate connection This theory explains that carbohydrate rather than protein is responsible for the increased levels of trytophan in the brain and eventual increased levels of serotonin. It is true that high-protein foods contain the necessary tryptophan and make it available to the bloodstream.

However, it cannot reach the brain without the help of carbohydrate which raises insulin levels. Insulin reduces the levels of amino acids, such as tyrosin, that are competing for limited access to the brain. Tryptophan, however, seems to be immune to the insulin response. Thus the sequence of increased carbohydrate, increased insulin, decreased amino acid levels is an advantage to tryptophan, the amino acid that is needed for increased levels of serotonin. If the objective is to stay awake and alert, it is best to concentrate on high-protein foods. If the objective is to become more relaxed, or to induce sleep, then high-carbohydrate foods would be emphasized. For most people, it would make sense to start the day with a high-protein breakfast. On the other hand, the evening meal might include high-protein *and* high-carbohydrate foods, increasing the chances of sounder sleep. High-protein foods include beef, cheese, cottage cheese, eggs, milk, nuts, yogurt. High-carbohydrate foods include apples, bananas, whole-wheat bread, fruit, oatmeal, and watermelon. See *carbohydrate, tryptophan, serotonin.*

carcinogenic Cancer producing.

carotene A pigment found in certain foods such as carrots and egg yolks, consisting of hydrocarbon; known as a provitamin it is converted by the body into vitamin A.

CAT scan *computerized axial tomography.*

catabolism The reduction of complex substances in living cells into simpler forms, with the release of energy. Compare with *anabolism.*

catecholamines The collective name for the neurotransmitters dopamine, norepinephrine, and epinephrine. These neurotransmitters are converted in the brain from tyrosine, an amino acid found in protein. The catecholamines induce wakefulness and suppress sleep. This highlights the importance of a high-protein breakfast, especially for those who suffer from fatique or depression. Carbohydrates have the opposite effect. Via the so-called carbohydrate connection, they enable tryptophan, another amino acid, to reach the brain where it converts into serotonin. Serotonin is a neurotransmitter which, among other effects, is associated with sleep. See *carbohydrate, carbohydrate connection, dopamine, epinephrine, norepinephrine,* and *tyrosine.*

catharsis Purging of the mind; the discharge of pent-up emotions (known as abreaction) such as anger, fear, love, hate, and so forth. Important for the treatment of anxiety, depression, and other mental/emotional problems.

CBC Complete blood count. See *blood count.*

cell The smallest basic structure of living material, consisting of a main mass known as cytoplasm, an outer membrane known as the cell membrane, and a nucleus which is the control center of the cell. See *blood count.*

central nervous system The brain and spinal cord; one of two main divisions of the nervous system, it is the main control center of the body and is responsible for the integration of information dealing with the peripheral nervous system. See *peripheral nervous system.*

cerebellum Often called the "little brain," it is the mass of nervous tissue located above and behind the medulla at the top of the spinal cord, which controls voluntary muscular activity.

cerebral cortex That part of the brain which is concerned with higher mental functions. The conscious center for perception and thought. It is divided into several functional regions and includes the sensory cortex, the motor cortex, and association areas. The cerebral cortex consists of an intricately folded grayish rind of tissue covering the cerebrum; it makes up about 40% of the brain and is composed of about 15 billion nerve cells. Perception, memory, thought, intellect, and mental ability all reside in the cerebral cortex, which has the power of voluntary control, choice, and direction, and has links with every part of the body. Proper use of the cerebral cortex enables people to succeed in staying alive as long as possible and as happily as possible.

cerebrum The largest part of the human brain divided into a right and left hemisphere, each of which is covered by the cerebral cortex.

change of life See *climacteric.*

characterologic neurotic depression See *neurotic depression.*

chlordiazepoxide Minor tranquilizer used for anxiety and marketed under the trade name of Librium.

chloride A compound usually consisting of only two elements, of which chlorine is one. A chemical conductor of electricity (electrolyte) chloride is found in blood serum together with other ions such as potassium, sodium, and others. Normal value in blood serum ranges from 98 to 109 mEq/L (98 to 109 mmol/L).

chlorpromazine A major tranquilizer marketed under the trade name Thorazine and frequently used in the treatment of agitated depression, psychotic disorders, and severe nausea and vomiting. See *tranquilizers.*

choline B-complex vitamin and fat emulsifier. Choline is important for nerve impulse transmission. It is necessary for the manufacture of the neurotransmitter acetylcholine. Also aids the healthy functioning of brain cells and the retention of mental function in older people. Choline is stress reductive, however, in very high dosages (3,000 mg/day or more) may cause depression.

chromium A mineral that is necessary for insulin effectiveness, the manufacture of the Glucose Tolerance Factor (GTF) and the regulation of blood sugar. Aids in the proper utilization of carbohydrates and the control of both hyper and hypoglycemia. Important in dietary treatment of depression.

chronic Continuing for a long time, or occurring with great frequency.

chronic depression See *atypical depression, dysthymia,* and *neurotic depression.*

climacteric The period of physical, mental/emotional, and hormonal changes that take place at the end of a woman's reproductive period, ending with the menopause and the cessation of reproductive capability. Popularly known as "change of life."

cognition The act or process of knowing. Cognition includes the ability to perceive, think, recognize, and remember.

compulsion Irresistible action to do something which the individual does not really wish to do, nor understands, but nevertheless feels impelled to do.

computerized axial tomography The examination of soft body tissues with an X-ray scanner that records "slices" of the tissues which are later integrated by a computer to provide a cross-sectional picture revealing pathological conditions if present. See *positron emission tomography (PET)*.

congenital   Present at birth.

Conn's syndrome   Adrenal cortex disorder often caused by a benign tumor releasing too much aldosterone. Consequently the salt-water balance is upset leading to symptoms of convulsions, muscular cramps, twitching, weakness, abnormal skin sensations, and other disturbances. See *adrenal cortex* and *aldosterone*.

corpus callosum   The bridge between the two brain hemispheres.

cortex   The outer part of an organ.

corticosteroid   Any of a group of hormones produced by the adrenal cortex, including glucocorticoids (cortisone, cortisol, corticosterone), and mineralocorticoids (for example, aldosterone), or their synthetic counterparts. Excessive production of corticosteroids by the body may lead to depression, while those taken as a medication may lead to euphoria. See *cortisol* and *ketosteroids*.

corticosterone   Adrenal cortex hormone; regulates salt retention.

cortisol   Adrenal cortex hormone; necessary for carbohydrate metabolism. High levels of cortisol increase the enzyme tryptophanase, which in turn lowers the amino-acid tryptophan, which then results in lower levels of the neurotransmitter serotonin, and perhaps depression. Low levels of cortisol, however, lead to excessive glucose utilization, which may be followed by hypoglycemia and perhaps depression. The normal blood plasma values for cortisol (hydrocortisone) are at 8:00AM, 10-15 ug/dl (300-700 nmol/L), and at 8:00PM, 4-13 ug/dl (110-350 nmol/L).

cortisone   Adrenal cortex hormone; necessary for carbohydrate metabolism.

creatine   A nitrogenous compound synthesized in the body and found in blood and muscle. Phosphorylated creatine (phosphocreatine) is a high energy source for muscle contraction.

creatinine   A substance obtained from creatine and creatine phosphate, and excreted in urine. Normal value in blood serum is 0.6 to 1.2 mg/dl.

Cushing's disease   An endocrine disorder resulting from excessive release of ACTH by the pituitary gland, which in turn leads to increased release of adrenal cortex hormones. Symptoms include high blood sugar, muscle weakness, and excessive fat on back, chest, and face. See *adrenal cortex* and *pituitary gland*.

Cushing's syndrome   An endocrine disorder resulting from excessive release of cortisol by the adrenal cortex. Symptoms include high blood pressure, weight gain, a moon face, excessive growth of body and facial hair in females (hypertrichosis), kyphosis, amenorrhea, muscular weakness, and an increase in the number of red blood cells. There are also many mental or emotional disturbances, including depression. See *adrenal cortex, cortisol,* and *hyperadrenocorticism*.

cyanocobalamin   Vitamin B_{12}. Also known as Cobalamin, it is essential for normal metabolism and the healthy functioning of the nervous system. Often a depression is directly related to a shortage of this vitamin. Deficiencies may be due to poor diet or nutrient malabsorption. B_{12} is used for the prevention and treatment of pernicious anemia. Strict vegetarians may have a special need for B_{12} supplementation.

cyclothymia Alternating moods of elation and dejection. Less severe than the alternating moods of euphoria and depression seen in bipolar-depressive illness. People who chronically demonstrate cyclothymia are said to have a cyclothemic personality. Cyclothymia is a low level, chronic, form of bipolar depression. Typically we find alternating depressive (gloomy, pessimistic, worrisome) and hyperthymic (cheerful, optimistic, vigorous) traits. Cyclothymia is less common than other chronic depressions such as atypical and neurotic depression. Cyclothymia may be a childhood or adolescent precursor of bipolar depression. See *personality disorder (cyclothymic personality)*.

D: vitamin Vitamin D is necessary for the absorption of calcium and phosphorus, healthy thyroid and parathyroid functioning, and has multiple other functions such as aiding the utilization of vitamin A. There are forms of vitamin D, namely calciferol, ergosterol, and viosterol.

deductive reasoning The process of arriving at conclusions by reasoning from the general to the specific based on known or assumed facts or events.

deficiency disease A disease arising from lack of essential nutrients, especially vitamins and minerals.

degenerative disorder Any disorder resulting in progressive lowering or loss of function.

déjà vu A sudden belief or impresion of great familiarity in a strange place or situation.

delusion A strongly held belief in violation of objective reality, that cannot be changed in spite of logical argument and evidence to the contrary. In psychotic individuals we may find the belief that the individual is an exalted personage (delusion of grandeur); the belief that the person is being plotted against (delusion of persecution); or the belief that chance happenings concern the individual (delusion of reference); the morbid belief that some body part is missing (delusion of negation); the belief that the self or external reality no longer exists (nihilistic delusion); a belief in one's own total unworthiness (depressive delusion), and many other forms. See *hallucinations, mental health,* and *psychosis.*

dementia Organic brain disorder leading to progressive mental decline. Symptoms include memory loss, reasoning difficulties, disorientation, personality changes, lack of personal care. At any age (but especially in the elderly) dementia may be the result of drug intoxication, metabolic conditions arising from poor diets, metabolic disease, or other correctible causes. Presenile dementia may be found in young or middle-aged people. It is important to carefully and properly evaluate each case and to make distinctions between Alzheimer's disease, Pick's disease, senile dementia, and other conditions. See *Alzheimer's disease, AIDS dementia complex, Pick's disease,* and *Senile dementia.*

dendrite A branch or treelike part usually with short fibers at the receiving end of a nerve cell, conveying messages to the nerve cell body.

dependence The reliance on others for comfort, nurturance, or assistance.

depersonalization A more or less pathological condition where a person loses awareness of his or her own identity or body. It may be associated with anxiety, depression, manic-depressive disorder or psychosis, or schizophrenia.

depressant   Any drug or other agent that diminishes a functional activity, especially a body part or system.

depression   A multifaceted body-mind-spirit stress disorder that can result from personal choice, physical disorders, loss of spiritual direction, or hereditary factors. In its simplest form depression is a negative emotive feeling, resulting from misperceptions and misbeliefs. As a multifaceted psychosomatogenic stress disorder we can identify both organic and nonorganic syndromes which are characterized by thought and mood disturbances as primary symptoms. As a general observation it can be said that depression is a disorder of the total person, a stress disorder, thinking disorder, and a complex disorder with many sources which are identifiable as physical variables, which ultimately may lead to loss of physical balance; emotional, mental, and social variables, that may lead to loss of psychological integration; and, spiritual variables that may lead to loss of spiritual direction.

Depression may be divided into two main divisions, namely endogenous and exogenous depression with scores of corresponding symptoms in babies, children, adolescents, and adults. Depression may be mild and temporary, moderate, or severe, and often long lasting. About 75% of all depressed people suffer from mild to moderately severe depressions that are caused by misperceptions and misbeliefs and do not require drug treatment. On the other hand, fifteen out of twenty different types of depression have a physical basis, pointing to various physical disturbances, many of these can be corrected by diet, exercise, and a more rational lifestyle in general.

Only about 10 to 15% of the depressed population are good candidates for drug therapy, while 100% of the depressed population may benefit by physical restoration, emotional re-education, and spiritual regeneration. By following a wholistic treatment plan which recognizes that depressions are always based on a combination of vulnerability and choice, paying proper attention to intelligence, training, education, opportunity, heredity, congenital, and other variables, as well as an individual's willingness to get well, it is possible to have victory over virtually any form of depression. The wholistic treatment of depression requires an evaluation and treatment of the total person, always remembering that the body is subject to the mind, that the mind is subject to God, and that every part of the mind is in some way influenced by, and dependent on the body. The national increase in depression is in part a reflection of an irrational and self-destructive society, where individual citizens work hard at creating conditions that are conducive to poor physical, mental, and spiritual health. It is important to make a distinction between depression and depressive illness. See *depressive illness.*

depressive illness   A severe, endogenous, usually genetically linked, depression. Included in depressive illness are *agitated* and *involutional depression,* but especially *unipolar depression* (other names are major depression, endogenous depression, melancholia, or psychotic depression), and *bipolar depression* (also known as manic-depression). Unipolar depression is believed to be inherited polygenically, and bipolar (manic) depression is believed to be inherited via single X-linked or autosomal dominant genes.

A diagnosis of *major depression* is made when the main features are a morbid sadness, hopelessness, and helplessness, with a duration of the episodes typically lasting from 3 to 9 months. The age of onset is usually in the 40s, affecting more women than men, who usually have a compulsive or passive dependent personality. In addition to the major depressive symptoms there need to be at least four of the following symptoms as well: (1) lack of appetite; (2) unplanned weight loss; (3) insomnia or hypersomnia; (4) agitation or retardation; (5) loss of energy; (6) feelings of worthlessness or self-blame; (7) slow or indecisive thinking; (8) thoughts of death or suicide. A person with major depression usually feels worse in the morning and better as the day goes on and has decreased sexual desire. Lithium is usually ineffective in the acute phase of major depression. The onset of major depression may be abrupt or insidious. A family history of alcoholism or unipolar illness is often found.

A diagnosis of *bipolar* (manic) *depression* is made when there is a documented history of an episode (or episodes) of both depression and mania. In the *manic phase* we typically find euphoria, excessive talkativeness, sleeplessness, irritability, easy distractibility, racing thoughts, rapid movements, incoherent thought patterns, and sometimes delusions of grandeur. In the depressive phase sadness, despair, hopelessness, self-criticism, slowness of movements, delusions of unworthiness or persecution, and suicidal thoughts. Bipolar depression phases are of a shorter duration than those found in unipolar depression. The onset in bipolar depression is often abrupt, starting in the 30s and is more commonly found in people with extroverted, cyclothymic, or compulsive personalities. A family history of alcoholism and bipolar or unipolar illness is often found. Lithium is the drug of choice in the treatment of bipolar depression. Manic depressed persons function very well in between acutely high or low periods. Many successful and famous people have suffered from bipolar depression, including Winston Churchill and Abraham Lincoln. The overwhelming majority of depressions (85 to 90%) do *not* constitute depressive illness. See *atypical depression, bipolar depression, dysthymia, endogenous depression, manic depression,* and *psychosis.*

depressive neurosis See *dysthymia.*

dereistic thinking Unrealistic and illogical thinking. If severe it may be a symptom of mental illness.

detoxification Reduction or removal of poisonous properties, or neutralizing of toxic effects.

dexamethasone A corticosteroid drug used primarily in the treatment of allergies, inflammatory conditions, and hormonal disturbances.

Dexedrine Trade name for dextroamphetamine; a central-nervous-system stimulant simular to amphetamine.

dextrose A monosaccharide, or simple sugar $(C_6H_{12}O_6H_2O)$, also known as dextroglucose or glucose.

diabetes An endocrine disorder in which excessive amounts of urine are passed. There is a major distinction between *diabetes insipidus* and *diabetes mellitus*.

diabetes insipidus A fairly rare metabolic disorder that is sometimes caused by damage to the pituitary gland by surgery, radiation therapy, other forms of trauma, or it may be due to lesions. Most of the time, however, the cause for the disorder is unknown. The main symptoms are the passing of large amounts of colorless urine and an unquenchable thirst. Effective treatment is usually obtained with synthetic antidiuretic hormone (ADH).

diabetes mellitus A fairly common metabolic disorder which is due to failure of the pancreas to produce needed insulin. High levels of glucose in the blood (hyperglycemia) and low absorption of glucose by the cells and liver. Symptoms include excessive urination, thirst, weakness, tiredness, loss of weight, tingling in hands and feet, urinary tract infections, blurred vision. The disorder can result from various other disorders such as acromegaly, hyperthyroidism, Cushing's syndrome, and pancreatitis.

Diagnostic and Statistical Manual of Mental Disorders. See *DSM III*.

diazepam A minor tranquilizer marketed under the trade name of Valium.

diencephalon The hind part of the forebrain which includes the hypothalamus, thalamus, metathalamus, and epithalamus.

diethyl tryptamine (DMT) A hallucinogenic synthetic substance.

differential leucocyte count The counting of specific types of white blood cells. See *blood count*.

dilantin An anticonvulsant drug.

disaccharides Carbohydrates such as sucrose, maltose, and lactose, consisting of double sugar molecules. In the digestive process they are broken down into single sugars, for example, *sucrose,* becomes glucose and fructose; *maltose* becomes glucose, and *lactose* becomes glucose and galactose.

discernment The ability to perceive and think clearly and to distinguish between two or more choices, facts, events, and so forth. For example the ability to discern what is good and what is bad.

disorder A derangement of physical, mental and/or spiritual health.

disorientation Mental confusion in regard to one's own identity, or of other persons and objects, or confusion in regard to time and place. The cause may be severe stress, drugs, physical disorders, and so forth.

dissociation A neurotic reaction to certain painful thoughts, emotions, and experiences, which are completely removed from consciousness, or separated from the rest of our conscious life. *Amnesia* and *somnambulism* are two common dissociative reactions. In *amnesia* people do not know who they are, or where they have come from. There is a total or partial loss of memory in regard to past experiences. Amnesia is usually the result of an experience that is so painful that it had to be blotted out of the memory. In *somnambulism* or sleepwalking, we find that people get up during their sleep and start walking about. Actually the person is in half-a-dream and half-a-waking state. While there is contact with the environment, it is part of a dream. Consequently any verbal response will be as part of the dream that the person is experiencing. *Multiple personality* is also a dissociative disorder. Here differing personality traits are so pronounced that it seems as if different people are living in the same body, each one being predominant at various times. See *neurosis* and *neurotic disorder.*

diurnal   Pertaining to daytime.

DNA   Abbreviation for "deoxyribonucleic acid," a complex chemical which contains the genetic code that is responsible for human development.

dopamine   An important chemical substance in the brain and elsewhere in the body. As a neurotransmitter dopamine is involved in the chemical transmission of nerve impulses. The dopamine hypothesis holds that excessive amounts of dopamine in the brain may lead to psychotic reactions, for example schizophrenia. Low levels of dopamine may be a causative factor in depression. See *neurotransmitters.*

doxepin   Tricyclic antidepressant drug marketed under the trade names of Adapin and Sinequan. See *antidepressants.*

DSM-III   *Diagnostic and Statistical Manual of Mental Disorders.* First adopted in 1952 as the official classification system of mental disorders by the American Psychiatric Association. Revised in 1968, in collaboration with the World Health Organization, it became known as the DSM-II. Revised again in 1980, it is now known as the DSM-III. Mood disorders described in this manual include:

1. *Manic disorder*
   hypomania
   hypomanic psychosis
   mania
   manic-depressive psychosis
      or reaction (hypomanic or manic)
2. *Major depressive disorder*
   depressive psychosis
   endogenous depression
   involutional melancholia
   manic-depressive psychosis
      (or reaction) depressed type
   monopolar (unipolar) depression
   psychotic depression
3. *Bipolar affective disorder*
   bipolar disorder (manic)
   manic-depressive psychosis, circular type (currently manic).
   bipolar disorder (depressed).
   manic-depressive psychosis, circular type (currently depressed).
   bipolar disorder (mixed).
   manic-depressive psychosis circular type (mixed).
4. *Manic-depressive psychosis*
   manic-depressive psychosis (unspecified)
   manic-depressive reaction or syndrome.
   manic-depressive psychosis (mixed).
5. *Unspecified and other affective psychoses*
   affective psychosis (unspecified)
   melancholia (unspecified)
   Mood swings (brief compensatory or rebound)

6. *Depressive type psychosis*
   psychogenic depressive psychosis
   psychotic reactive depression
   reactive depressive psychosis
7. *Atypical affective disorders*
   atypical bipolar affective disorder
   manic-depressive psychosis, circular type.
   atypical manic disorder
   atypical depressive disorder
8. *Neurotic depression*
   anxiety depression
   depression with anxiety
   depressive reaction
   neurotic depression
   reactive depression
9. *Affective personality disorders*
   affective personality disorder
   chronic hypomanic personality disorder
   depressive character or personality
   cyclothymic personality
10. *Depressive reactions*
    brief depressive reaction
    grief reaction
    prolonged depressive reaction

dysfunction   Malfunctioning, disturbance, impairment, or otherwise abnormal functioning of a body part or organ.

dysfunctional abreaction   The inappropriate and counterproductive release of emotional tension through excessive acting out, verbalization, and reflecting on the past.

dysthymia   Also known as *dysthymic disorder* or *depressive neurosis*. Dysthymia is a moderately severe, chronic, subclinical form of unipolar depression. Mental health specialists who use the *DSM-III* (see Glossary), will only make this diagnosis if the depression is at least of *two years duration,* with normal moods lasting only a few days, weeks, or at the most a few months. The depressive periods are marked by either a noticeably depressed mood or loss of interest in almost all regular activities; *at least three specific depressive symptoms* are present during these moods (for example, inability to sleep or too much sleep, lack of energy, fatigue, loss of a sense of personal worth, less effective or productive, less able to think or clearly concentrate, irritable or excessively angry, unresponsive to praise or rewards, tearfulness, crying, thoughts of death or suicide, less talkative than usual, pessimism, brooding, self-pity, social withdrawal), and absence of psychotic features. And if superimposed on a previously existing disorder then this must be clearly different than the person's usual mood. Tricyclic antidepressants (Pertofrane/Norpramin) and lithium carbonate have been used in the treatment of dysthymia. See *atypical depression* and *neurotic depression*. (Compare with *depressive illness*.)

dysthymic disorder   See *dysthymia*.

E: vitamin   Fat soluble vitamins (tocopherols). They are important for blood cell production and reproductive function. Tocopherol is an alcohol with the properties of vitamin E and is obtained from wheat germ oil. Synthetic vitamin E is known as A (alpha) tocopherol. Vitamin E is an anti-oxidant, antisterility, and anticoagulant vitamin, and has multiple functions. Good sources for vitamin E include eggs, nuts, soybeans, and vegetable oils.

echolalia   The automatic and meaningless repetition of another person's words. Usually a symptom of mental-emotional disturbance.

ECT   See Electroconvulsive Shock.

edema   Swelling caused by abnormally large amount of fluids in spaces between cells.

effectors   Those muscles or glands that cause muscular contraction or glandular secretion, or any structure or gland that causes activity in a muscle or gland.

efferent   Any nerve or blood vessel that carries "outward," that is away from the center. Refers specifically to blood or nerve vessels that carry blood or impulses away from a central location. For example a nerve that carries impulses from the brain to a gland, muscle, and so forth.

efferent neuron   Neuron which carries impulses from the central nervous system.

ego   An individual's conscious self, or rational part of the personality.

electroconvulsive shock   Also known as electroconvulsive therapy (ECT), electroshock, or shock therapy. Used in the treatment of some mental disorders, specifically in cases of severe depression. A brief convulsion results from the passing of a very quick (less than one-half a second) electric current. This leads to unconsciousness and convulsions (involuntary muscle contractions), with the patient awakening in a short period of time. Much controversy surrounds this practice which is now used less and less, as it is being replaced by drug therapy.

electrolyte   Any substance in the body that dissociates into ions and becomes capable of conducting an electric current. Electrolytes such as calcium, potassium, and sodium need to be available in well-balanced amounts in the human body. The normal balance may be affected by glandular dysfunction, illness, and/or malnutrition.

emotion   A complex state of pleasant or unpleasant arousal. An emotion is a feeling state (emotive feeling), however, it cannot be separated from physical changes occurring in the body involving the central nervous system, endocrine system, gastrointestinal system. An emotive feeling is a conscious experience and the outcome of perceptions and mental evaluations, all of which are greatly conditioned by heredity and environment. Especially learning (education, training, and experience) plays a major part in the formation of emotions such as anger, hate, love, and so forth.

emotional centers   The hippocampus, septum pellucidum, and amygdala are the emotional centers. They are located in the so-called limbic system of the brain.

emotional depletion   Shallow and flat emotional responses; the absence of strong, healthy, and lively emotions.

emotional distortions The exaggerated and inappropriate expression of emotive feelings.

emotional re-education The process described by Dr. Maultsby, the founder of Rational Behavior Therapy, which enables an individual to replace less desirable habits with more desirable ones. The process has five steps, namely, *intellectual* insight (we know what to do and why); *correct practice* (the actual or vicarious practice of the new behavior); *cognitive dissonance* (we know something is right but it still feels wrong); *emotional insight* (we know something is right and it feels right); *personality trait formation* (the new behavior has become habitual).

emotional repression The repression of such emotions as anger, depression, fear, guilt, and hate, and their disguised expression in psychosomatic illnesses, such as anorexia nervosa, asthma, digestive disorders, high blood pressure, obesity, migraine headaches, rheumatoid arthritis, and many others.

empathy The ability to understand and to some extent share the emotions and experiences of another person.

encephalitis Inflammation of the brain.

endocrine glands Ductless glands (such as the pituitary, thyroid, pancreas) that secrete their substances (hormones) directly into the blood stream for the purpose of finding specific organs and producing necessary effects. Improper functioning of the endocrine glands may lead to many disorders, including depression.

endocrine system The network of glands that, together with the nervous system, coordinates and regulates many of the important functions of the body. The major endocrines and their main hormones are: *adrenal cortex* (glucocorticoids); *adrenal medulla* (adrenaline); *anterior pituitary* (growth hormone (STH); *gonads* (testosterone in males, and estrogen, progesterone in females); *pancreas isles of Langerhans* (insulin); *parathyroid* (parathyroxin); *pineal* (melatonin); *posterior pituitary* (vasopressin); *small intestine* (secretin); *stomach* (gastrin); *thymus* (thymosin); *thyroid* (thyroxin).

endogenous Proceeding from within, for example, as developed within an organism.

endogenous depression Depression caused primarily by biochemical and genetic factors, and only secondarily by psychological factors. Since depressions always involve perceptions and cognitions, there are no purely physical depressions. See *depressive illness*.

endorphins Natural brain chemicals that are believed to play a role in the reduction and elimination of pain and increasing pleasant feelings. See *enkephalins*.

enkephalins Natural brain chemicals that are believed to play a role in the direction of mental activity, behavior, and the body's immune system in the battle against disease. See *endorphins*.

enzyme A protein substance manufactured in cells which causes other processes (for example digestion and respiration) to proceed more rapidly.

eosinopenia Decreased number of eosinophils.

eosinophil White blood cell. Important for resisting some infections.

eosinophil count   The normal count is 100-300 mm³, or 1-3% of the total white blood cell count.

epilepsy   Neurological disorder characterized by convulsion, loss of consciousness, and abnormal behavior. The cause of epilepsy is often unknown, but may include trauma to the head, brain tumors, chemical imbalances, and so forth.

epinephrine   More commonly known as adrenaline, it is a hormone manufactured by the adrenal medulla, a powerful stimulant secreted in times of strong emotion. Epinephrine causes many physiological changes such as increased blood sugar, blood pressure, heart rate, and breathing, and stimulation of the heart muscle, as well as constricting of blood vessels. Epinephrine plays a major role in those depressions (and other disorders) that are related to *hypoglycemia*. Epinephrine also plays a role as a *neurotransmitter*. See *adrenergic, alarm reaction, hypoglycemia,* and *neurotransmitters.*

Equanil   Trade name for the tranquilizer meprobamate.

erythrocytes   Red blood cells containing hemoglobin and transporting oxygen. The normal range of the number of red blood cells in the male is from 4.600.000 to 6.200.000 in one cubic milliliter of blood (4.6-6.2 mil/mm³, and from 4.200.000 to 5.400.000 in one cubic milliliter of blood in the female (4.2-5.4 mil/mm³).

essential amino acids   Those amino acids which cannot be manufactured by our bodies and must be obtained from protein. The essential amino acids are: isoleucine, leucine, methionine, phenylalanine, threonine, tryptophan, histidine, lysine, and valine.

EST   See *electroconvulsive shock.*

estrogen   Female hormones (including estradiol, estrone, and estriol) which are produced by the ovaries. Small quantities of estrogen are manufactured by the adrenal glands and testes. Synthetic preparations are used in the treatment of premenstrual depression (tension), the menopause, and so forth.

euphoria   Exaggerated feeling of well-being which may be found in a manic person. In general it is a heightened feeling of optimism.

exacerbate   Increase in seriousness of an illness or disorder.

excessive stress   The amount of stress the human organism is unable, and/or unwilling to deal with.

exhaustion stage   The third stage in the general adaptation syndrome (stress syndrome), and one of the leading physical sources of depression. It is caused by adrenal exhaustion, as a result of prolonged stress. Adrenal exhaustion may lead to various disorders. See *alarm stage, general adaptation syndrome, hypoadrenalism* and *resistance stage.*

exocrine glands   Glands with a duct or ducts.

exogenous   Something that is derived from external sources, that is, from outside the body. Exogenous depression has external (environmental) sources.

fatty acids   Those organic (carbon-containing) substances that give fats different flavors, textures, and melting points. They are the building blocks of many fats (which contain only one molecule of glycerine, but three molecules of fatty acids). There is a difference between saturated and unsaturated fatty acids. *Saturated fatty acids* are found primarily in animal fats, the use of which may lead to high cholesterol levels in the blood and possible coronary artery and other disorders. *Unsaturated fatty acids* are divided in *monounsaturated fatty acids,* as found in almonds, chicken, and olive oil, and *polyunsaturated fatty acids* as found in corn, fish, safflower and soybean oil. The Wellness Diet recommends a diet high in polyunsaturated fatty acids, and low in saturated fatty acids, so as to achieve low-serum cholesterol levels and other health benefits.

flat affect Abnormal emotional response, where hardly any emotion is expressed regardless of the quality and/or quantity of the stimuli.

fluphenazine Tranquilizer sometimes prescribed for certain psychotic disorders, specifically in the treatment of schizophrenia, as well as for the management of behavioral complications sometimes found in persons with mental retardation. Adverse reactions include blood abnormalities, liver toxicity, and hypotension.

flurazepam Minor tranquilizer often used in the treatment of insomnia. Marketed under the trade name *Dalmane.* The drug is not recommended for children, pregnant women and those with known hypersensitivity to it, or a number of other physical and/or emotional problems. Severely depressed persons should not use this drug. Adverse reactions include daytime sleepiness, dizziness, and drug dependence.

folic acid Antianemia vitamin. Necessary for growth and division of blood cells. One of the B-complex vitamins, it is essential not only for cell growth but also for reproduction. Folic acid works as a co-enzyme with vitamins B_{12} and C in the metabolism of protein and the manufacture of hemoglobin in red blood cells. Folic acid (folate) is also important for amino acid and sugar utilization. It is stress reductive and a deficiency may lead to depression.

follicle stimulating hormone (FSH) A hormone released by the anterior pituitary gland, which stimulates the ripening of the follicles in the ovaries and the formation of sperm in the testes.

food allergy Many people have hypersensitive reactions to certain food substances (usually a protein). Physical symptoms may include diarrhea, bronchial asthma, colitis, nausea, rhinitis, vomiting, and many others. Mental/emotional symptoms may include anger, anxiety, *depression,* restlessness, irrational behavior, violence. Most allergic reactions are due to cane sugar, cow's milk products, eggs, corn, soy products, and yeast. Many other allergic reactions are due to chocolate, citrus fruits, fish, tomatoes, and other common products.

forebrain That portion of the adult brain which is the farthest forward part of the brain. The forebrain consists of the diencephalon (epithalamus, thalamus, hypothalamus, and ventral thalamus) and the two cerebral hemispheres. The forebrain controls sensation, perception, emotion, learning, thinking, and other functions.

free association The uncontrolled release of thoughts and emotions. A method used to enable a person to express any thought or emotion in the hope of freeing repressed experiences and allowing them into conscious awareness.

frontal lobe The forward part of the cerebral cortex, located behind the forehead. The frontal lobe is associated with higher mental functions such as reasoning, planning, and so forth, as well as with personality-trait formation.

frontal lobe syndrome Brain syndrome of an organic nature. We may find lack of concern, initiative, and good feelings, and other major personality changes due to lesions of the frontal lobe.

fructose A simple sugar (monosaccharide) found in fruits, honey, berries, and vegetables. Fructose is the sweetest of all sugars, yet it seems the safest for human consumption. Different sugars and starches have different effects on our blood sugar levels. Surprisingly, fructose causes a lower rise in blood sugar levels than glucose (dextrose), sucrose. Amazingly, fructose causes an even lower rise in blood-sugar levels than is obtained from such complex carbohydrates as bread and potatoes. Fructose, like other carbohydrates, has four calories per gram. While refined carbohydrates such as sucrose are not recommended on the Wellness Diet, the prudent use of "small" amounts of fructose is allowed.

galactose Simple sugar (monosaccharide) derived from milk sugar. It is absorbed in the intestine, converted into glycogen by the liver, and stored there for future glucose needs of the body.

gamma globulin See *immunoglobulins.*

ganglion Collection of nerve cells and synapses.

gastric lipase Digestive enzyme produced by the pancreas and the glands of the small intestine. It is necessary to break down fats into glycerol and fatty acids during the digestive process.

general adaptation syndrome (G.A.S.) General stress syndrome, which highlights the fact that our bodies can adapt only for so long and for so much. Under continued stress the body shows specific reactions which are described as the alarm, resistance, and exhaustion stages. During the *alarm stage* we find increased heart rate, the widening of bronchial tubes, and so forth, to increase our energy levels. During the *resistance stage* we find (with the help of increased secretions of the anterior pituitary and adrenal cortex) that the body fights to maintain normal blood chemistry. There is increased sodium and water retention, and increased energy for the long-term battle of counteracting stress. In the *exhaustion stage* we find that the body can no longer resist the stressors and illness (even death) may result.

genetic Pertaining to heredity.

gigantism Excessive size usually the result of oversecretion of growth hormone by the pituitary gland.

globus hystericus Feeling of a lump in the throat due to functional disturbance of certain muscles and nerves. Caused by emotional difficulties, in particular anxiety and fear.

glucagon A (polypeptide) hormone, secreted by the pancreas, which stimulates the conversion of glycogen to glucose by the liver, and increases blood sugar levels. Glucagon preparations may be used by injection in the treatment of severe low blood sugar.

glucocorticoid A common name used to describe any of several hormones that are secreted by the adrenal cortex. Included are cortisol, cortisone, and corticosterone. The glucocorticoids play a major role in helping the body to fight fatigue and stress; however, continued high levels of cortisol will lead to physical as well as mental/emotional problems. High levels of cortisol are found in about half the people who suffer from endogenous depressions and highlights the hypothesis that depression is a stress disorder. See *cortisol*.

glucose   a simple sugar found in many fruits as well as in animal tissues and fluids. It is an essential nutrient for man, and the main energy source for living organisms. Glucose is absorbed from the intestines into the blood-stream, and is the "only" energy source for the brain. When this energy source fluctuates too much, a number of physical and mental/emotional symptoms may occur. When blood sugar levels fall below acceptable limits, as in the case of hypoglycemia (low blood sugar), we may encounter a number of emotional difficulties, of which "depression" is but one. See *hypoglycemia*.

glucose tolerance test   The oral glucose tolerance test is widely used to check on the body's ability to effectively metabolize carbohydrates. Proper levels of glucose are maintained in the body through the actions of several hormones, mainly glucagon and insulin. Following a period of fasting (usually overnight) the blood glucose level is measured. After the ingestion of 100 grams (more commonly 75 grams) of glucose, the blood glucose levels are checked first after 30 minutes, then hourly for a five (5) and sometimes six (6) hour period. This test will help to show if a person suffers from hyperglycemia (diabetes) or hypoglycemia (low blood sugar), and may also provide helpful data in the diagnosis of such disorders as pituitary deficiency, hypoadrenocorticism, anorexia nervosa, and many others. The glucose tolerance test is normal when the fasting blood glucose level is between 80-120 mg/dl, less than 180 mg/dl at the first hour, and less than 140 mg/dl at the second hour, and in the normal range (80-120 mg/dl) for the third and remaining hours. Ideally the glucose level returns to the normal range, or a normal fasting level, at the second hour and remains there for the duration of the test. See *glucagon* and *insulin*.

glucosuria   Abnormal condition of glucose in the urine.

glycogen   The chief form of stored carbohydrate in the body. Glycogen is stored mainly in the liver and secondarily in muscles. In case of need the glycogen is easily hydrolized (broken down) to glucose.

gonadotropic hormones   Hormones that are synthesized and released by the pituitary gland and stimulate the gonads (testes or ovaries). We distinguish follicle stimulating hormone (FSH), and luteinizing hormone.

gonads   The glands that produce gametes (sex cells); the testes in the male and the ovaries in the female.

grief reaction   The prime example of reactive (moderate) depression. It results from a reaction (interpretation) to significant losses, often involving romance, marriage, or death, but also financial losses, leaving familiar surroundings. Bereavement and loss may make an individual with a genetic predisposition more vulnerable to depressive illness.

growth hormone   The hormone synthesized, stored and released by the anterior pituitary gland. Growth hormone, also known as GH, or somatotropin, is important for protein synthesis and stimulates the growth of long bones in arms and legs.

growth hormone releasing factor (GHRF)   A substance secreted by the hypothalamus which in turn stimulates the anterior pituitary gland to release growth hormone (GH).

Haldol   Trade name for the major tranquilizer haloperidol.

hallucination   The sensory impression of something that has no basis in objective reality, that is, does not actually exist. A hallucination is a false perception and may be of an *auditory nature* (hearing voices or noises) or of a *visual nature* (see objects that are not present in actuality). Hallucinations are often found in schizophrenia; however, they may also occur as the result of head injuries, delirium (from organic brain disease), various toxic states (as alcohol) or from legal and/or illegal drugs. Many of the drugs given for depression, for example, the so-called tricyclic antidepressants (including Amitril, Pertorfane, Adapin, Tofranil, Pamelor, and many others) may result in adverse reactions, of which hallucination is but one. See *delusion, mental health,* and *psychosis.*

hallucinogen   A substance or drug (legal or illegal) that excites the central nervous system and causes mental/emotional changes (including hallucinations), physical changes, including increase in blood pressure, body temperature, and pulse. A common diagnostic indicator is the dilation of the pupils of the eyes. Hallucinogens include lysergic acid diethylamide (LSD), mescaline, peyote, and phencyclidine.

halo effect   The tendency to place a global rating on a person based on one particular trait.

haloperidol   Major tranquilizer marketed under the trade name of Haldol.

healing imagery   Substitute mental practice (in lieu of actual practice) of wholesome self-talk, and desired feelings and behavior, and to be applied to future situations.

hematocrit   The volume percentage of red blood cells in whole blood. Normal range for males: 40-45%, and for females: 37-47%. See *blood count.*

hemispheres   The lateral (side to side) halves of the cerebrum and cerebellum. See *brain.*

hemoglobin   An important substance found in red blood cells and consisting of an iron containing (nonprotein) pigment (heme) and a protein (globin). Hemoglobin transports oxygen to every cell in the body and carries carbon dioxide from the cells. Normal range of hemoglobin for males: 14-18 grams per deciliter (14-18 g/dl), and females: 12-16 grams per deciliter (12-16 g/dl).

hereditary   Any quality, disorder, trait, characteristic, or potential, that is passed on from parents to offspring through the genes.

hereditary potential   Any genetic (inborn) factors or possibilities for development, that may occur when environmental conditions are favorable. A person may have hereditary potential for a certain type of depression, but without certain environmental conditions the illness may not occur, or will occur in varying degrees of severity, length, and number of occurrences. In human behavior we always deal with an interplay of heredity and environment, that is vulnerability and choice, of which the latter is usually the more important.

heredity See *hereditary*.

Hexadrol Trade name for dexamethasone which is an anti-inflammatory substance.

hexose Any of a class of sugars that contain six carbon atoms, for example glucose and fructose.

hippocampus That structure of the brain which is an important part of the limbic system, and identified among other things with olfactory sensitivity, the regulation of emotion, and transferring information from short-term memory to long-term memory. The hippocampus, together with the septum pellucidum, and amygdala are considered the emotional centers of the brain.

holistic See *wholistic*.

homeostasis The balanced state, or tendency to stability, in the normal physiological state of the body. Homeostasis is controlled primarily by the endocrine and nervous systems of the body, and involves such conditions as body temperature, heart rate, respiration, metabolism, electrolyte balance, and so forth. When homeostasis is lost a variety of physical and mental/emotional disorders may ensue, of which depression is but one.

hormones Secretions of the endocrine glands that enter into body fluids and are transported to other organs where specific metabolic effects are produced. Hormones have a strong effect on various functions of the body, human emotions, and behavior.

human chorionic gonadotrophin (HCG) The hormone manufactured by the placenta in early pregnancy and necessary to maintain that pregnancy. It is found in the urine of pregnant women.

Huntington's chorea An inherited physical and mental disorder that is characterized by progressive rapid jerking of the limbs (known as chorea), as well as mental deterioration, confusion, and psychotic behavior. Huntington's chorea is considered an autosomal dominant disease, which means it is passed on by a single dominant gene. Symptoms appear most frequently between ages 30 and 50.

hydrochloric acid An acid that is an essential part of gastric juice.

hydrocortisone The chief glucocorticoid produced by the adrenal cortex, commonly known as cortisol. See *cortisol*.

hydrogenation The process whereby hydrogen is introduced into compounds. When oils are hydrogenated, they become solid fats.

hyperactivity A childhood condition characterized by excessive movement and restlessness, and an inability to control this. It may be part of the so-called "attention-deficit syndrome," which is more common among boys than girls, with short attention span, other learning problems, and behavioral difficulties.

hyperadrenalism See *Cushing's syndrome*.

hyperadrenocorticism See *Cushing's syndrome*.

hyperaldosteronism See *aldosteronism*.

hypercalcemia Excessively high concentration of calcium in the blood. This may be the result of several disorders including hyperparathyroidism. The condition leads to muscle pain and weakness, loss of appetite, and other symptoms.

hyperglycemia Excessively high concentration of glucose in the blood, usually associated with diabetes mellitus.

hyperinsulinism The excessive secretion of insulin due to overactivity by the islet cells of the pancreas, or the use of too much insulin in diabetic conditions.

hyperkalemia Excessively high concentration of potassium in the blood. the condition leads to diarrhea, muscle weakness, nausea, and other symptoms.

hyperparathyroidism Excessive production of parathyroid hormone by the parathyroid glands. This condition, also known as von Recklinghausen's disease, may be caused by parathyroid disease, or other problems including below normal blood calcium levels. The disorder may lead to hypercalcemia. See *hypercalcemia.*

hyperpituitarism Excessive secretion of pituitary hormones, usually due to the overactivity of the anterior lobe of the pituitary gland. This may lead to abnormal enlargement of the extremities (acromegaly) or excessive body size (gigantism).

hypersensitivity reaction See *allergy.*

hyperthyroidism Excessive activity of the thyroid gland which results in an increased metabolic rate, and autonomic nervous system disturbances. The cause may be found in tumors, overgrowth of the gland, or goiter, which in turn may be caused by a lack of iodine in the diet. See *metabolism.*

hyperventilation Excessive breathing rate which may lead to excessive oxygen levels in the blood and deficient levels of carbon dioxide. Caused by breathing too frequently, or deeply, as the result of anxiety, exercise, fever, pain, or numerous other conditions, including emphysema and hyperthyroidism.

hypervitaminosis Physical and/or mental disorders resulting from excessive intake of vitamins. Special caution is required in the use of all vitamins, and especially A and D.

hypoadrenalism In less severe cases analogous to hypoadrenocorticism, which is due to a lessening of secretions of hormones by the adrenal cortex. In more severe cases we find a failure of function of the adrenal cortex and more serious symptoms, such as, abnormal mineral levels in the body, anorexia, fatigue, increased bronzelike pigmentation, intolerance for cold, weight loss, etc. The latter is commonly known as Addison's disease. See *Addison's disease.*

hypoadrenocorticism See *hypoadrenalism.*

hypocalcemia Excessively low levels of calcium in the blood. May result from lack of vitamin D, kidney disorders, hypoparathyroidism, and other causes.

hypoglycemia Excessively low levels of glucose in the blood. There are many possible physical and mental/emotional symptoms including anger, anxiety, depression, dizziness, headaches, palpitations, and sleep disturbances. There are two categories, *reactive* or functional (exogenous) *hypoglycemia,* and *spontaneous* (endogenous) *hypoglycemia.*

Reactive hypoglycemia is usually caused by the excessive consumption of refined carbohydrates leading to rapid formation of excessive glucose, followed by excessive insulin production—also known as functional hypoglycemia. Other causes include postgastrectomy (alimentary hypoglycemia) or delayed insulin response in early maturity-onset diabetes mellitus (late hypoglycemia). The overwhelming majority of people with hypoglycemia have the reactive (functional) type.

There are also two saccharides that inhibit the output of glucose by the liver, namely fructose (in hereditary fructose intolerance) and galactose (in case of galactosemia). Reactive hypoglycemia may also result from taking excess insulin, alcohol, or drugs that cause excess *glucose utilization* including EDTA, manganese, Mebanzaine, Oxytetracycline, Propranolol, alcohol, and phenylbutazone, or drugs that cause *deficient glucose production* including alcohol, aspirins, aminobenzoic acid, Haldol, and Thorazine (chlorpromazine).

Spontaneous hypoglycemia (in the fasting state) results from an endogenous metabolic process and includes tumors of the beta cells of the islands of Langerhans (insulinomas). These tumors are usually benign, and constitute one of the main causes of fasting hypoglycemia. Not only insulinomas but also a *deficiency of contrainsulin hormones* may lead to endogenous hypoglycemia. Contrainsulin hormones are cortisol, glucagon, growth hormone, epinephrine, and thyroid hormones. Other mechanisms that increase the utilization of glucose include exercise, fever (infectious disease), pregnancy and large tumors (such as a sarcomas). Spontaneous hypoglycemia may also result from deficient glucose production due to liver disease, hepatic enzyme defects, (enzymes necessary for glycogen mobilization or release), and other causes. Any type of hypoglycemia warrants medical attention. This is especially so in the case of spontaneous (endogenous) hypoglycemia. See *glucagon, glucose,* and *glucose tolerance test.*

hypokalemia Excessively low levels of potassium in the blood which may result in physical weakness and heart problems. Adrenal tumors, inadequate food intake, and diuretics may cause the condition.

hypomania A nonpsychotic moderate form of unwarranted elation. Manifested in excessive excitability, irritability, anger, a decreased need for sleep, and increased sexual interest.

hypoparathyroidism Underfunctioning of the parathyroid glands and resultant low calcium levels in the blood with physical and mental-emotional symptoms, including muscle spasms, nervousness, and depression.

hypotension Low blood pressure which may be due to excessive fluid loss and other conditions. Low blood pressure may also result from hypoadrenalism. See *hypoadrenalism.*

hypothalamus That part of the limbic system of the brain that directly controls the endocrine and autonomic nervous systems, and controls numerous body functions such as hunger, thirst, temperature. The hypothalamus is greatly influenced by the neocortex (or thinking portion) of the brain. The hypothalamus is involved with emotion, motivation, and sexual behavior.

hypothesis   A proposed explanation, which can either be a provisional opinion or a highly probable assumption, based on well-established facts.

hypothyroidism   Underactivity of the thyroid gland. May lead to such problems as myxedema and depression. See *myxedema*.

hypovitaminosis   Any condition that results from lack of vitamins in the diet.

hysteria   Emotional disorder characterized by wild excitability and conversion reactions where mental/emotional difficulties are changed into such bodily disturbances as blindness, numbness, and so forth. See *personality disorders*.

iatrogenic   Any condition caused by medical intervention. The term is often used for adverse or side effects of medical treatment. It is estimated that about 5 million people have an adverse drug reaction within a given year in the USA.

iatrogenic depression   Those depressions that sometimes result from taking various medications (or food supplements) including:

amantadine	guanethidine
benzodiazepines	haloperidol
calcium (in excessive amounts)	indomethacin
carbamazepine	ioniazid
chloramphenicol	levodopa
choline (in excessive amounts)	methsuximide
cortisone preparations	methyldopa
cycloserine	methysergide
digitalis	oral contraceptives
digitoxin	phenylbutazone
digoxin	procainamide
diphenoxylate	progesterones
estrogens	propranolol
ethionamide	reserpine
fluphenazine	sulfonamides

See *iatrogenic drug abuse*.

iatrogenic drug abuse   The "addiction" to legal drugs, originally prescribed for a legitimate physical, and/or mental/emotional problem. The drugs involved are usually prescribed for the reduction of stress. In this category we may find, for example, the benzodiazepine drugs such as Ativan, Centrax, Dalmane, Librium, Paxipam, Restoril, Serax, Tranxene, and Xanax. The most widely known and used, as well as abused, of the benzodiazepines is Valium. The latter has been among the more controversial drugs in recent medical history. It is believed that a person may become addicted to Valium (or any of the other benzodiazepines), even at prescribed doses, if taken for only a few months. A commonly accepted requirement for addiction is based on (1) increased tolerance, and (2) withdrawal symptoms, and as such we must include *amphetamines, barbiturates,* and *tranquilizers.* Withdrawal from amphetamines or taking excessive doses of barbiturates may lead to depression. Among possible side effects to the use of tranquilizers we also find depression.

id According to psychoanalytic theory, the unconscious part of the personality.

ideation Refers to thought processes and in particular the formation of concepts, ideas, and images.

identification The process of identifying with someone or something. Specifically adopting the attitudes, beliefs, characteristics, habits, traits, of other persons. The identification with a parent or other significant person is important in the development of appropriate sex roles, and other specific personality traits.

illusion A false impression, and/or interpretation of anything that is perceived by the senses. All human beings experience illusions, or misinterpretations of facts and/or events. Illusions are more frequently encountered by persons who suffer from mental/emotional difficulties, for example, depression. See *delusions* and *hallucinations.*

imagery The formation of vivid mental pictures through the use of normal thought processes. See *healing imagery.*

imipramine Tricyclic antidepressant medication marketed under such trade names as Imavate, Janimine, Presamine, SK-Pramine, and Tofranil.

immune system Bone marrow, thymus gland, and lymphoid tissue working together in a complex protective system against disease producing organisms and foreign substances. The process involves the production of antibodies and activation of specific white blood cells.

immunoglobulins Specific antibodies (Ig) distinguished as IgA, IgD, IgE, IgG, IgM produced by lymph tissue against disease-producing organisms and foreign invaders.

infundibulum The funnel-shaped part of the brain that connects the hypothalamus and pituitary gland.

innate Existing from birth.

inositol Anti-eczema and hair-loss vitamin. Important for fat metabolism, and necessary for the formation of the emulsifier lecithin. Inositol acts as a natural tranquilizer and is stress-reductive.

insight The instant of discerning the true nature of something, in particular concerning mental/emotional matters.

insomnia Difficulty falling asleep, staying asleep, or having disturbed sleep.

insulin Hormone produced by the beta cells of the islands of Langerhans in the pancreas gland. It is essential for regulating sugar metabolism. See *diabetes.*

insulinase Enzyme responsible for the breakdown of insulin in the body.

insulinoma An insulin-producing tumor (of the beta cells in the islands of Langerhans) of the pancreas gland. Symptoms may include episodic loss of consciousness and many of the symptoms of excessively low blood sugar. See *glucose tolerance test, hypoglycemia,* and *insulin.*

insulin coma therapy See *insulin shock.*

insulin shock 1. The treatment of serious mental disturbances by the administration of insulin which results in a period of profound unconsciousness (coma), which is followed by a period of clear perception and understanding. The latter period is then used for psychotherapy.
2. A mild form of insulin shock may also result from an overdose of insulin, unsatisfactory food intake, and excessive exercise. The symptoms are those commonly found in hypoglycemia, such as, nervousness, pallor, sweating, trembling, and irritability. Untreated the condition may lead to convulsions and death.

insulin tolerance test An indirect test of anterior pituitary and adrenal cortex function. The test is rarely used today.

intellect The capacity to perceive and comprehend.

intelligence The ability to perceive, comprehend, and rationally apply experiences.

internalization The unconscious integration of the attitudes, beliefs, and values of others into one's own value system. See *Perceptual-cognitive field.*

islands of Langerhans Cell clusters within the pancreas gland. Alpha cells produce glucagon; beta cells produce insulin; other cells produce pancreatic peptide. See *glucagon* and *insulin.*

islets of Langerhans See *islands of Langerhans.*

isocarboxazid Monoamine oxidase inhibitor, marketed under the trade name Marplan. The product inhibits monoamine-oxidase and is sometimes used to treat depression when tricyclic medications are contraindicated or have proven ineffective. Other monoamine oxidase inhibitors (MAO) include pargyline HCL, phenelzine sulfate, and tranylcypromine. See *monoamine oxidase* and *monoamine oxidase inhibitors.*

isoleucine One of the eight essential amino acids. See *amino acids.*

jamáis vu The sudden sensation of being unfamiliar with everyday surroundings. Usually a symptom of temporal lobe epilepsy. See *déjà vu.*

Janimine Trade name for the tricyclic antidepressant imipramine-hydrochloride. Used primarily for moderately severe depression with anxiety attacks.

ketogenic Capable of conversion into ketone bodies. See *ketosis.*

ketonuria Excessive amounts of ketone bodies in the urine. Ketones are organic chemicals resulting from oxidation of alcohol. They consist of a carbon-oxygen group (CO). Included are acetone and acetoacetic acid.

ketosis An abnormal condition with excessive production of ketone bodies, usually due to an imbalance of fat metabolism as found in uncontrolled diabetes mellitus or starvation. Untreated, ketosis may lead to ketoacidosis, with symptoms of mental confusion, nausea, vomiting, and eventually coma and death.

ketosteroids The so-called 17-ketosteroids found in normal urine include certain adrenocortical and adrogenic hormones. *Increased* levels of ketosteroids may be found in adrenal hyperplasia (an abnormal increase of normal cells), and Cushing's syndrome. *Decreased* levels of ketosteroids may be found in hypothyroidism. Normal values in adult males range from 10-18 mg/24 hrs, and in adult females from 6-15 mg/24 hrs. After age 50 the excretion of ketosteroids decreases, and by age 65 may be as low as 4-8 mg/24 hrs, in both males and females. Ketosteroids are often low in hypoadrenocorticism (common symptoms include fatigue, nervousness, depression). See *Cushing's syndrome, hypoadrenocorticism,* and *hypothyroidism.*

Korsakoff's syndrome An organic brain disorder also known as Korsakoff's psychosis. Most likely caused by vitamin B_1 (thiamine) deficiency (which leads to degenerative changes in the thalamus), resulting from excessive alcohol use. Treatment requires improved nutrition and large doses of vitamin B_1. Symptoms include disorientation and the inability to learn new information with good recall of past events.

lactose A disaccharide ($C_{12}H_{22}O_{11}$) consisting of glucose and galactose and found in milk. See *disaccharides.*

laissez faire Nonintervention in the affairs of others, especially in economic affairs.

lecithin A fat emulsifier, consisting of a yellow-brown organic compound (phospholipids), which is found in plant tissues (such as soybeans), and such foods as egg yolk and liver. Lecithin contains choline, inositol, phosphoric acid, fatty acids, and glycerol. Choline is necessary for the manufacture of the neurotransmitter acetylcholine (which plays a role in memory, mood, and perception). See *choline,* and *inositol.*

leucine An essential amino acid. See *amino acid.*

leucocytes White blood cells. See *blood count.*

leucopenia Excessive decrease of white blood cells.

libido The sexual drive.

limbic system Popularly known as the feeling portion of the brain. The limbic system includes the hippocampus, cingulate gyrus, and amygdala, and plays a major role in sexual arousal and our emotions.

lithium Also known as lithium carbonate and marketed under various trade names including Carbolith, Cibalith-S, Eskalith, Eskalith CR, Lithane, Lithizine, Lithobid, Lithonate, and Lithotabs. Lithium is used mainly for the treatment of the manic stage of bipolar depression, and to help reduce the frequency and severity of other manic states. Lithium acts on the central nervous system and helps to provide more stable emotions. *Adverse effects* that may be encountered with this major tranquilizer include kidney damage and salt and water retention. *Side effects* include fainting, frequent urination, irregular pulse, troubled breathing, increased thirst, mild nausea, palpitations, tiredness, trembling of hands, bloating of stomach, weakness, and weight gain. The use of lithium may also lead to low thyroid function, which may result in dry skin, loss of hair, hoarseness, swelling of neck, feet, and/or lower legs, and an unusual sensitivity to cold. Many factors may interfere with the proper use of lithium including allergies, low salt or low sugar diets. It is *not* recommended to use caffeine products such as coffee, tea, while on lithium. Many medications are also contraindicated when on lithium including:

aminophylline

amphetamines

anti-inflammatory analgesics (for example, diflusinal, fenoprofen, ibuprofen, indomethacin, meclofenamate, mefenamic acid, naproxen, oxyphenbuta-zone, phenylbutazone, piroxicam, sulindac, and tolmetin).

caffeine

carbamazepine

chlorpromazine

diuretics

dyphylline

haloperidol

oxtriphylline

sodium bicarbonate

sodium chloride

theophylline

thyroid medications

tranquilizers

Lithium must be taken exactly as directed by the attending physician. Usually verbal as well as printed instructions are provided to the person who is taking lithium. Lithium is found in normal blood serum. The therapeutic range (normal values) is from 0.5 to 1.2 mEq/L.

loxapine   Tranquilizer marketed under the trade name of Loxitane and used in the treatment of schizophrenia.

LSD   See *lysergic acid diethylamide.*

luteinizing hormone (LH)   Hormone secreted by the anterior pituitary gland which in turn stimulates the ovaries and testes to secrete sex hormones.

lymphocytes   Type of white blood cells found in the lymph nodes, spleen, thymus gland, bone marrow, and gut wall. Normal value is 20-30% of the total white blood count. See *blood count.*

lysergic acid diethylamide   An illegal hallucinogenic drug commonly known as LSD. See *hallucinogen.*

lysine   Essential amino acid. See *amino acid.*

magnesium   An essential mineral for normal body functioning, believed important in the prevention and treatment of depression.

major affective disorders   See *DSM-III.*

major depression   Deep and lasting depression, sometimes with psychotic symptoms. See *depressive illness.*

malnutrition   Unsatisfactory nutritional condition which may result from unbalanced, or otherwise unhealthy diets, and/or an inability to properly absorb and assimilate foods.

maltose   A disaccharide ($C_{12}H_{22}O_{11}$) consisting of two molecules of glucose and found in germinating cereal seeds (grains).

manganese An essential mineral for normal body functioning. Especially important for normal muscle and nerve functions.

mania Mental/emotional condition characterized by intense, uncontrolled excitement and not resulting from specific stimuli.

manic Very excited, hyperactive, and/or irritable.

manic-depression A depressive condition characterized by severe mood swings, alternating between periods of euphoria and extreme sadness, or consisting of both mania and depression. Although an endogenous disorder, there are often exogenous factors that precipitate an attack. Lithium has been found helpful to reduce the severity and frequency of manic episodes. The more appropriate current name of manic-depression is *bipolar depression*. When the mood swings occur simultaneously the condition is known as manic-depression, mixed type. When the mood swings occur only individually, they are known as manic-depression, manic type (euphoric), or manic-depression, depressed type (extreme sadness). See *bipolar depression, depressive illness,* and *DSM-III.*

manic-depressive psychosis See *psychosis.*

marasmus Emaciation and wasting of subcutaneous tissue and muscle due to severe malnutrition, found especially in institutionalized young children.

Marplan Trade name for the antidepressant drug isocarboxazid.

masked depression Especially when depression is equated with weakness people may hide their depression behind heroic fronts of feigned happiness and well-being. This may occur especially among children and adolescents, as well as among members of religious groups where depression may erroneously be seen as a lack of testimony or faith. Often we find minimal changes in mood with major changes in behavior or psychosomatic problems, which in essence help the individual hide a depression. Gastrointestinal and cardiac symptoms are often indications of masked depression. Manic disorders are sometimes seen as the ultimate forms of masked depression.

medulla oblongata The lowest part of the brain stem found at the top of the spinal cord.

megadose Generally referring to large doses of certain preparations, such as, vitamins and minerals.

megavitamins A general term for large quantities of specific nutrients. Special care is required in taking megadoses of vitamins. See *avitaminosis, choline, vitamin,* and *vitamin withdrawal.*

melancholia Extreme depression and sadness. See *bipolar depression, depression, DSM-III,* and *manic depression.*

menopause The period of life when menstruation stops. This is normally between the age of 40 and 55. In addition to common symptoms such as dryness of vaginal membranes, hot flashes and palpitations, we find crying spells, depression, fatigability, insomnia, irritability, lassitude. See *climacteric.*

mental disorder Any disorder of perceptions, thoughts, feelings, behavior, and/or memory. Mental disorders may be acquired, congenital, or hereditary. They include "neurosis," where perception of reality is retained, and "psychosis" where perception of reality is often lost. See *neurosis,* and *psychosis.*

mental health   Mentally healthy persons are able and willing to deal to their satisfaction with conflicting factors (such as needs and desires versus realities) within themselves, and/or their environments. As such, they are relatively comfortable with themselves, others, and objective reality. They especially refrain from placing irrational (self-defeating) demands on themselves, other people, and/or the larger environment. Major *obstacles* to good mental health include: poor physical health; poor nutrition; negative childhood conditions and experiences; unsatisfied physical, psychological, and/or spiritual needs; lack of positive self-esteem; acute social-environmental stresses; grave social injustices with corresponding lack of opportunities; excessive physical, psychological, and/or spiritual stress; common irrational ideas in self and society; innate and/or acquired tendency toward self-defeating thinking, feelings, and/or behavior. The three dimensions of good mental health are rational, realistic, and positive thinking. See *positive thinking, rational thinking,* and *realistic thinking.*

meprobamate   A minor tranquilizer marketed under such trade names as Acroban, Bamate, Coprobate, Equanil, Meprocon, Meprospan, Miltown, Pax 400, Robamate, Saronil, SK-bamate.

mercury   A chemical element. Acute mercury poisoning may produce serious physical symptoms including abdominal pain, vomiting, and bloody diarrhea. Chronic mercury poisoning may produce such symptoms as loosening of the teeth, hypertrophied gums with easy bleeding, incoordination, tremors, and depression. It is believed that mercury poisoning can result from leaking fillings in the teeth.

metabolism   The chemical and physical changes and processes, such as nutrient distribution, energy production, and waste elimination, taking place in the body. Metabolism involves a constructive, building-up phase, and a destructive, breaking-down phase. See *anabolism,* and *catabolism.*

methionine   An essential amino acid and the main amino-acid source of organic sulphur. Methionine assists in the breakdown of fats and is important for the liver and digestive system. See *amino acid.*

mineralocorticoids   Those hormones (for example, Aldosterone) produced by the cortex of the adrenal glands and that are responsible for the regulation of salt (sodium retention and potassium loss), blood volume, and water balance. See *aldosterone, corticosteroid,* and *glucocorticoid.*

minerals   Inorganic substances. A number of minerals are essential for physical and mental health. In the body we find the following essential "bulk" minerals (expressed in percentage of body weight): calcium (1.5%), phosphorus (1%), potassium (0.35%), sulfur (0.25%), sodium (0.15%), chlorine (0.15%), magnesium (0.05%), and silicon (0.05%), as well as the following essential "trace" minerals (in amounts smaller than 0.01% of body weight): arsenic, barium, boron, bromine, chromium, cobalt, copper, fluorine, iodine, iron, manganese, molybdenum, rubidium, selenium, strontium, vanadium, and zinc. Nonessential trace minerals found in the body include:

aluminum, cadmium, gold, mercury, tin, lithium. A diet lacking in certain minerals, and/or malabsorption may lead to mineral deficiencies.

mineral supplement A food supplement for the treatment and/or prevention of possible mineral deficiencies in the body. Ideally a person's mineral needs are satisfied by a wholesome diet. Unfortunately, modern diets are often lacking in essential minerals, and multiple mineral supplementation is a rational solution. Single deficiencies are often hard to identify and require the assistance of experts such as nutritionally oriented physicians. It is usually consisidered best to use a well-balanced multiple mineral supplement, rather than only one or more specific minerals. If a well-balanced supplement is taken it will also be easier for experts to identify any remaining deficiencies. Specific minerals that play a role in certain disorders have been identified, for example in the case of *depression,* it has been found that calcium, chromium, magnesium, manganese, and zinc may play a direct or indirect part. Regardless of origin, type, or severity of the depression, and regardless of other treatment forms, whether with or without drugs, and/or counseling, it is important to consider taking a well-balanced multiple mineral supplement (as well as a vitamin and amino-acid-complex supplement). The often recommended daily amounts of specific minerals for depression are calcium 1000-1500 mg; chromium 50-200 mcg; magnesium 500-750 mg; manganese 2.5-5 mg, and zinc 30-45 mg.

minor tranquilizers See *tranquilizers.*

monoamine oxidase (MAO) Enzyme found in body tissues, and in particular, the nervous system and liver. Monoamine oxidase causes the oxidation of monoamines. See *oxidation* and *monoamines.*

monoamine oxidase (MAO) inhibitors Those drugs that act as inhibitors of the enzyme "monoamine oxidase," and used in the treatment of depression. Included are Marplan, Nardil, and Parnate. By inhibiting the monoamine oxidase enzyme, these drugs are believed to increase the availability of certain neurotransmitters. Because of dangerous food and drug interactions the MAO inhibitors require close medical supervision and specific instructions for their use. See *tyramine.*

monoamines Amines with only one amino group, that is, the central neurotransmitters dopamine, epinephrine, norepinephrine, and serotonin. See *amine, monoamine oxidase inhibitors,* and *neurotransmitters.*

monocytes White blood cells that are important in dealing with bacteria and tissue debris. Normal value is 2-6% of the total white cell count. See *blood count.*

monosaccharides Sugars made up of single molecules, but different molecular structures. Included are glucose, fructose, and galactose. See *fructose, galactose,* and *glucose.*

motor neuron See *efferent neuron.*

multiple personality See *personality disorders.*

myxedema A dry swelling with abnormal deposits of mucin in the skin and other tissues. The condition is caused by hypothyroidism. Commonly seen are swollen lips and thickened nose. Also a more general syndrome of thyroid deficiency is seen with fatigue, intolerance for cold, weight gain, and so forth. See *hypothyroidism*.

narcissistic Any activity and/or interest which leads to excessive self-love and self-absorption, with irrational and unrealistic self-appraisals, and with little or no regard for other people. See *personality disorders*.

narcotic Drugs derived from opium or synthetically made. They are often used for the relief of pain or the induction of mood changes. Included are codeine, heroin, meperidine, and morphine.

neocortex See *cerebral cortex*.

nerve One or more bundles of connecting nerve fibers that transmit impulses to and from the brain and spinal cord to specific body regions.

nervous system The complex network of brain, spinal cord, and nerve cells, that is responsible for the regulation and coordination of body activities. The nervous system is subdivided into three systems. See *autonomic nervous system, central nervous system,* and *peripheral nervous system*.

neuron Individual nerve cell, the basic unit of the nervous system. Also see *neurotransmitters,* and *synapse*.

neuropeptides Brain chemicals consisting of simple proteins that have great effects on moods and behavior. Brain peptides seem to regulate the activities of other neurons, especially in regard to emotion, hunger, memory, mood, pain, pleasure, and sexual behavior.

neurosis A mild to moderate, usually intermittent, mental-emotional, and behavioral disturbance. It is characterized by unrealistic, pessimistic, and/or irrational thoughts, feelings, and/or behaviors. Often present is misinterpretation of reality. Common neurotic disturbances include anxiety, excessive use of defense mechanisms, compulsions, depression, obsessions, and phobias. Sources of neurosis include physical, mental, emotional, sociocultural, and spiritual factors. Especially childhood experiences and conditions may have led to inflexible behavior patterns of anger, defensiveness, hostility, narcissism, self-centeredness, selfishness, and/or self-righteousness, but also self-effacing patterns. In addition, we frequently find that negative experiences, unfulfilled needs, and powerful emotions are repressed (or suppressed) leading to numerous physical, and/or emotional problems. The term "neurosis" is becoming outdated. See *psychosis*.

neurotic depression A chronic subclinical form of unipolar depression, also known as reactive depression. It may have resulted from one or more incompletely remitted episodes of unipolar depression. The depression is usually related to stressful, unhappy, negative, and hurtful events, including physical disorders, interpersonal losses, or irreconcilable marital conflict. Symptoms include chronic low self-esteem, dysphoric mood, manipulative suicidal gestures, extreme sensitivity to alcohol and for sedative-hypnotics (barbiturates, minor tranquilizers, chloral hydrate). The depression often responds to supportive treatment. If symptoms of borderline personality disorder are also present, the diagnosis might be atypical depression. Re-educative (cognitive) therapy is an ideal treatment form. See *dysthymia, atypical depression,* and *neurotic disorder*. Compare with *depressive illness*.

neurotic disorder Mental disorders for which no physical cause can be found. Included are *anxiety disorders* (generalized anxiety, phobias, and obsessive-compulsive behavior); *somatoform disorders* (somatization disorder—previously known as hysteria, and *conversion disorders*—previously known as hysterical conversion reactions); *dissociative disorders* (amnesia, fugue, and multiple personality); and *affective disorders* (nonpsychotic mood disorders that are characterized by severe mood fluctuations of mania and depression). A neurotic disorder is unacceptable to the individual, and may be chronic or recurrent.

neurotransmitters A chemical substance secreted by neurons that affect the transmission of an impulse by crossing the synapse between nerves, or nerves and muscles. Neurotransmitters include: (1) *monoamines* such as acetylcholine, dopamine, histamine, epinephrine, norepinephrine, and serotonin (5-hydroxytryptamine); (2) *amino acids* such as GABA (y-aminobutyrate), glycine, glutamate, and parnate. See *amino acid, monoamine oxidase inhibitors,* and *synapse.*

neutrophils White blood cells which fight infection by engulfing bacteria and tissue debris. Normal value is 60-70 percent of the total white cell count. See *blood count.*

niacin One of the B-complex vitamins (also known as B_3) and necessary for a healthy brain and nervous system. Depression is one of the deficiency symptoms of B_3.

nonorganic Not containing any matter of plant or animal origin.

nonrapid eye movement (Non-REM) The larger period (75 percent) of normal sleep when dreaming and rapid eye muscle contractions are absent. See *rapid eye movement.*

norepinephrine A hormone secreted by the neurons and which acts as a neurotransmitter. Also a hormone secreted by the medulla of the adrenal gland and especially released during times of low blood pressure, strong emotions, and other stresses. Norepinephrine, also known as noradrenaline, constricts small blood vessels, slows the heart rate and raises blood pressure. Norepinephrine is one of the two principal hormones of the adrenal medulla. The other hormone is epinephrine which is more powerful and accounts for about 20 percent of the medulla's secretions. Norepinephrine accounts for about 80 percent of the medulla's secretions. Low levels of norepinephrine may be a causative factor in depression. See *epinephrine.*

nortriptyline A tricyclic antidepressant, marketed under the trade name of Aventyl and Pamelor. Often prescribed for depression with anxiety.

nutrient A substance such as carbohydrates, fats, proteins, vitamins, minerals, and water that must be obtained from the diet in order to maintain health, life, and reproduction.

objectivity Freedom from bias, opinion, prejudice, and so forth, and as such, based on things external to the mind.

obsessions Persistent or recurrent ideas which a person believes cannot be prevented. Frequently involves a strong urge to some kind of action.

obsessive compulsive disorder An abnormal condition characterized by the presence of anxiety, preoccupation with recurrent irrational ideas, and/or

the compulsive performance of ritualistic and seemingly unavoidable behaviors. See *neurotic disorder.*

oral glucose tolerance test (OGTT)   See *glucose tolerance test.*

organic mental disorder   Also known as organic brain syndrome, and consisting of any mental/emotional problem resulting from identifiable temporary or permanent physiological or genetic factors, including the aging
process, disease, drugs, poisons, trauma. See *dementia.*

ornithine   Amino acid obtained from arginine. Ornithine helps to stimulate
the immune system, aids the healing process, and is linked to arginine in
the release of growth hormones. See *amino acid,* and *growth hormone.*

orthomolecular   The prevention and treatment of physical, and/or men-
tal/emotional problems by adjusting levels of substances, such as, amino
acids, minerals, and vitamins, normally found in the body. Especially the
use of mega (large) doses of nutrients.

oxidation   Chemical process by which a substance combines with oxygen
and thus creating another form.

palpitations   Fast heart beats which may result from a variety of causes,
including allergies, emotional stress, heart problems, low blood sugar, and
so forth.

pancreas   A large elongated compound gland situated behind the stomach
and between the spleen and duodenum. The pancreas is both an endocrine
and exocrine gland. The internal secretions (hormones) of the endocrine
gland are insulin, (produced by the beta cells) and glucagon (produced by
the alpha cells). The alpha and beta cells form aggregates known as the
islets of Langerhans. Both insulin and glucagon enter directly into the
bloodstream. The external secretion of the exocrine gland, called pancreatic
juice, is emptied into the duodenal (first portion) part of the small intestine
via the so called pancreatic duct. Pancreatic juice contains water, salt, and
several enzymes including trypsin and chymotrypsin, which are necessary
for the breakdown of fats, proteins and starches (polysaccharides). See *diabetes, endocrine glands, enzyme, exocrine glands, hormones, hyperglycemia,
hypoglycemia,* and *insulin.*

panic disorder   Chronic high levels of anxiety with sudden incidents of
unfocused highly intense panic. The disorder may have mental, emotional,
and/or physical underlying causes. Tofranil is a medication that is helpful
in many cases. It does not seem to help with anticipatory anxiety or agoraphobia. See *anxiety.*

pantothenic acid   Also known as vitamin B_5 it is important for carbohydrate metabolism and the production of hormones of the adrenal cortex.
Lack of vitamin B_5 may lead to depression and other problems.

paranoia   A rare mental disorder characterized by a well-systematized, persistent, and often elaborate, logical delusional system of thinking, which
centers on delusions of grandeur and/or persecution. See *delusion.*

paranoid   Resembling paranoia.

paranoid certainty   A paranoid schizophrenic's confidence and assurance
about a delusion in spite of all objective evidence to the contrary.

paranoid schizophrenia   A rare mental disorder characterized by delusions of grandeur and/or persecution, as well as gross disturbances of perceptions, thoughts, feelings, and actions.

paranoid state Temporary paranoid delusions sometimes resulting from excessive stress.

parasympathetic nervous system One of the two divisions of the autonomic nervous system, consisting of nerve fibers leaving the brain and spinal cord. The parasympathetic nervous system controls most of the essential functions of life, such as, stimulating peristalsis (the progressive wave of contraction and relaxation of the alimentary canal), the induction of bile and insulin secretion, dilation of peripheral blood vessels, and contracting bronchioles, pupils, and esophagus. The parasympathetic nervous system in most instances is antithetic to the functions of the sympathetic nervous system. See *nervous system,* and *sympathetic nervous system.*

parathyroid glands Two pairs of small endocrine glands that are attached to (or imbedded within) the thyroid gland, and which are responsible for the maintenance of normal blood calcium levels, and neuromuscular function. A decrease in blood calcium stimulates the parathyroid glands to release parathyroid hormone (PTH). Both parathyroid and thyroid glands work together in a negative feedback control system to regulate blood calcium levels. See *calcium, parathyroid hormone,* and *thyroid gland.*

parathyroid hormone (PTH) A hormone produced by the parathyroid glands which is essential for the regulation of blood calcium and phosphorus levels, and important for blood clotting and neuromuscular functions. See *parathyroid glands.*

paresis, general Mental disturbance caused by damage of brain nerve cells.

Parkinson's disease A progressive neurologic disorder found in middle-aged and elderly people which is marked by rigidity, resting tremor, shuffling gait, stooped posture, expressionless face, depression, and other signs and symptoms. Also known as Parkinsonism.

pepsin Stomach enzyme necessary for the digestion of protein.

perception The process of becoming aware of something and/or identifying facts and/or events, and/or determining meaningful relations between objects. Perception usually refers to the transformation of sensations into cognitions. See *perceptual-cognitive field.*

perceptual-cognitive field All the perceptions and cognitions within a person's awareness. Also known as field of awareness, or phenomenal field.

perceptual defect A serious interfering with recognizing and interpreting sensory stimuli.

peripheral nervous system All parts of the nervous system outside the brain and spinal cord. This includes the cranial nerves, the spinal nerves, sensory neurons, and the autonomic nervous system. The peripheral nervous system is responsible for carrying information to and from the Central Nervous System. Basically there are two divisions, namely the somatic system, which is responsible for carrying messages to and from the sense organs and skeletal muscles, and the autonomic system which regulates internal organs and glands. The autonomic system is divided into the sympathetic and parasympathetic systems. See *autonomic nervous system, parasympathetic nervous system,* and *sympathetic nervous system.*

personality disorders   While it is true that any person, regardless of personality type, can become depressed, it is important to recognize that certain personality types may predispose to certain illnesses. For example, about half of the people suffering from *bipolar depression* have so called cyclothymic personalities, while unipolar depression is more common in persons with dependent personalities. This does not mean, however, that personality types and various types of depression are necessarily related. It is perhaps even more urgent to recognize that various conditions such as depression and a personality disorder can and often do exist side by side. Failure to recognize a personality disorder is often to the detriment of both the sufferers and those who deal with them in a professional or social way. Personality disorders belong to any of a group of rather firmly (chronic) fixed maladjustive behavioral responses to external and/or internal stress, which always involves suffering for the individual and/or others. Personality disorders are characterized by (1) *lack of insight;* (2) *resistance to change;* and (3) *rigid behavior patterns.* These are often identifiable from early adolescence onward. Individuals with personality disorders usually believe that their problems are caused by others, and this leads to frequent conflict with the environment as well as self-defeating and self-destructive lifestyles. Those who are suffering from personality disorders find it difficult, if not impossible, to learn from experience, and we commonly find denial of responsibility, blaming others, excessive use of fantasy, exaggerating of minor physical problems, lack of concern about failure to perform adequately (in school, at home, or on the job), and delinquent, and other immature behaviors. The following are a few of the more common personality disorders:

antisocial personality: Also known as psychopathic or sociopathic personality. The person can distinguish between right or wrong, however, does not care about others, or the consequences of his or her behavior. Antisocial personalities may range from mild to severe, and includes people who are often intelligent and well liked, and the behaviors may range from fraud to violence. The antisocial personality is formed at an early age and well established by early adolescence. Characteristic behaviors include inability to forego immediate gratification, low frustration tolerance, and excessive rationalizations. Interpersonal relations may be charming; however, alcoholism, drug addictions, promiscuity, and sexual deviations are often found.

avoidant personality: Characterized by excessive need for acceptance, respect, and understanding, and distress over inability and/or difficulty in establishing and/or maintaining comfortable interpersonal relationships. There is an excessive fear of starting relationships without numerous guarantees of unconditional acceptance. The avoidant personality is extremely sensitive to criticism which is interpreted as rejection, and a "wall" is formed around the personality to protect the ego.

borderline personality: Chronically self-defeating people with very intense, dramatic—if not histrionic—interpersonal relationships, depressive moods (see *atypical depression*), excessively low self-esteem, self-destructive behaviors, confused sexual identity, abusive—excessively demanding—episodes with crying, screaming, and swearing. Exogenously induced rapidly alternating moods, vague physical problems, disturbed formal thought processes, and—under pressure—brief psychotic delusionary and hallucinatory episodes.

cyclothymic personality: Sometimes confused with those who suffer from bipolar depression; however, there are distinct differences. While the cyclothymic personality suffers from both high and low mood fluctuations, there is no known organic cause, nor necessarily specific external events. Nevertheless, up to one-half of the people who suffer from bipolar depression are found to have cyclothymic personalities. The mood swings are fairly regular and predictable. Either depression or elation may be prevalent. The cyclothymic personality is often charming, creative, intelligent, and interesting. In some persons either the depressive or the euphoric cycle is more dominant, with the other cycle often going unnoticed. Unlike the bipolar depressed person, we find that cyclothymic personalities do not suffer from extremes in mood swings and while often difficulties arise in interpersonal relationships, they do function adequately in society.

dependent personality: The dependent personality is characterized by low self-esteem and fearfulness of being alone. Hysterical behavior is commonly found, and direct or indirect manipulation may be involved by placing their own needs ahead of the needs of others on whom they depend.

explosive personality: This personality type must be seen as distinct from explosive outbursts that may occur in any personality type as the result of organic conditions such as hypoglycemia, severe lack of sleep, or other excessively stressful conditions. The explosive personality type frequently, if not regularly, responds to minor stressful situations in an extremely exaggerated manner. In addition, we find critical, authoritarian, argumentative, and aggressive behaviors. The explosive personality does not form close relationships, thus we find very few, if any, friends. Other people are frequently used in order to attain personal goals.

hysterical personality: The hysterical personality suffers from seemingly uncontrollable outbursts of emotion or fear, and a variety of disorders ranging from excessive suspicions to hysterical numbness, blindness, and wild psychotic-type behaviors. Basic to the personality we find excessively self-centered behavior, aimed at overcoming an all-abiding lack of self-esteem, grounded in gross emotional immaturity. Hysterical personalities are often perfectionistic, vain, theatrical, and childish. Much of the hysterical behavior centers on overcoming a perpetual fear of rejection and to gain and/or maintain control over their environments. While hysterical personalities rarely form deep emotional attachments, they are forever searching for affection. Essentially dependent on others, they also have the characteristics of the dependent personality, which rarely stands by itself in any case. Sexually seductive behavior is sometimes found with corresponding difficulties in marital and other relationships. Manipulation via threats, ranging from breaking up a relationship to suicide gestures and attempts, are all aimed at controlling others in the environment. In addition to dependent-personality traits we also find narcissistic-personality traits. These multiple personality traits, plus the hysteric's ability to present either a positive or negative side, may lead to the diagnosis of multiple personality, while in essence we are dealing with various aspects of the hysterical personality. Unfortunately the hysterical personality has great difficulty with insight, is given to self-pity, self-blame, other-pity, and other-blame, and these exogenous factors, plus a sooner or later deranged hormonal system (including perhaps excessive cortisone output) may lead to various forms of depression. Treatment of the hysterical personality is difficult, but the wholistic approach, with a major emphasis on emotional re-education, and a loving, but structured environment, will prove beneficial.

inadequate personality: The inadequate personality is outwardly often an agreeable person, but, on closer examination will be found rather ineffective and lacking in positive motivation toward self and/or others. Emotionally, mentally, and/or socially immature, the inadequate personality does not seem to benefit a great deal from education, experience, or training. The inadequate personality is all too often content with a status-quo, and to just drift along.

multiple personality: An extremely rare form of dissociative (hysterical) disorder. The latter is a rare condition in itself and thus very few people exist who truly suffer from multiple personality. In multiple personality two or more distinct personalities are found in the same person. Two types of multiple personalities can be identified. In the first we speak of "alternating personality." Here two personalities alternate, but are unaware of the thoughts and behaviors of the other. In the second type we speak of "dominant" or "subordinate" personalities. Here the primary or dominant personality may have no awareness of the secondary or subordinate personality. The latter, however, is fully aware of the dominant (and less acceptable) personality. Personality transitions usually come about under stress and may last for short or long periods of time. See *hysterical personality.*

narcissistic personality: Inordinately concerned with self-importance, the narcissistic personality frequently suffers from mood swings, especially when hoped for achievements do not materialize. Being overly sensitive to criticism, and fearing both failure and rejection, the narcissistic personality works overtime at trying to control his or her environment. Narcissistic personality traits are frequently found in other personality types, such as the hysterical personality. Real or perceived physical ailments are commonly found. Failure to maintain manipulative control, and real or perceived rejection, may lead to depression.

obsessive-compulsive personality: The obsessive-compulsive personality suffers from a highly exaggerated sense of duty, and shows patterns of rigid, overly inhibited, and perfectionistic behaviors. There is an excessive need to control every aspect of the environment, especially at work and at home. Being extremely cautious, the obsessive-compulsive personality has great difficulties in making decisions, is rather slow and methodical in most tasks, and after a decision has been made may continue to evaluate and analyze its merit. Marriage may continuously be postponed, not only because of difficulty in making a decision, but, also because of fear of giving up control over any aspect of one's personal life, and an awareness of a basic inflexibility that makes it difficult to adapt to a new lifestyle. Early childhood experiences of obsessive-compulsive personalities may show rather compliant, obedient, and overall good behaviors. Especially at work the obsessive-compulsive personality is dependable and reliable, but interpersonal relations often suffer greatly. Under stress the obsessive-compulsive personality may have a tendency to depression.

paranoid personality: Hostility, jealousy, oversensitivity, and suspiciousness are typical characteristics of paranoid personalities. Unacceptable internal conflicts and hostilities are often transferred to others, leading to aggressive behaviors and consequently rejections. Suffering from low self-esteem, the paranoid personality assumes that others hold the same opinion, feels disliked, and suffers from the misbelief that others laugh and talk about him or her. Because of the suspiciousness a vicious cycle develops, where the person becomes more and more isolated and feels persecuted. It is possible to have a paranoid personality without ever suffering from paranoia. See *paranoia.*

passive-aggressive personality: Two types can be identified. The first is marked by *passive-dependency,* characterized by helpless, overly dependent behavior and procrastination. The second is marked by *passive-resistance,* characterized by obstinate, sullen, and obstructive behaviors. Underlying passive-aggressive behaviors are (1) strong feelings of anger; (2) fear of its expression; (3) passivity to prevent its expression. There may be superficial compliance, with concomitant obstructionism. Under stress, passive-aggressive personalities have a tendency to depression.

schizoid personality: Schizoid personalities are often unfriendly, remote, and emotionally detached. As children they do not participate in the games of other children, isolate themselves, and do not confide their feelings. The schizoid personality is introverted, solitary, distant, emotionally cold, and withdrawn. Much time is spent in daydreams, fantasy, and imaginings, with an absence of closeness to others. While there is no personality disintegration (as found in those suffering from schizophrenia) this may nevertheless develop in the future. About one-third of schizoid personalities will come to suffer from schizophrenia. See *schizophrenia.*

schizotypal personality: In this personality disorder many of the behaviors found in schizophrenics are manifested, such as magical thinking and paranoid ideation. While these behaviors are more marked than in schizoid personalities, they are not severe enough for a diagnosis of schizophrenia. See *schizoid personality,* and *schizophrenia.*

pet scan See *positron emission tomography.*

pH A scale measuring the levels of acid or alkaline in a solution. On this scale 7 is neutral, above 7 alkaline, and below 7 acid. Normal values in our blood must be slightly alkaline.

phenelzine Monoamine oxidase inhibitor, marketed under the trade name of Nardil and used in the treatment of depression. See *monoamine oxidase inhibitors.*

phenobarbital An anticonvulsant and sedative drug. Often used in the treatment of some forms of epilepsy, and less frequently as a sedative in the treatment of anxiety. Excessive doses may lead to depression. See *barbiturates,* and *iatrogenic drug abuse.*

phenomenon An observable and sometimes extraordinary circumstance, fact, or event.

phenothiazine A major tranquilizer effectively used in the symptomatic treatment of schizophrenia by blocking dopamine receptors. See *dopamine, neurotransmitters, schizophrenia,* and *tranquilizers.*

phenylalanine A naturally occurring amino acid which is essential for optimal growth in children and for protein metabolism. Phenylalanine increases the production of norepinephrine by the brain, enhances mental alertness, elevates moods, often gives relief for chronic back pain, and has been used in countering depression. Phenylalanine, a natural food product obtained from protein, may well be as effective as certain medications for depression, (for example, imipramine), and without the many adverse and side effects that are part of drug treatment. Phenylalanine is contraindicated, however, for those who suffer from high blood pressure, pregnant, and lactating women, and those who take MAO inhibitor or tricyclic antidepressant drugs. See *amino acid, imipramine, norepinephrine,* and *phenylketonuria.*

phenylketonuria A genetic metabolic disorder which is marked by an inability to convert phenylalanine into tyrosine due to a deficiency in the liver enzyme phenylalanine hydroxylase. See *amino acid, phenylalanine,* and *tyrosine.*

pheochromosytoma A small vascular tumor of the adrenal medulla or sympathetic paraganglia, which disturbs the secretions of epinephrine and norepinephrine, resulting in such symptoms as headaches, high blood pressure, increased heart rate, and palpitations. The diagnosis of pheochromosytoma is related to such signs and symptoms as intermittent anxiety attacks (with corresponding high blood pressure, resulting from the increased secretion of epinephrine and norepinephrine), nausea, and vomiting. A twenty-four hour urine collection may also be checked for norepinephrine-meta-epinephrine excretions. See *adrenal glands, anxiety, epinephrine, panic disorder,* and *norepinephrine.*

phobia An anxiety disorder marked by intense and unrealistic fears of certain objects or situations. See *anxiety, neurosis,* and *panic disorder.*

phosphorus A solid nonmetallic element which has more functions than any other mineral in the human body. Phosphorus compounds are found in the tissues of animals, humans, and plants. Most of the phosphorus (about 80%) in humans is located in the bones and teeth, and the rest is located in soft tissue cells. Phosphorus is essential for calcium, glucose, and protein metabolism. The phosphorus in blood consists of several different compounds, for example, inorganic phosphate, and ester phosphate. Food sources high in phosphorus include cod, beef, Brewer's yeast, chicken, milk, and yogurt. The normal values of inorganic phosphorus in adults is 2.5-4.8 mg/dl. In young children this may be 25-50% higher. In hypoparathyroidism the value of phosphorus goes up slightly, while in hyperparathyroidism the level may be as low as 2 mg/dl. See *hyperparathyroidism, hypoparathyroidism,* and *minerals.*

Pick's disease   A rare form of presenile dementia in middle-aged people.

pineal gland   Also known as epiphysis (or pineal body), the gland is found between the two cerebral hemispheres at the back of the skull. The pineal gland secretes melatonin. It is believed that undersecretion of melatonin (due to lack of sunlight or other causes) may lead to a form of depression known as seasonal affective disorder (SAD).

pituitary gland   The pituitary is a pea-sized endocrine gland, located beneath (and attached to) the hypothalamus, consisting of an anterior lobe (adenohypophysis), and a posterior lobe (neurohypophysis). The pituitary gland is known as the master gland because it produces, stores, and releases hormones that stimulate other endocrine glands. For example, the *adenohypophysis* secretes thyroid stimulating hormone, gonadotrophins, growth hormone, prolactin, lipotropin, and melanocyte-stimulating hormone. The *neurohypophysis* secretes oxytocin, and vasopressin, which after being synthesized by the hypothalamus, is stored in the pituitary for future release. Many nerve pathways from the brain lead to the pituitary gland, and consequently the pituitary is greatly and directly influenced by brain activity, including cognitive processes, and especially via the hypothalamus also by emotional processes. The pituitary is a direct link in many psychosomatic (mind-body) disorders. Perceptions and cognitions within the cerebral cortex directly affect the limbic system, and in turn—via the hypothalamus—the pituitary gland. The pituitary is responsible for so-called secondary stress responses, while the hypothalamus, which also has a direct link with the adrenal medulla, is responsible for so-called primary stress responses. The pituitary plays a key role in physical and mental health. See *endocrine glands, endocrine system, hyperpituitarism, hypothalamus, limbic system, mental health.*

placebo   An inactive substance that has been substituted for a drug.

polysaccharide   A complex carbohydrate that can be changed into monosaccharides. See *monosaccharides.*

polyunsaturated   An organic compound, that is, a fatty acid with more than one double bond. Polyunsaturated pertains especially to fats of animal or vegetable origin that will result in low cholesterol. See *fatty acids.*

positive thinking   Positive thinking is synonymous with faith, and as such it is confident, constructive, definite, expectant, optimistic, and sure, rather than destructive, doubtful, and skeptical. These are characteristics of negative thinking. Positive thinking is one of the three dimensions of good mental health, the other two are rational thinking and realistic thinking. Psychologically based depressions result from loss of psychological integrity, that is the absence and/or inability to make positive as well as rational and realistic choices in daily life. See *rational thinking,* and *realistic thinking.*

positron emission tomography   A computerized radiographic technique which is used for the evaluation of metabolic activity in different tissues, and in particular in brain tissue. Glucose with radioactive oxygen injected into the body will after uptake by functioning neurons, slowly metabolize while giving off radioactive emissions (gamma rays). Via computer analysis, these emissions will eventually become color-coded images. Because metabolic activity in damaged brain tissue is markedly reduced, there will also be a marked reduction—or absence—of radioactive emissions. PET scans are used for the diagnosis of various brain damage disorders. Also see *metabolism,* and *computerized axial tomography (CAT).*

posterior pituitary gland   See *pituitary gland.*

potassium   A metallic element which is vital for health and life. Found primarily in the cells of the body, potassium has many essential functions, such as helping with the conversion of glucose to glycogen, stimulating nerve impulses for muscular contractions, and (together with sodium) to help regulate body fluids. Deficiency symptoms of potassium include edema, muscular weakness, nervousness, and tachycardia (abnormally rapid heartbeat). Treatment for potassium deficiency may include the administration of potassium chloride. Normal value in blood serum is 3.5-5.6 mEg/L. See *minerals.*

predisposition   An inclination, or tendency, to be susceptible to certain physical and/or psychological disorders. This tendency may be *genetic,* or *acquired* because of environmental factors, especially in relation to lifestyle. The predisposition may result from, or be enhanced by, such factors as lack of food, lack of specific nutrients, such as, amino acids, minerals, vitamins, or malnutrition, caused by the excessive use of junk foods, addictive substances, lack of exercise, sleep, and so forth. Other environmental factors may include lack of love, self-esteem, spiritual direction. A higher-than-average predisposition to certain nongenetic disorders may be found in some families. See *hereditary potential, heredity,* and *malnutrition.*

premenstrual depression   See *premenstrual syndrome.*

premenstrual syndrome (PMS)   A physical and mental/emotional condition that affects many women seven to ten days preceding menstruation, and in some cases for a few days after menstruation has started. Premenstrual syndrome (PMS) is also known as premenstrual tension. About 50% of all women of child-bearing ability suffer mild to severe problems associated with the menstrual cycle. To speak of premenstrual syndrome is a misnomer, not only because some women may also suffer for a day or two after menstruation has started, but also because a few women even after the menopause or removal of the uterus still suffer from PMS. It has been noted that PMS may have a direct effect on people in the immediate environment of the sufferer, in particular husband and children, whose mood disturbances and psychosomatic problems often correspond dramatically to those of the wife and mother.

The menstrual cycle is regulated (timed) by the hypothalamus, which is a part of the brain's limbic (feeling) system. It is to be remembered that the hypothalamus to a very great extent comes directly under the control of the neocortex (thinking) part of the brain. It is the hypothalamus that sends messages to the pituitary gland, which controls all the functions of the endocrine system, including that of the ovaries. The overall control of the menstrual cycle takes place by four hormones, namely FSH and LH secreted by the pituitary gland, and estrogen and progesterone secreted primarily by the ovaries. To understand PMS requires a basic knowledge of the menstrual cycle, the endocrine system, and the interrelationship of body and mind. The menstrual cycle is a continuously repeated series of events lasting from 21-35 days for women from puberty to menopause (altered only by disease, oral contraceptives, pregnancies, and so forth) and requiring a somewhat precarious balance of various hormones.

The process starts with the release of (1) *FSH* (by the pituitary); followed by (2) *estrogen* (ovary); followed by (3) *LH* (pituitary); followed by ovulation; and (4) *progesterone* (corpus luteum). As FSH (follicle stimulating hormone) enters the bloodstream it induces a follicle (undeveloped egg) in the ovary to fully develop (ripen). At this point estrogen is manufactured by the ovary and enters the bloodstream to alert the pituitary gland to halt the manufacture of FSH. Now as the estrogen level builds up in the bloodstream the pituitary begins to manufacture LH (luteinizing hormone). Once in the bloodstream LH induces ovulation, which signals the fully developed egg to leave the ovary and enter into the fallopian tube.

It is the space that has been vacated by the fully developed egg that now becomes the so-called *corpus luteum* (yellow body) which starts to produce progesterone. The latter's functions include: (1) tell the pituitary to halt production of FSH and LH; and (2) tell the womb to thicken its mucus membrane lining (endometrium). If fertilization does not take place, then the corpus luteum breaks down and progesterone is no longer produced. This drop in progesterone alerts the pituitary to once again produce FSH and start the menstrual cycle anew.

The fact that more women than men suffer from depression and related problems is due (to some extent at least) to the menstrual cycle and various disturbances resulting from related endocrine dysfunctions. Estrogen and progesterone not only act as simple messengers in the menstruation cycle, but also affect breasts, skin, smooth muscle tissue of blood vessel walls and intestines, and brain chemistry. The latter in turn plays a major role in various emotional problems such as anxiety and depression. All of the endocrine glands work in close harmony with each other and whenever any part of it fails, it affects the entire system, and thus body and mind. Estrogen and progesterone are steroids manufactured by the cortex of the adrenal glands. The steroids play a major role in maintaining the proper balance of water and minerals, glucose levels, and cortisone levels (which is crucial for inflammatory, infectious, and allergic conditions). Dysfunction of the pituitary, ovaries, adrenals, but also of any other part of the endocrine system, may play a direct part in premenstrual tension, for example, prolactin (a hormone produced by the pituitary gland), is necessary for the growth and development of the female mammary glands, and the stimulation of milk production after childbirth. The excessive production of prolactin is sometimes treated with bromocriptine (Parlodel), and lack of progesterone with natural or synthetic progesterones.

Causes of PMS include: (1) a disturbance of the progesterone-estrogen ratio; (2) low levels of vitamin B_6; (3) magnesium deficiency; (4) prostaglandin imbalance; (5) Central Nervous System malfunctions; (6) improper nutrition; and (7) other forms of excessive stress.

Symptoms of PMS include: abdominal pain, appetite changes, aggressiveness, anxiety, backache, bloated or distended abdomen, colds susceptibility, confusion, constipation, cramps, depression, edema, forgetfulness, headache, irritability, joint pains, lethargy, low blood sugar, nervousness, restlessness, salt retention, skin eruptions, swollen and painful breasts, tiredness, water retention, weepiness, and weight gain.

Medical treatment for PMS may include the administration of natural or synthetic progesterone. *Nonmedical treatment* often includes: proper nutrition (Wellness Diet), food supplements (especially vitamins A, B_6, C, folic acid, as well as primrose oil), rest, relaxation, exercise (especially walking), and emotional re-education. There are also excellent self-help books, as well as specialty clinics that deal exclusively with PMS. Premenstrual syndrome is only one of several physical sources of depression (such as, candida albicans, hypoglycemia, hypothyroidism, and hypoadrenocorticism) found in many women.

It is important to realize that there is a major difference in the physical makeup of women, and that—in general—their vulnerability for depression is greater than in men. However, in spite of this vulnerability, women are generally found to be more rational than men. See *anterior pituitary gland, anxiety, candidiasis, depression, emotional re-education, endocrine system, hypothalamus, hypoglycemia, hypothyroidism, hypoadrenocorticism, follicle stimulating hormone, glucocorticoid, luteinizing hormone, limbic system, mental health, mineralocorticoids, mineral supplement, pituitary gland, estrogen, progesterone, prolactin, vitamin supplement, wellness diet.*

presenile dementia   See *Alzheimer's disease.*

preservatives   Substances added to medications, foods, or food supplements to prevent spoilage.

prochlorperazine   A major tranquilizer, strong antipsychotic, and anti-nausea medication, marketed under the trade name of Stemetil. Used primarily for severe nausea and vomiting and sometimes in the treatment of certain mental disorders, for instance, schizophrenia.

proctor nocturnis   Night terror.

progesterone   A steroid hormone secreted primarily by the *corpus luteum* of the ovary, during pregnancy by the placenta, as well as by the adrenal cortex and testes in small amounts. Progesterone prepares the inner lining of the womb for pregnancy. If fertilization takes place, progesterone stops the release of eggs from the ovary. Natural and synthetic progesterone is used in oral contraceptives. Low levels of progesterone have been identified with premenstrual syndrome (PMS). See *premenstrual syndrome.*

prognosis Prediction.

projection A defense mechanism by which some people unconsciously attribute their own shortcomings and unacceptable thoughts, feelings, and actions to others. It functions as a defense against repressed anxiety and as a means of self-justification.

prolactin A hormone of the anterior pituitary gland which is necessary for development of the female mammary glands and for lactation. See *premenstrual syndrome*.

prostaglandin One of a group of naturally occurring hormonelike fatty acids found in small amounts in many tissues of the body, as well as in body fluids, for example, semen and menstrual fluid. Prostaglandins are important for many body functions including the endocrine and nervous systems.

protein Any of a group of complex nitrogenous organic compounds, consisting of carbon, hydrogen, oxygen, and nitrogen, found in all living cells, and essential for life. Normal value of total protein in blood serum is 6-8 g/dl.

protein bound iodine (PBI) The iodine found in thyroxin and thyrocalcitonin that is bound to the plasma protein "thyroxin-binding globulin (TBG)," is known as protein bound iodine or PBI. Normally there is a fairly constant amount of PBI in a person's blood, ranging from 4-8 micrograms PBI per 100 milliliters of blood. PBI is used as an index of thyroid hormone secretion and helpful in diagnosing thyroid disorders. See *hyperthyroidism, hypothyroidism, thyrocalcitonin, thyroid gland, thyroid hormones, thyroid stimulating hormone (TSH),* and *thyrotropin releasing factor (TRF)*.

protriptyline A tricyclic antidepressant medication sold under the trade name of Vivactil and sometimes prescribed for moderately severe endogenous depressions.

psilocybin A hallucinogen. See *hallucinogen*.

psychogenic Originating in the mind. Psychogenic refers to diseases, disorders, or symptoms of a psychological (rather than a physical) origin.

psychomotor Related to the motor affects of mental processes, especially those conditions where muscular activity is affected by a cerebral disturbance.

psychomotor retardation Slow physical and mental responses, such as slowness of thought, speech, and movement.

psychopath A person who does not seem to make a distinction between right and wrong, nor to feel guilty about his or her antisocial behavior. A psychopath is an unstable individual with an apparent inability to fully realize or care about the results of his or her actions, or to be committed to social mores and ethics. Although there is an absence of deep emotional feelings, there may not be a specific mental disorder. Also see *personality disorders*.

psychosis A psychological disturbance or mental state characterized by detachment from objective reality, usually involving severely disturbed emotions, delusions, and hallucinations, and at times by severe personality disintegration and grossly disturbed interpersonal relationships. The psychotic person replaces reality with imaginary thoughts and ideas and does not generally recognize there is something seriously wrong with changing fantasy into reality. The psychoses include: *schizophrenia; manic-depressive psychosis* (an extreme form of manic depression with hallucinations, delusions of grandeur, persecution, and so forth); *involutional psychosis* (including *involutional melancholia,* marked by anxiety, agitated depression, weeping, moaning, intense feelings of guilt, worthlessness; of having injured others, having committed grievous sins, needing to be punished, deserving to be destroyed, and knowing that this will happen; imaginary illnesses, and suicide attempts, and *involutional paranoid reaction,* marked by agitation, fear, and delusions of persecution, with people trying to poison or kill the sufferer); *psychotic depressive reaction,* which is more of an exogenous, rather than an endogenous nature, and is a reaction to some fact or event in the past or present environment. It is marked by thought disturbances, delusions, and hallucinations related to guilt or worthlessness, and difficulty to function adequately in the environment; *organic psychoses due to changes in the brain; oneiroid psychosis,* marked by excessive dreamlike confused state (characteristic also of schizoid personalities); and *schizoaffective psychosis,* which is marked by both manic-depressive and schizophrenic symptoms. The major features of a psychosis are withdrawal from reality, hallucinations, delusions, severely disturbed emotions, and personality disintegration. The treatment of psychosis includes psychoactive drugs, psychotherapy, and major lifestyle adjustments, including appropriate nutrition, food supplements, and so forth. See *bipolar depression, delusion, depression, DSM-III, hallucinations, mental health, neurosis, paranoid schizophrenia,* and *schizophrenia.*

psychosomatic   Pertaining to mind and body. Usually refers to physical symptoms and disorders, resulting from excessive psychological stress.

psychosomatogenic   Originating in both mind and body.

psychotic depression   See *depressive illness.*

pyridoxine   Also known as vitamin B_6 it is important for carbohydrate, protein, and fat metabolism: the production of hormones in the central nervous system; the conversion of tryptophan into niacin (vitamin B_3); and the production of the neurotransmitter serotonin, and so forth. The need for pyridoxine is increased by elevated levels of estrogen. Birth control pills may lead to serious deficiency of pyridoxine and depression. The treatment of premenstrual tension often includes the administration of pyridoxine. See *estrogen, metabolism, neurotransmitters, niacin, premenstrual syndrome, serotonin,* and *tryptophan.*

rapid eye movement   The period of sleep marked by rapid eye muscle contractions, by dreaming, and by changes in brain wave, muscle, and respiratory activity, usually lasting no more than 30 minutes, and alternating with so-called nonrapid eye movement periods of sleep. Involves approximately 25% of a person's normal sleep. See *nonrapid eye movement.*

rational thinking   Rational thinking is synonymous with reason, and as such it is analytical, appropriate, explanatory, objective, and logical; it involves an emphasis on the validity and reliability of one's own thoughts. Rational thinking is life enhancing, objective, goal achieving, allows persons to feel how they want to feel, and keeps them, whenever possible, out of unwanted trouble. Rational thinking requires the objective insight and philosophical acceptance of the fallibility of all people, as well as a personal commitment to stay alive as long and as happily as possible. Rational thinking is marked by a desire for scrupulous honesty, the acceptance of personal accountability, and responsibility for one's own perceptions, thoughts, feelings, and actions. It emphasizes the need to continuously evaluate and update one's thoughts, feelings, and actions with a special emphasis on "choice." Rational thinking is one of the three dimensions of good mental health; the other two are positive thinking and realistic thinking. Psychologically based depressions (and many other emotional disorders) result from loss of psychological integrity, that is the absence and/or inability to make rational as well as positive and realistic choices in daily life. See *positive thinking,* and *realistic thinking.*

rationalization The justification of one's behavior by explaining away shortcomings and avoiding responsibility. A common defense mechanism to prevent loss of social approval and self-esteem.

reactive depression Often used in lieu of exogenous, mild, moderate, or neurotic depression. Reactive Depression is the opposite of—and more common than—depressive illness. See *depressive illness.*

realistic thinking Realistic thinking is synonymous with factual thinking, that is, the representation of objects and life as they really are. Realistic thinking zeros in on the requirements of an external situation, is productive, and aids problem solving. Realistic thinking is concrete, practical, and real, and consequently is marked by its nonspeculative nature, dealing with facts rather than assumptions. Realistic thinking often involves the postponement of short-term pleasures, satisfactions, or rewards, in order to achieve certain long-term goals. Realistic thinking is one of the three dimensions of good mental health; the other two are positive thinking and rational thinking. Psychologically based depressions (and many other emotional disorders) result from loss of psychological integrity, that is the absence of and/or inability to make realistic, as well as rational and positive choices in daily life. See *positive thinking,* and *rational thinking.*

receptor The endings of a sensory nerve which is specially adapted to detect various changes in the environment and to trigger impulses in the sensory nervous system. Receptors detect chemicals, lights, sounds, and so forth.

recommended dietary allowances (RDA) The amount of nutrients that the National Research Council believes are essential for life in most "healthy" individuals. Those who have nutritional deficiencies or specific disorders may need considerably higher amounts under the supervision of a physician, registered dietician, or other qualified health practitioner.

repression A defense mechanism by which painful, guilt producing, or otherwise unacceptable thoughts, feelings, and memories are excluded from conscious awareness, often resulting in abnormal behavior. See *emotional repression.*

reserpine A drug extracted from the rauwolfia plant, marketed under many trade names, including Arcum-RS, Randxin, Rau-Sed, Serpasil, and SK-Reserpine. The drug is used primarily for the treatment of high blood pressure. Unfortunately, there are sometimes adverse effects, including impotence and depression. The drug is believed to affect the storage sites of norepinephrine in the nerve endings of the sympathetic nervous system. While less norepinephrine leads to a relaxation of the blood vessel walls, and thus a lowering of blood pressure, it also may lead to impotence and depression. Reserpine is contraindicated for those who suffer from depression, and it must not be taken concurrently with MAO inhibitors. See *monoamine oxidase inhibitors*.

resistance stage The second stage of the stress syndrome, which is also known as the General Adaptation Syndrome. Under stress the anterior pituitary gland and the adrenal glands provide increased hormonal secretions to maintain normal blood chemistry and bodily functions. Continued stress will lead to adrenal exhaustion and such conditions as hypoadrenocorticism (hypoadrenalism), with such manifestations as anxiety, depressions, etc. See *general adaptation syndrome*.

riboflavin Also known as vitamin B$_2$. Riboflavin has many functions, including the metabolism of carbohydrates, protein, and fat, the proper functioning of the Central Nervous System; necessary for tryptophan metabolism; and helpful in reducing the extremes of depression. Deficiency symptoms include cracks in the corners of the mouth, dizziness, numbness in arms and legs, as well as depression.

Ritalin Brand name for methylphenidate, a Central Nervous System stimulant, which has been used and abused in the treatment of hyperactivity in children, in whom the drug paradoxically has a calming effect. When used in adults it has a stimulating effect, possibly through the release of the neurotransmitter norepinephrine. See *hyperactivity*.

saccharide One of a large series of carbohydrates, including starches, and various sugars such as disaccharides (double sugars), monosaccharides (single sugars), and polysaccharides (multiple sugars). See *carbohydrate, dextrose, fructose, galactose, hexose, maltose,* and *sucrose*.

saturated fatty acids All fats that are in a solid state (except coconut oil) at room temperature. Foods high in saturated fatty acids include all animal fats such as beef, lamb, pork, and veal, and all milk products such as butter, cheese, and cream. A healthy diet is low in saturated fatty acids, and high in unsaturated fatty acids. Diets high in fatty acids are dangerous to health, causing excess calories, blood fats, and blood cholesterol, leading to increased risk of hardening of the arteries, heart attack, stroke, and other disorders. See *unsaturated fatty acids*.

schizoid Resembling to a mild degree some of the symptoms of schizophrenia. A schizoid personality is characterized by perfectionism, self-consciousness, feelings of isolation, loneliness, and an inability to form close personal relationships. Schizoid personalities are afraid of closeness and intimacy, and often seem distant and emotionally cold. See *personality disorders*.

schizophrenia Any of a group of psychiatric disorders characterized by disintegration of intellectual and emotional processes, withdrawal from reality, social isolation, seriously impaired perceptions, illogical thoughts, inappropriate feelings, and bizarre, often regressive behaviors. Commonly found are delusions, hallucinations, and rambling speech. Schizophrenic persons frequently believe that their thoughts, feelings, and actions are controlled by other people, leading to social withdrawal. Schizophrenia is the result of both hereditary and environmental factors, including excessively stressful childhood experiences, sociocultural influences, and biochemical factors. While there is an apparent genetic predisposition, this does not mean that helpful treatment is not available. Much success is attainable with a thorough plan of physical and psychological treatment, including the major tranquilizers, antidepressants, psychotherapy, and orthomolecular (nutritional) therapy. Schizophrenia may be mild, moderate, or severe. Types of schizophrenia include:

1. *catatonic schizophrenia,* marked by motor disturbances and excitement
2. *hebephrenic schizophrenia,* marked by adolescent, or early adulthood onset, shallow, and inappropriate emotions, giggling, silly behaviors, and hypochondriasis
3. *paranoid schizophrenia,* marked by serious delusions, usually of grandeur, or persecution, and often accompanied by hallucinations
4. *reactive schizophrenia,* marked by acute onset due to early childhood conditions
5. *simple schizophrenia,* marked by slow onset and progression, apathy, lack of initiative, withdrawal, and personal ineffectiveness

senile dementia Serious mental impairment resulting from physical deterioration of the brain, beginning—for the first time—in advanced age. Senile dementia is not related to cerebral vascular disease or injury. Symptoms include apathy, agitation, confusion, confabulation, irritability, major personality changes, and memory loss. Sometimes senile dementia is misdiagnosed in persons suffering from nutritional deficiencies, or who live in isolated and stimulation deprived environments, or are taking excessive medications, or suffering from other stressful conditions. Senile dementia is to be distinguished from Alzheimer's disease, which is an organic disorder. A person who suffers from senile dementia will admit that he or she is suffering from a loss of intellectual ability, while Alzheimer's patients will deny this. Senile dementia is the logical outcome of physical and psychological factors, which often may successfully be treated with appropriate medicines, and other measures for anemia, systemic illnesses, endocrine dysfunctions, electrolyte imbalances, and so forth. People of advanced age may benefit greatly by a Wellness Diet of whole, natural foods, food supplements (which is to include lecithin), mild exercise, recreation, and if necessary, occupational, physical, and psychological therapies, as well as spiritual assistance. See *AIDS dementia complex, Alzheimer's disease, dementia, Huntington's disease,* and *Pick's disease.*

serotonin A substance found naturally in the brain and intestines and which plays multiple roles for the maintenance of good physical and mental health. For example, it narrows blood vessels in case of injury and also reduces inflammation. Serotonin plays a role in the regulation of appetite, aggression, sleep, mood, pain, and the stimulation of the female sex drive. For example, low levels of serotonin may not only lead to depression, but also to a reduction of sexual desire in women. Serotonin is manufactured in the body, but only when there is a satisfactory amount of the essential amino acid tryptophan present in the intestines. Low levels of serotonin are believed to be a source of endogenous depression. To increase the levels of serotonin in the brain (where it functions as a neurotransmitter) several approaches may be taken. Physicians frequently prescribe socalled monoamine oxidase inhibitor (MAOI) drugs. These drugs inhibit (slow down) the use of an enzyme called "monoamine oxidase." The latter is responsible for the metabolism (oxidation) of serotonin in the brain. Retarding the oxidation process results in an increase of the neurotransmitter serotonin and a decrease in depression. Physicians also may prescribe socalled tricyclic (and other) antidepressant drugs. Some of these, for example, Amitril and Elavil, increase the serotonin levels, while others, for example, Aventyl and Tofranil, increase both serotonin and norepinephrine levels in the brain. There is another way of increasing both serotonin and norepinephrine levels in the brain by a more natural means. A food supplement, the amino acid DL-Phenylalanine, has similar effects on mood elevation. This highlights the relationship between food and mood and the necessity for proper nutrition. As stated before, the manufacture of serotonin in the body depends on tryptophan which cannot be manufactured by the body and must be obtained from protein in our diet. Certain foods are naturally high in serotonin: avocados, bananas, eggplant, pineapple, and plums. The effectiveness of drug treatment can be measured both subjectively by how well the person feels, and objectively by urinalysis. The normal value of serotonin excretion in the urine is 2 to 9 milligrams in a 24-hour period (2-9 mg/24 hr). This test might also be helpful in the diagnosis of an endogenous depression related to low levels of serotonin. The use of monoamine oxidase inhibitors and antidepressant drugs lowers the levels of serotonin in urine excretion, proving their effectiveness in slowing down amine metabolism. See *amino acids, antidepressants, imipramine, MAO inhibitors, norepinephrine, neurotransmitters, phenylalanine,* and *tryptophan.*

stimulants Substances that promote temporary excitation of a body part, or system, in particular the Central Nervous System. Stimulants include amphetamine, caffeine, nicotine, theobromine, and theophylline. Stimulants are stressful because they alert the *hypothalamus* to send messages to the adrenal glands and to activate the fight or flight mechanism. They increase sugar production, which is quickly followed by a drop in sugar levels, creating a self-defeating cycle of physical and emotional ups and downs. Temporary mood elevation created by stimulants are always followed by a more serious mood depression.

stimulus Any object or event that provokes a response in sensitive cells, tissues, and so forth. For example, odors excite olfactory receptors. A stimulus is either adequate or inadequate to provoke a response.

stress More appropriately called stress-response. Dr. Hans Selye, the "father" of stress theory, maintains that stress is the nonspecific response of the body to any demand (whether pleasant or unpleasant) for adaptation.

Life is not possible without stress; however, we can make a distinction between good stress (eustress) and bad stress (distress). There is no life without stress. Everything we do is the result of physical, psychological, and/or spiritual stress. Only *excessive* stress that becomes a problem, may lead to disease and even death. Normal stress is simply any condition to which body and mind must adapt or adjust. It is important to recognize that "potential" stressors can only become "actual" stressors if body and/or mind are so predisposed or persuaded. Consequently, what is excessive stress for one person, or at one given time, may not be excessive stress for another person, or at another time. One of the major sources of stress in modern society is found in nutritional deficiencies, caused by inadequate or dangerous diets, which play havoc with normal chemistry. The resulting biochemical imbalances are all too frequently treated symptomatically with drugs, without dealing with underlying causes. Inadequate levels of hormones, glucose, and neurotransmitters, leading to numerous physical and mental disorders, including depression, are all too often caused by excessive stress. The adrenal glands, also known as the stress glands, are particularly susceptible to excessive stress.

As stressful situations develop, these glands are continually called upon to provide the necessary corrective responses. If "alarm" calls become excessive, and the glands do not get an opportunity to restore themselves, they will eventually become unable to secrete essential hormones. Proper diet, food supplements, exercise, rest, recreation, emotional re-education, (to include rational, realistic, and positive thinking), and other common-sense measures are necessary for the treatment and the prevention of excessive stress. Excessive stress may cause as much as 85% of all physical and psychological disorders, including such common problems as anxiety, biochemical imbalances, and depression. Also see *anxiety, biochemical, depression, emotional repression, emotional re-education, epinephrine, excessive stress, general adaptation syndrome, glucocorticoid, glucose, hypoadrenalism, hypoglycemia, mental health, mineral supplement, neuropeptides, neurotransmitters, norepinephrine, positive thinking, predisposition, rational thinking, realistic thinking, serotonin, sympathetic nervous system, tranquilizers, vitamin supplement.*

stressor Any condition, fact, or event requiring adaptation or adjustment.

superego An individual's conscience. See *ego,* and *id.*

suppression The voluntary and conscious process of dismissing from consciousness unpleasant thoughts, feelings, and memories. See *Repression.*

sympathetic nervous system One of two divisions of the autonomic nervous system that activates the body in response to high levels of physical, or mental/emotional stress, for example, extreme cold, violent effort, strenuous exercise, fear, rage, etc. See *autonomic nervous system,* and *parasympathetic nervous system.*

symptom Any indicator that there is a possibility of a physical, psychological, and/or spiritual disorder. *Symptoms* are only subjective indicators, while *signs* are objective indicators of possible disorders. See *syndrome.*

synapse A microscopic gap between two nerve cells (neurons), or a nerve cell and a muscle (neuromuscular junction). Whenever a nerve impulse reaches the tip of an axon-terminal, certain brain chemicals, called neurotransmitters, will be released. Nerve impulses are primarily electrical events, but communication between the nerve cells are chemical events. Brain chemicals consist of *monoamines,* such as, acetylcholine, dopamine, histamine, epinephrine, norepinephrine, and serotonin; and *amino acids,* for example y-aminobutyrate (GABA), glycine, glutamate, and parnate. When neurotransmitters cross the synapse between two neurons they may either excite or inhibit the next nerve cell. Each of these cells is connected to as many as 10,000 other cells. A single nerve cell may, at any given time, receive messages from hundreds, or even thousands, of other nerve cells. In order to serve the brain's estimated 100 billion nerve cells there are 100 trillion synapses, creating "endless" possible pathways between the nerve cells. See *amines, amino acids, monoamines, neurons,* and *neurotransmitters.*

syndrome   A group of signs and/or symptoms that provide a clinical picture of physical and/or psychological conditions.

synergistic   The increased and beneficial effect obtained through the joint action of treatment modalities; including the increased effectiveness obtained when certain drugs or vitamins are taken together.

systemic   Affecting the entire body, rather than only certain parts.

tactile   Pertaining to, or affecting the sense of touch.

tardive dyskinesia   A disorder of the nervous system characterized by uncontrollable twitches of facial and other muscles, speech disturbances, and tics. The person suffering from tardive dyskinesia may flail his/her arms about, be very agitated, grimacing, and/or depressed. Tardive dyskinesia may result from prolonged use of antipsychotic drugs. However, it has been reported that some patients who, along with the drugs, also received vitamins B_3, B_6, C, and E, did not develop this neurological disorder. It is assumed that most likely vitamin B_6 was responsible for the prevention of the tardive dyskinesia. Treatment for tardive dyskinesia, with sometimes encouraging results, has been undertaken with lecithin. Lecithin contains choline, which eventually raises the acetylcholine levels in the brain. It is thought that acetylcholine counteracts the brain's hypersensitivity to dopamine. See *acetylcholine, choline, dopamine, lecithin, neurotransmitters, niacin,* and *pyridoxine.*

taurine   Amino acid, which functions as a major neuroinhibitor, slowing down the transmission of nerve impulses from one cell to another. Important for proper functioning of brain and nervous system, and helpful for anxiety and hyperactivity.

testosterone   A male sex hormone and responsible for development of secondary sexual characteristics. Testosterone is secreted by the interstitial cells of the testes, and small quantities also by the adrenal glands and ovaries of women.

thalamus   One of two large, egg-shaped masses of gray matter, located at the base of the cerebrum. Sensations of pain, pressure, and temperature originate in the thalamus. The thalamus is a relay center for sensory impulses to the cerebral cortex.

theobromine A weak stimulant found in cocoa.

theophylline A weak stimulant found in tea leaves.

thiamine Vitamin B_1. Among other factors, important for proper functioning of brain and nervous system. Aids the immune system, tranquilizes,
relieves depression caused by B_1 deficiency.

Thorazine Brand name for the major tranquilizer chlorpromazine. See
tranquilizers.

threonine Amino acid which is important for collagen, elastin, and enamel
protein. Aids proper functioning of the liver. See *amino acid.*

thymus An endocrine gland located behind the sternum and important for
the proper functioning of the lymphatic and immune systems.

thyrocalcitonin Hormone secreted by the thyroid gland which is responsible for the regulation of blood calcium levels. See *hypercalcemia,* and
hypocalcemia.

thyroid function tests There are many thyroid function tests, including
PBI, Serum total T4, T3 Resin uptake, free thyroxine (T4) index, etc. A
rather common test is the thyroxine-binding index (TBI), of which the normal values in blood serum are 0.90 - 1.11. Lower TBI values may indicate
hyperthyroidism, and higher values (above 1.11) may indicate hypothyroidism. See *hyperthyroidism,* and *hypothyroidism.*

thyroid gland Large endocrine gland, at the base of the neck, consisting of
two lobes, one on each side of the trachea (windpipe) and connected by an
isthmus. The hormones of the thyroid gland, among other things, regulate
the rates of metabolism and body growth. See *thyroid function tests,* and
thyroid hormones.

thyroid hormones The thyroid gland secretes two hormones, namely thyroxine (T3), which is important for increasing the rate of cell metabolism,
and triiodothyronine (T4), which is more biologically active than thyroxine.
Excess of thyroid hormones leads to *thyrotoxicosis,* and shortage of thyroid
hormone leads to *myxedema.* See *hyperthyroidism, hypothyroidism, thyroid
function tests, thyrotoxicosis,* and *myxedema.*

thyroid stimulating hormone (TSH) Hormone secreted by the anterior
pituitary gland and responsible for the release of thyroid from the thyroid
gland. TSH, in turn, is directed by thyrotropin releasing factor (TRF).

thyrotoxicosis Condition caused by the secretion of excessive thyroid hormones, and characterized by anxiety, tremor, rapid heart beat, increased
appetite, weight loss, and intolerance for heat. May be caused by thyroid
overactivity, benign or nonbenign tumors, or Grave's disease (exophthalmic
goiter). See *hyperthyroidism.*

thyrotropin releasing factor (TRF) Hormone released by the hypothalamus and responsible for directing the release of TSH by the anterior pituitary gland. See *hypothalamus* and *thyroid stimulating hormone.*

tocopherol See E: Vitamin.

Tofranil Brand name for the tricyclic antidepressant imipramine.

toxicity The poisonous effects found in people who have ingested a substance, or substances, above their level of tolerance.

trace mineral   Essential elements needed only in minute amounts to sustain life.

tranquilizers   Those drugs that calm or quiet agitated and anxious people. A distinction is made between major and minor tranquilizers, as follows:

Major Tranquilizers

They have sedative as well as antipsychotic properties, which, among other things, aim at reducing, or eliminating, delusions, hallucinations, and other psychotic symptoms. The major tranquilizers include:

Carbolith (lithium)   Phenergan
Compazine (prochlorperazine)   (promethazine)
Eskalith (lithium)   Prolixin (fluphenazine)
Haldol (haloperidol)   Promapar (chlorpromazine)
· Lithane (lithium)   Serentil (mesoridazine)
Lithonate (lithium)   Stelazine (trifluoperazine)
Lithotabs (lithium)   Temaril (trimepazine)
Mellaril (thioridazine)   Thorazine (chlorpromazine)
Navane (thiothixene)   Trilafon (perphenazine)
Permitil (fluphenazine)

Minor Tranquilizers

They have no antipsychotic properties and are used primarily for anxiety and other nervous conditions. The minor tranquilizers include:

Ativan (lorazepam)   Serax (oxazepam)
Centrax (prazepam)   Tranxene (clorazepate)
Dalmane (flurazepam)   Valium (diazepam)
Librium (chlordiazepoxide)   Xanax (alprazolam)

See *anxiety, delusions, hallucinations, iatrogenic drug abuse, lithium, neurosis* and *psychosis.*

tricyclic antidepressants   See *antidepressants.*

trypsin   A digestive enzyme involved in protein digestion.

tryptophan   Amino acid. A natural tranquilizer, tryptophan is important for mood stabilization and promotes restful sleep. May also be helpful to relieve depression caused by serotonin deficiency. See *amino acid,* and *serotonin.*

tyramine   An amine found in products such as beer, cheese, chocolate, cola drinks, wine, and so forth. The effect of tyramine on the body is similar to epinephrine, which is released by the adrenal medulla in response to hypoglycemia, and also increased blood pressure. The latter is especially dangerous for individuals who are taking MAO inhibitors, and they need to obtain a listing of all products that are high in tyramine and abstain from them. See *adrenal glands, epinephrine, hypoglycemia,* and *MAO inhibitors.*

tyrosine   Amino acid. Important for the production of dopamine, epinephrine, and norepinephrine, and in the treatment of depressions. Tyrosine must not be taken together with tryptophan as it is believed that tyrosine may compete with carrier molecules for transport from blood capillaries to brain neurons. The other two amino acids often used in the treatment of depression are DL-Phenylalanine and Tryptophan. See *amino acid, carbo-hydrate connection, depression, norepinephrine, phenylalanine,* and *tryptophan.*

unipolar depression   A major depression characterized by a single or re-current depressive episode. See *DSM-III* and *depressive illness.*

unsaturated fatty acids   Fats that are in a liquid state at room tempera-ture. *Monounsaturated* fatty acids are found in such foods as almonds, chicken, and olive oil, while *polyunsaturated* fatty acids are found in such foods as corn, fish, safflower, and soybean oil. Unsaturated fatty acids are important for a healthy diet. See *saturated fatty acids.*

valine   Amino acid. Important for treatment of amino acid deficiencies caused by drug addictions.

vasopressin   A hormone secreted by the posterior pituitary gland, known as antidiuretic hormone (ADH), because it increases the reabsorption of water by the kidneys, which prevents excess water loss from the body. Vasopressin is also important as a blood vessel constrictor. See *pituitary gland.*

viral   Caused by a virus. The latter is a minute particle without independent metabolism and only capable of reproducing itself within living cells.

Vistaril   Brand name for the tranquilizer hydroxyzine. See *tranquilizers.*

vitamin   Any of a group of organic substances found in foods and which are essential for specific and vital functions in the cells and tissues of the body. Virtually all of the vitamins have to be obtained from the diet, since the body cannot synthesize them. Shortage of specific vitamins may lead to physical and/or mental/emotional disorders. Vitamins are water soluble, with the exception of A, D, E, and K, which are fat soluble and more readily build up to toxic levels in the body. Some vitamins may also interfere with certain drugs or may aggravate certain physical disorders. See *avitaminosis, megavitamins,* and *vitamin withdrawal.*

vitamin withdrawal   Deficiency symptoms may appear when a person sud-denly stops taking vitamin and mineral supplements, especially if so-called megadoses have been used for a prolonged period of time. As a rule it is best to gradually reduce the doses. In any case, megadoses of food supplements should only be taken under the supervision of physicians or other health experts.

white blood cell   A cell without hemoglobin and which helps the body de-fend itself against disease. See *blood cell, blood count,* and *leukocytes.*

wholistic   Pertaining to the total person, body, mind, and spirit. The whol-istic approach is concerned with the evaluation and treatment of the total person, as well as the integration of healing systems, the preservation of wellness, and prevention of illness.

withdrawal   Separating oneself from the environment due to lack of inter-est, or in response to perceived dangers, or other stressful situations. With-drawal may be manifested in apathy, boredom, lethargy, and so forth. Withdrawal is a term frequently used for the stressful and sometimes dan-gerous physical changes that take place when a person discontinues the use of substances to which he, or she, has become addicted, such as alcohol, barbiturates, narcotics, stimulants, and so forth. Even caffeine, nicotine, and sucrose withdrawal may lead to unpleasant physical and mental/emotional changes, and may require the assistance of health professionals.

xanthine oxidase An enzyme found in the fat globules of cow's milk. Some physicians believe that when milk is homogenized, the fat globules are changed into such small units, that they pass into the blood stream and create dangerous deposits in the arterial walls.

yeast Single-celled fungi commonly used to ferment carbohydrates. Brewer's yeast is used for beer brewing and the manufacture of other alcoholic beverages as well as baking bread. Dried yeast is a by-product of beer brewing and frequently used in the manufacture of B-complex vitamins. Individuals who are prone to yeast infections and related problems, for example, depression caused by Candida Albicans, must abstain from yeast. See *candidiasis*.

zinc A metallic element which is essential for normal metabolism, especially phosphorus. Zinc helps maintain normal blood sugar levels, and has multiple other functions. Zinc is one of five minerals that have been found helpful in the reduction of stress and the treatment of *depression*. The other minerals are calcium, chromium, magnesium, and manganese. See *calcium, chromium, magnesium, manganese, minerals,* and *mineral supplement*.

References

Abrahamson, E. M., and Pezet, A. W. *Body, Mind, and Sugar.* New York: Avon Books, 1977.

Adams, P. W., et al. "Depression and Oral Contraceptives." *Lancet.* 1:7879, August 31, 1973, pp. 516–17.

————. "Effect of Pyridoxine Hydrochloride, Vitamin B6, on Depression Associated with Oral Contraceptives." *Lancet.* 1:7809, April 28, 1973, pp. 897–904.

Airola, Paavo. *Are You Confused?* Phoenix, AZ: Health Plus Publishers, 1971.

————. *Cancer: Causes, Prevention and Treatment.* Phoenix, AZ: Health Plus Publishers, 1972.

————. *How to Get Well.* Phoenix, AZ: Health Plus Publishers, 1974.

————. *Hypoglycemia: A Better Approach.* Phoenix, AZ: Health Plus Publishers, 1977.

American Medical Association Family Medical Guide, The. New York: Random House, 1982.

Baker, Don, and Nester, Emery. *Depression.* Portland, OR: Multnomah Press, 1983.

Ballentine, R. M. Jr. "The American Diet and the Health of Our Youth." *Elementary School Guidance and Counseling,* 1979, 14, 149–155.

Bargmann, Eve, and Wolfe, Sidney M. *Stopping Valium.* New York: Warner Books, 1983.

Bauer, J. *Clinical Laboratory Methods.* St. Louis: C. V. Mosby Company, 1982.

Beck, A. *Cognitive Therapy and the Emotional Disorders.* New York: New American Library, 1979.

Berger, Stuart M. *Dr. Berger's Immune Power Diet.* New York: New American Library, 1985.

Bergman, Jerry. "Mankind—The Pinnacle of God's Creation." *Christians in Education.* 2:1, 1985. Costa Mesa, CA: National Association of Christian Educators.

Blackburn, Bill. *What You Should Know About Suicide.* Waco, TX: Word Books, 1982.

Brandon, Nathaniel. *The Psychology of Self-Esteem.* Los Angeles: Nash Publishing Corporation, 1969.

Brandt, Frans M. J. "The Causes of Depression." *Journal of the National Council of Psychotherapists.* Vol. XIII:14, London, 1986.

————. "The Classification of Personality Disorders." *Journal of the National Council of Psychotherapists.* Vol. XIV:2, London, 1987.

————. *A Guide to Rational Weight Control.* Oscoda, MI: Wesselhoeft Associates, 1980.

————. "How to Heal Depression." *Journal of the National Council of Psychotherapists.* X:2, London, 1983.

————. *A Rational Self-Counseling Primer.* Kelsale Court, Saxmundham, Suffolk, England: Institute for Rational Therapy, 1979.

————. "Rational Self-Counseling: Thinking About Our Thinking." *Journal of the National Council of Psychotherapists,* VII:4, London, 1980.

————. "The Signs and Symptoms of Depression." *Journal of the National Council of Psychotherapists.* Vol. XIII:14, London, 1986.

————. "The Treatment of Depression." *Journal of the National Council of Psychotherapists.* Vol. XIII:15, London, 1986.

————. *The Way to Wholeness.* Westchester, IL: Crossway Books, Good News Publishers, 1984.

————. "What Is Depression?" *Journal of the National Council of Psychotherapists.* Vol. XII:11, London, 1985.

Brennan, R. O. *Nutrigenetics.* New York: New American Library, 1977.

Bricklin, Mark. *The Practical Encyclopedia of Natural Healing.* Emmaus, PA: Rodale Press, 1983.

————. *The Natural Healing Annual.* Emmaus, PA: Rodale Press, 1985.

————. and William Gotlieb, Eds. *Understanding Vitamins and Minerals.* Emmaus, PA: Rodale Press, 1984.

Brodie, H. Keith. "New Hope for the Depressed." *U.S. News & World Report,* January 24, 1983.

Brown, Robert S., Ramirex, Donald E., and Taub, John J. "The Prescription of Exercise for Depression." *The Physician and Sports Medicine,* 6:12, December 1978, McGraw-Hill, Inc.

Burns, D. *Feeling Good: The New Mood Therapy.* New York: William Morrow, 1980.

Burroughs Wellcome Company. *A Compendium of Medical Tables.* Triangle Park, NC: 1978.

Burton, Robert. *The Anatomy of Melancholy.* New York: Tudor Publishing Company, 1927.

Bylinski, G. *Mood Control.* New York: Charles Scribner's Sons, 1978.

Chaitow, A. "Your Body's Unwelcome Guests." *Alternative Medicine Today,* U.K.: July, 1984.

Cheraskin, E., and Ringsdorf, W. M., with Brecher, A. *Psychodietetics: Food as the Key to Emotional Health.* New York: Stein & Day, 1975.

Cleave, T. L. *The Saccharine Disease.* New Canaan, CT: Keats Publishing, Inc., 1974.

Coca, Arthur F. *The Pulse Test.* New York: Arco Publishing, Inc., 1979.

Cousins, Norman. *Anatomy of an Illness.* New York: Bantam Books, 1981.

Demaray, Donald E. *Laughter, Joy, and Healing.* Grand Rapids: Baker Book House, 1986.

Diagram Group, The. *The Brain: A User's Manual.* New York: Berkley Books, 1982.

Diamond, John. *Your Body Doesn't Lie.* New York: Warner Books, 1980.

Evans, D. L. "Organic Psychosis Without Anemia or Spinal Cord Symptoms in Patients with Vitamin B12 Deficiency." *American Journal of Psychiatry.* 140:2, February, 1983, pp. 218–220.

Eysenck, H. J. "The Classification of Depressive Illnesses. *British Journal of Psychiatry,* 1970, 117, 241–250.

Faelton, Sharon. *The Allergy Self-Help Book.* Emmaus, PA: Rodale Press, 1983.

————. *The Complete Book of Minerals for Health.* Emmaus, PA: Rodale Press, 1981.

Fieve, Ronald R. *Moodswing.* New York: Bantam Books, 1975.

Flint, Thomas, and Cain, Harvey D. *Emergency Treatment and Management.* Philadelphia: W. B. Saunders Company, 1975.

Forbes, Alex. *The Bristol Diet.* London: Century Publishing House, 1984.

Fredericks, C., and Goodman, H. *Low Blood Sugar and You.* New York: Constellation International, 1974.

Fromm, Erich. *The Heart of Man.* New York: Harper & Row, 1964.

Geddes, Jim. *The Bright Side of Depression.* Nashville: Broadman Press, 1986.

Gelenberg, A. J. "Tyrosine for the Treatment of Depression." *American Journal of Psychiatry.* 137:5, May 1980, pp. 622–623.

George, Bob. "There's No Need to Be Depressed." *Moody Monthly,* February, 1982.

Gerras, Charles. *The Complete Book of Vitamins.* Emmaus, PA: Rodale Press, 1977.

Ghadirian, A. M., et al. "Folic Acid and Depression." *Psychosomatics: Journal of the Academy of Psychosomatic Medicine,* 21:11, November 1980.

Gillespie, R. D. "Clinical Differentiation of Types of Depression." *Guy Hospital Rep.,* 1929, 79, 306–344.

Greist, John H., and Jefferson, W. *Depression and Its Treatment.* New York: Warner Books, Inc., 1985.

Haneveld, G. T. ed. *Elseviers Medisch Onderzoekgids.* Amsterdam: Elsevier, 1982.

Hauck, Paul A. *Overcoming Depression.* Philadelphia: The Westminster Press, 1976.

Hausman, Patricia. *The Right Dose.* Emmaus, PA: Rodale Press, 1987.

Hirschfeld, Herman. *Your Allergic Child.* New York: ARC Books, Inc., 1964.

Huggins, Hal A. "Mercury Toxicity." *Your Good Health,* 2:7, New Canaan, CT: Keats Publishing, Inc., 1984.

Hurst, L.A. "Classification of Psychotic Disorders From a Genetic Point of View." *Acta Genetica Medica,* 11, 1962. 321–332.

Josephson, Emanuel M. *Prevention,* July 1955, Rodale Press, Emmaus, PA.

Kaplan, Harold I., and Sadock, Benjamin J. *Comprehensive Textbook of Psychiatry/IV.* Baltimore: Williams & Wilkins, 1985.

Kirschmann, John D., and Dunne, Lavon, J. *Nutrition Almanac.* New York: McGraw-Hill Book Company, 1984.

Klerman, G.L. "Clinical Research in Depression." *Archives of General Psychiatry,* 24, 1971, 305–319.

Kline, Nathan S. *From Sad to Glad.* New York: Ballantine Books, 1974.

Kunin, Richard. *Mega-Nutrition.* New York: New American Library, 1980.

LaHaye, Tim. *How to Win Over Depression.* Grand Rapids: Zondervan, 1974.

Lange, J. (1926). Cited in Kendell, R. E. *The Classification of Depressive Illnesses.* London: Oxford University Press, 1968.

Langer, Stephen E. *Solved: The Riddle of Illness.* New Canaan, CT: Keats Publishing Company, 1984.

Lesser, Michael. *Nutrition and Vitamin Therapy.* New York: Bantam Books, 1981.

Lewinsohn, P. M. and Shaffer, M. "Use of Home Observations as an Integral Part of the Treatment of Depression: Preliminary Report and Case Studies." *Journal of Consultant Clinical Psychology,* 37, 1971, 87–94.

Light, Marilyn Hamilton. *Homeostasis Revisited*. Troy, NY: Adrenal Metabolic Research Society of the Hypoglycemia Foundation, 1981.

————. ed. *Hypoadrenocorticism*. Troy, NY: Adrenal Metabolic Research Society of the Hypoglycemia Foundation, Inc., 1980.

Lloyd, Charles W. "Endocrine Factors in the Emotional Development of Women." *Physiologic Basis for Emotional Disorders in Women*. New York: Ayerst Laboratories, 1973.

Long, James W. *The Essential Guide to Prescription Drugs*. New York: Harper & Row, 1985.

MacFayden, Heather Wood. "The Classification of Depressive Syndromes." *Journal of Clinical Psychology*. Vol. 31:3, July 1975, Brandon, VT.

Mackarness, Richard. *Chemical Victims*. London: Pan Books, 1980.

————. *Not All in the Mind*. London: Pan Books, 1976.

Mandell, Marshall, and Scanlon, Lynne Waller, *Dr. Mandell's 5-Day Allergy Relief System*. New York: Pocket Books, 1980.

Maultsby, Maxie C., Jr. *Coping Better Anytime, Anywhere*. Englewood Cliffs, NJ: Prentice-Hall, Inc., 1986.

————. *Rational Behavior Therapy*. Englewood Cliffs, NJ: Prentice-Hall, Inc., 1984.

McCoy, Kathleen. *Coping With Teenage Depression*. New York: New American Library, 1982.

Mears, Frederick, and Gatchel, Robert J. *Fundamentals of Abnormal Psychology*. Chicago: Rand McNally College Publishing Co., 1979.

Medical Letter on Drugs and Therapeutics, The. New Rochelle, NY: 28:721, August 29, 1986.

Menninger, William C. *Newsweek,* December 8, 1958.

Merck Manual of Diagnosis and Therapy, The. Rahway, NJ: Merck Sharp & Dohme Research Laboratories, 1982.

Mindell, Earl. *Earl Mindell's Vitamin Bible*. New York: Warner Books, 1985.

Morgan, Marie. *Breaking Through*. Minneapolis: Winston Press, 1983.

Nash, David T. *Medical Mayhem*. New York: Walker and Company, 1985.

Newbold, H. L. *Mega-Nutrients for Your Nerves*. New York: Berkley Books, 1975.

Norris, Ronald V. *PMS-Premenstrual Syndrome*. New York: Berkley Books, 1985.

Nutrition News. December 1983. Pomona, CA.

Padus, Emrika. *Your Emotions and Your Health*. Emmaus, PA: Rodale Press, 1986.

Page, Melvin. *Your Body Is Your Best Doctor*. New Canaan, CT: Keats Publishing, 1972.

Pearce, Ian C. B. *The Holistic Approach to Cancer.* Boturick, Alexandria, Dunbartonshire, Great Britain: R. Findlay, 1983.

People's Medical Society, *Newsletter,* Emmaus, PA: Rodale Press, 1986.

Philpott, William H., and Kalita, Dwight K. *Brain Allergies: The Psychonutrient Connection.* New Canaan, CT: Keats Publishing, Inc., 1980.

Physicians' Desk Reference. 41st ed. Oradel, New Jersey: Medical Economics Company, 1986.

Post, F. "The Management and Nature of Depressive Illness in Late Life: A Follow-through Study." *British Journal of Psychiatry,* 121, 1972, 393–404.

Powell, Lenore S., and Courtice, Katie. *Alzheimer's Disease.* Reading, MA: Addison-Wesley Publishing Company, 1983.

Prevention. Emmaus, PA: Rodale Press, January 1985.

Robinson, C.H. "Nutrition Education—What Comes Next?" *Journal of the American Dietetic Association,* 69, 1976, 126–132.

Rodale, J. I. *Best Health Articles from Prevention,* Rodale Books, Inc., Emmaus, PA: 1967.

——— . *Happy People Rarely Get Cancer,* Rodale Books, Inc., Emmaus, PA: 1970.

——— . *Rodale's System for Mental Power and Natural Health.* Englewood Cliffs, NJ: Prentice-Hall, Inc., 1966.

Rodin, Gary. "Depression in the Medically Ill: An Overview." *American Journal of Psychiatry,* 143:6, 1986, 696–705.

Ross, Harvey M. *Fighting Depression.* New York: Larchmont Books, 1975.

Selye, Hans. *Stress Without Distress.* New York: New American Library, 1974.

——— . *The Stress of Life.* New York: McGraw-Hill, 1978.

Schwab, Laurence. "Can Poor Nutrition Lead to Suicide?" *Let's Live.* Los Angeles, CA: January 1984.

Sheinkin, David and Schachter, Michael. *Food, Mind, & Mood.* New York: Warner Books, 1980.

Stevens, Laura J. *The Complete Book of Allergy Control.* New York: Pocket Books, 1982.

Stearns, Frederic. *Anger.* Springfield, IL: Charles C. Thomas, 1972.

The Medical Letter on Drugs and Therapeutics. New Rochelle, NY: 28:721, August 29, 1986.

Tintera, J. "Endocrine Aspects of Schizophrenia: Hypoglycemia or Hypoadrenocorticism." *Journal of Schizophrenia.* 1:3, 1967.

——— . "The Hypoadrenocortical State and Its Management." *New York State Journal of Medicine.* 55:13, 1955.

——— . "Stabilizing Homeostasis in the Recovered Alcoholic Through Endocrine Therapy: Evaluation of the Hypoglycemia Factor." *Journal of American Geriatrics Society.* 14:2, 1966.

————— , and Lovell, H. "Endocrine Treatment of Alcoholism." *Geriatrics*. 4:5, 1949.

————— , and Lovell, H. "Hypoadrenocorticism in Alcoholism and Drug Addiction." *Geriatrics*. 6:1, 1951.

Van Den Berg, J. H. *Kleine Psychiatrie*. Nijkerk, Holland: G. F. Callenbach B.V., 1966.

Van Praag, H. M. "The Vulnerable Brain: Biological Factors in the Diagnosis and Treatment of Depression." In V.W. Rakoff, H.C. Stancer, & H.B. Kedward. *Psychiatric Diagnosis*. New York: Brunner-Mazel, 1977.

Walsh, Maryellen. *Schizophrenia*. New York: Warner Books, 1985.

Weller, Charles. *How to Live With Hypoglycemia*. New York: Jove Books, 1977.

White, Kristin. *Diet and Cancer*. New York: Bantam Books, 1984.

Whittlesey, Marietta. *Killer Salt*. New York: Avon Books, 1978.

Wittrock, M. C. *The Human Brain*. Englewood Cliffs, NJ: Prentice-Hall, Inc., 1977.

Worthington-Roberts, B., and Breskin, M. M. *Journal of the American Dietetics Association*, 84:7, July 1984, pp. 795–800.

Wright, Jonathan. *Dr. Wright's Book of Nutritional Therapy*. Emmaus, PA: Rodale Press, 1979.

————— . *Dr. Wright's Guide to Healing With Nutrition*. Emmaus, PA: Rodale Press, 1984.

Yacenda, John. *Let's Live*. Los Angeles, CA: February 1984.

Yudkin, John. *Sweet and Dangerous*. New York: Wyden Publishers, 1972.

Subject Index

Psychomotor, 329; retardation, 329
Psychopath, 329
Psychosocial depression, 45, 194
Psychosomatic, 69, 330
Psychosomatogenic, definition of, 26, 330
Psychotic depression, 21, 44, 231, 330; depressive reaction, 43
Ptomaines, 242
Ptyalin, 242
Pyridoxine, 330

Quadracyclic antidepressants, 234

Raffinose. *See* Monosaccharides
Rapid eye movement (REM) sleep, 131–32, 330
Rational thinking, 20, 79–80, 330–31
Reactions, maladaptive. *See* Allergy
Reactive depression, 43, 45, 194, 331. *See* Hypoglycemia
Realistic thinking, 80, 331
Recommended food sources in the treatment of depression, 248–52
Reconciliation, 167–69, 172
Recreation, need for, 133–34, 136
Refined carbohydrates, 61, 202, 212; avoidance of, 109, 112
Relaxation exercise, 133
Rennin, 242
Repentance, 166
Repression, 331
Reserpine, 22, 196, 233, 331–32
Resistance stage. *See* General adaption syndrome (G.A.S.)
Rest and relaxation, 129–34, 136
Reticular formation, 233; stimulation of, 232
Riboflavin, 332
Right thinking, 75–78, 86, 140–42, 158
Ritalin, 332

Saccharide, 332
SAD. *See* Seasonal affective disorder
Sadness, 19, 20, 42, 43, 58, 62, 76, 195, 196
Salivary amylase, 242
Salvation, 165–67
Saturated fatty acids, 332
Schizoid, 332
Schizophrenia, 103, 332–33
Schizophrenic depression, 43, 45, 189, 199
Seasonal affective disorder (SAD), 21
Secondary depression, 45, 195–96
Selenium, 241

Self-analysis, 144–47; examples of, 142–45, 151–56; formula, 142–43, 145–46
Self-blame, 22, 43, 74
Self-centeredness. *See* Narcissistic depression
Self-counseling, 138, 139–47
Self-defeating attitudes, 69–70, 139–40, 177; beliefs, 69–70, 177; thinking, 21, 22, 30, 42–43, 69–70, 73, 139, 146
Self-enhancing behavior, 146; thinking, 22, 64, 73
Self-help for depression, 137–58
Self-induced depression, 137–40, 177, 183
Self-medication, dangers of, 102
Self-pity, 22, 42, 43, 47, 74
Self-talk, 70–71, 140–47; versus group-talk, 140–41
Senile dementia, 333; depression, 45, 196–97, 199; psychosis, 197
Septum pellucidum, 211
Serotonin, 57, 66, 209, 219, 226, 228, 232, 261, 268, 333–34
Serum alkaline phosphate, 100
Severe depression, 20, 43–44, 231, 233–35
Sex drive, food, depression, and, 210–11
Shock treatment, 26
Side effects of drugs, 101–02
Simmond's disease, 222, 228
Sinequan, 26, 233, 234
Single parent blues. *See* Psychosocial depression
Singular approach, 20, 22, 23, 25, 26, 175, 177; versus wholistic approach, 173–80
SK-Amitriptyline, 234
SK-Pramine, 234
Sleep, 130–32; difficulties, 43, 132
Slowness of movement. *See* Psychomotor retardation
Sodium, 100, 110, 241
Somatotrophic hormone (STH), 206
Sound decision making, rules for, 144–45; eating, 210–14
Speed. *See* Amphetamines
Spiritual depression, 45, 83–93, 197–98; regeneration, 161–71; sources of depression, 83–93; stress and depression, 174; treatment of depression, 161–71; treatment progress chart 172; value system, 94; variables, 34, 35
Starch, 238, 239, 242
Stimulants, 104, 334
STP. *See* Psilocybin
Stress and depression, 21, 26, 27–30, 65–